TWENTIETH CENTURY VIEWS

The aim of this series is to present the best in
contemporary critical opinion on major authors,
providing a twentieth century perspective on
their changing status in an era of profound
revaluation.

Maynard Mack, *Series Editor*
Yale University

Anthony and Viola Winner

MALRAUX

A COLLECTION OF CRITICAL ESSAYS

Edited by

R. W. B. Lewis

Prentice-Hall, Inc., *Englewood Cliffs, N. J.*

Current printing (last digit):

12 11 10 9 8 7 6 5 4

© 1964 BY PRENTICE-HALL, INC.

ENGLEWOOD CLIFFS, N.J.

LIBRARY OF CONGRESS CATALOG CARD NO.: 64-14537

Printed in the United States of America—C

P 54800
C 54801

To Joseph Frank

Table of Contents

Introduction:
Malraux and His Critics

by R. W. B. Lewis

I

"Malraux is interested in painting," Maurice Blanchot remarked in 1950, "but we know that he is also interested in man." What is beguiling about the remark is not only its deceptive simplicity—in an essay not otherwise notable for simplicity—but the ordering of its key terms. Blanchot, to be sure, was engaged at the moment in appraising Malraux's interest in painting as reflected by *La Psychologie de l'Art* (*The Psychology of Art*); even so, his formulation was and, I think, remains essentially correct, especially as he continued: "To save one through the other—[Malraux] was unable to resist this great temptation."

Not many readers were as quick to grasp the intimate relation between Malraux's supposedly new concern with the total world of art forms and his abiding concern with the condition and the destiny of man. Writing in 1957, Armand Hoog remembered "the outburst of surprise . . . and bafflement that accompanied the publication, in 1947, of the *Musée Imaginaire*," the first part of *La Psychologie de l'Art*. "More than one critic," Hoog said, "marveled, however admiringly, that such an excellent novelist should turn into an art historian." No novelist of his generation had been more closely associated, in the vague consciousness of the reading public, with the raw violence of contemporary events. Malraux had dramatized the 1926 uprising in Canton in *Les Conquérants* (*The Conquerors*) in 1928[1]; his own penetration of the Siamese jungle with something of the tribal warfare going on there in *La Voie Royale* (*The Royal Way*) in 1930; another and larger phase of the Chinese revolution (*Man's Fate*) in 1933; aspects of brutality and enslavement in Nazi Germany in *Le Temps du Mépris* (*Days of Wrath*) in 1935; the Spanish Civil War in *L'Espoir* (*Man's Hope*) in 1937; and, most recently, a poison-gas attack on the German-Russian front in the First World War, preceded by a glance at the Young Turk revolutionary movement before that war and framed by memoirs of the Second World War, in *Les Noyers de l'Altenburg* (*The*

---

[1] Dates are those of the first French edition.

1

Walnut Trees of Altenburg) in 1943. No writer, not even Hemingway, could seem less likely to the unknowing to devote himself to researches into Sumerian or Gothic art.

But the surprise occasioned by Malraux's art studies was due of course, as Hoog says, to an inattentive reading of the novels just mentioned, and to popular ignorance of Malraux's several interrelated careers. It is now clear—and most of the essays in this volume testify to the fact—that there is an astonishing unity to everything Malraux has written, one is inclined to add everything he has done, since his first significant book, a sort of epistolary novel bearing the Spengler-echoing title *La Tentation de l'Occident* (*The Temptation of the West*) in 1926. A main element of that unity has been a persistent preoccupation with art—with works of art and the cultures they comprise and express—and with the role of art in a generally "absurd" universe. It was Malraux who, in *La Tentation de l'Occident,* introduced the word "absurd" into the modern philosophical vocabulary in a contention that, to the eye of modern man, the universe appeared fatally bereft of meaning, because of the loss of compelling and explanatory religious belief and, with it, the collapse of any direction-giving concept of man: because of the successive "deaths" of the idea of God and the idea of man. Most of Malraux's novels have been symbolic assaults upon history, in an endeavor to wrest from history a persuasive definition of human nature and a dependable guide and measure of human conduct; while in his life Malraux has been committed to intensive action and to what Gaëtan Picon calls "the myth of the great individual" as sources, perhaps of insight, but certainly of compensation. But he has also and ever more strenuously been committed to the great art work as performing, more satisfactorily yet, these same functions. If Malraux evidently still believes in the efficacy of the master, he believes even more in the saving power of the masterpiece.

The play of these terms—man, the absurd, action, history, and art— has been constant in Malraux's writing from the beginning. But before criticism could explore their use, it had to get beyond a prior misapprehension—namely, that Malraux was primarily a chronicler of contemporary revolutions, a skillful journalist of the political and economic upheavals peculiar to his age.

II

Leon Trotsky posed the issue in 1931 when he said about *Les Conquérants:* "The book is called a novel. What in fact we have before us is a fictionalized chronicle of the Chinese revolution during its first period, the Canton period." Trotsky had an uncommonly quick perception of literature; he was among the first, a couple of years later, to detect the achievement of Ignazio Silone's *Fontamara*—in which, he said, revolutionary passion was raised to the level of art. He felt that *Les Con-*

quérants was itself a work of considerable art and made some acute and generous observations about its beauty of narrative. But he felt that the author's revolutionary passion was flawed; that Malraux's effort to give a faithful portrait of insurrectionist China had been (in Trotsky's word) corrupted, both by an "excess of individualism" and by "esthetic caprice." Even in retrospect, the charge (which Trotsky supported with considerable and pressing detail) is not without substance and pertains to a wider problem: for there has always been a sort of murky imbalance between Malraux's political affinities (the presumptive ones in his novels and the actual ones—Communist and then Gaullist—in his life) and his stated or implied beliefs about literature. Nonetheless, Malraux had reason to say, in answer, that his book was not intended and should not be judged as a fictionalized chronicle, and that, in effect, it was just the individualism and the esthetics that made it a novel. As to the former, the book's stress was placed "on the relationship between individual and collective action, not on collective action alone." As to the latter, Malraux made the crucial remark that the novel was dominated, not by considerations of doctrinal loyalty and historical inclusiveness, but by the vision, the way of looking at things—in Malraux's French, by *"l'optique"*— proper to the novel as an art form. The entire critical "problem" of Malraux—the "Malraux case," as some French commentators have called it—lies, implicit but bristling, in this early exchange.

Still, when *Les Conquérants* was followed by a fuller narrative of the Chinese revolution, the betrayal and defeat of the Communist effort to seize Shanghai in *La Condition Humaine,* and that by an account (manifestly firsthand in part) of the Spanish Loyalist rebellion in *L'Espoir,* it became generally agreed that Malraux, even more than Silone or Koestler, was *the* novelistic historian of the great social agitations of the century. However original he might be as a craftsman, his subject, it was agreed, was the specific contemporary battle between Socialism and Capitalism: "The central struggle of modern times," according to Haakon Chevalier in his introduction to his own English translation of *L'Espoir,* "—the struggle of a dying order with the forces within it that are molding a new world." That opinion, too, now strikes us as limited rather than misguided, and limited exactly in its failure to see Malraux's passionate hostility to limitations. For Malraux's heroes, as Joseph Frank has observed, "were never simply engaged in a battle against a particular social or economic injustice; they were always somehow struggling against the limitations of life itself and the humiliation of destiny." The Socialist revolts loomed, in Malraux's view, as instances, urgently important in themselves, of a much grander revolt; and he took them as occasions for depicting in fiction the revolt of man against his spiritually and intellectually hemmed-in condition. This was why Malraux's writing had so immense an impact during the Thirties upon the rebellious spirits of so many different countries with their so different modes and objects and strategies of revolt, and why he was able to enlist a far-flung loyalty that has persisted with a sometimes unsubdued fierceness.

Malraux's main characters really are protagonists: that is, etymologically, primarily combatants. What they do about the human condition is to take arms against its historical embodiments; and they will go to the ends of the earth to seek them out. The point has been noticed more than once: Garine, son of a Swiss father and a Russian mother, comes in *Les Conquérants* to southern China; Perken, in *La Voie Royale,* literally as well as psychologically *heimatlos* (his native state, Schleswig-Holstein, has been annexed by Denmark), probes uncharted areas of Siam on a crusade against death; in *La Condition Humaine* and *L'Espoir,* persons from many nations gather in Shanghai and Madrid, as they actually did, at the moment of supreme historical crisis; the Alsatian Vincent Berger, in *Les Noyers de l'Altenburg,* pursues a mirage of Ottoman nationalism through central Asia. Berger's mission is a failure: the holy war he believes in is not to be kindled; but the others find and take part in the (losing) battle of their deepest desire. In short, and the commonplace is worth repeating since it applies more unequivocally to Malraux than to any other modern novelist, Malraux's heroes make their test of life in those places and times where human experience is most intensified, where indeed it has become most decisively embattled.

But as they do so, we move with Malraux into perplexities which, if not wholly philosophical in nature, are at least sources of logical anxiety. Time and again, Malraux has implied that it is in *action* that the strong-willed individual may hope to find not only assuagement but revelation. Victor Brombert reminds us that many of Malraux's key personages are intellectuals, former university professors and the like, but intellectuals who for the most part have lost faith in the values of ideas as such and who have come to distrust the pure exercise of mind. They have therefore abandoned the contemplative or the teaching life and have turned to some arena of explicit action—usually by attaching themselves to a revolutionary cause undergoing trial by warfare—in search of some truth more vital than the truth of ideas. It is a belligerent version of the perennial pragmatic strategy. Nicola Chiaromonte remarks that Malraux "pushed to its extreme consequences the modern pragmatic impulse which tends to see in the world of action the only reality, and, what is more, to reject any proposition which cannot be directly translated into a force, an act, or series of acts." The word "modern" might well be replaced by the phrase "ancient and traditional," for it has always been the hallmark of the pragmatist that he sees "in the world of action the only reality." Customarily, moreover, the pragmatic temper not only rejects propositions that cannot be translated into actions; it also dispenses with any branch of thought and despises any activity of mind that is not involved with—cannot be tested by—human experience. So it is that *history*—that is, precisely, "the world of action"—history in both its first and second intentions, as a series of actual events and as the record of events: history, in the usual pragmatic scheme, takes the place of metaphysics and of any independent theory of knowledge. The tumult of history becomes the one accessible context of truth and value; and inspecting it, the pragmatist has often been able to disclose some developing and meaningful shape, some gratifying or alarming design of things past and passing and to come. His chart of that design is the pragmatist's account of reality. The very troubling question about Malraux and for Malraux is whether he has ever managed to suggest in his fiction any such disclosure.

But Malraux is or has been a novelist, a person dedicated (as he told Trotsky) to *l'optique* of fiction rather than that of history or philosophy. The literary issue here is at least as complex as the philosophical one, and goes far beyond the confines of an introductory essay. It has to do with that level of a work of literature—that is, of any work that aspires to such a level—on which the literal incidents and characters, the actual clashes and conversations, can be seen enacting an allegory of some large and generalized historical process—a process in which an entire social order may be caught up, or even a whole world; and a process which may or may not be "true" in the perspective of a scientific historian. In Conrad's *Nostromo,* for example, the various convulsions that rend and then reshape the little South American republic of Costaguana, the assortment of plots and purposes, the interaction of a host of ambitions and devotions all secrete an appalling myth of modern economic, political, moral, and even religious history. It is the history, most generally, of the devious and yet absolute conquest by "material interests" of the spirit and energy of modern man; more particularly, of the process by which material interests, trusted and supported as a source of order and justice in a repressive and unstable backward society, bring in their own brand of intolerable injustice and repression and thus assure further unheavals in the future.[2] One looks in vain for so powerful a pattern in *Les Conquérants* or *La Condition Humaine,* or *L'Espoir,* or in the three taken together. Nor can one make out in those novels the tremendous and still more emphatic kind of historical pattern (the inevitable spawning of nihilism by liberalism in mid-nineteenth century Russia) set forth in *The Possessed.* Nor, at an opposite extreme of fictional stress, do we find the sort of far-away but sizable implications about social and moral history that exist somewhere in the depths of James's *The Golden Bowl.*

Malraux's dilemma, if dilemma it be, is caused in part by the very subject—contemporary historical violence—which he has been brave

---

[2] In *Politics and the Novel* (1957), Irving Howe credits *Nostromo* not only with dramatic significance but with historical accuracy and even prescience. It verifies, says Mr. Howe—"in the limited way a novel can verify anything"—"Leon Trotsky's theory of the 'permanent revolution,' "; and, on the level of actual history, it describes in advance what would be "a basic pattern of Latin American politics."

enough to deal with. When, as in *La Condition Humaine*, he remains faithful to the historical outcome of the struggle, he concludes with a disaster which is not, *within the novel*, invested with any particular significance. But when, as in *L'Espoir*, he shapes historical fact to his fictional purposes (by concluding with the Loyalist victory at Guadalajara), he suggests an outcome and a meaning other than those history was already bleakly providing. Chiaromonte, who makes this latter point, relates it to what he describes as Malraux's evasion of "the implications of tragedy"; but I am not so sure. *L'Espoir* is problematic; but it may well be that in most of his novels, Malraux, far from evading the implications of tragedy, was resolutely facing up to something more terrible yet—to the absence of tragedy as a discernible and determining form at work in modern historical experience. Needless to say, one great way to find and to make evident an illuminating design within the confusions of history is to subject the course of the events in question to the organizing power of the tragic imagination. Herman Melville did exactly that when he confronted the turbulence of the American Civil War in his loosely epic volume of war-poems, *Battle-Pieces*. Most of those poems were written while the war was still in progress; but looking back both at the war and the poems after the pacification, Melville (in a prose supplement) could draw upon Aristotle's definition of tragedy in the *Poetics* to define the war as a "great historic tragedy" which he prayed had not "been enacted without instructing our whole beloved country through terror and pity." But Malraux has not felt or envisaged the civil wars he has participated in as genuine tragic actions—not, at least, on any scale beyond that of a few driven and defeated individuals.

The importance, indeed the artistic and spiritual "value," of those individual destinies should not be minimized. It is true, as several critics have noticed, that there are no really evil figures in Malraux's novels: no persons who either are evil through some private wayward impulse or who represent the force of some evil principle in the universe. But it is not true, as Claude-Edmonde Magny would have us believe, that Malraux has never created a character who "changes and really grows." Malraux does not concentrate his narrative on the change and growth of an individual psyche with the patience, say, of a Flaubert or a Proust. Change, in Malraux's fiction, is a regular phenomenon, but it occurs spasmodically, with earthquake speed and shock, and almost always during moments of greatest intensity. Tchen in *La Condition Humaine* has grown into an altogether different phase of being before the novel is ten pages old; Vincent Berger's very soul turns over in the midst of the apocalypse on the plains of Russia. And in fact, all those persons whom Frohock has called "neophytes" (the narrator of *Les Conquérants,* Claude Vannec in *La Voie Royale,* Kassner in *Le Temps du Mépris* and so on) change and grow to a greater or lesser degree, and in fits and lurches; and the mark of their development is the acquisition of insight. It is an insight, customarily, into the solitary, mortal, spiritually blinded, and fundamentally helpless condition of individual man; and with it, a conviction about the supreme value of human companionship, "virile fraternity." This is one of the great themes of contemporary fiction, and no writer has handled it more efficiently (and influentially) than Malraux. But these insights do not arise, so to speak, as the lesson of history: for example, as its tragic import. They are much rather the individual human response to history's failure to deliver any lesson at all.

That failure is acknowledged with devastating rhetoric in the extraordinary debate that occupies the center of Malraux's last novel, *Les Noyers de l'Altenburg*. Here Malraux's entire personal and fictional endeavor, the whole "action" of his life and his novels over two decades, is recapitulated in terms of intellectual discourse, when the question of the definable nature of man is posed as a question about the continuity and coherence of the *history* of man. The debate seems at least, via the somber climactic speech of the anthropologist Möllberg, to set the seal on incoherence as the only fact, as it were the truthless truth, discoverable in history. One might still turn to human fraternity as a form of consolation, on the edge of this abyss of meaning. But had no other truth been seized from the plunge into action, the long encounter with history?

III

In one perspective, the answer has to be in the negative. Insofar as it aimed at anything more than sheer nervy excitement, the pragmatic impulse had been defeated along with the revolutionary causes in which it had variously exerted itself. Contemporary history had proven to be as shapeless and discordant as the vast history of human cultures so bleakly examined by Möllberg; from neither could those passionately sought after explanations be extracted. But if Malraux's pragmatic strategy had failed, what we might call his Romantic strategy had been faring a good deal better; and in another perspective, the perspective of art, a very different and decidedly affirmative answer had long since begun to issue. Malraux had learned—the hard way, as the saying goes—and had shown his characters learning that, in E. M. Forster's phrase, human history "is really a series of *dis*orders"; but he had also learned with Forster that "[Art] is the one orderly product which our muddling race has produced." Perhaps he had always known this. It is implicit in a part of his reply to Trotsky; and it is even more implicit in his developing style. For, as Geoffrey Hartman remarks, from *La Condition Humaine* on 'the style itself intimates the author's freedom from the law to which his world remains subject, so that if the idea of Man remains inseparable from the idea of tragedy"—or, as I would prefer to say, of incoherence and absurdity, seen perhaps as tragic fatalities—"the idea of the artist pairs with the idea of freedom."

About this contention, however, there has been a significant disagree-
ment: significant because it bears upon the nature and degree of Malraux's own artistic achievement, and on the relation between it and the
absurdities he has confronted in his subject matter. Mme. Magny, for
example, before registering her deep disapproval of what she takes to be
Malraux's message, warmly and brilliantly praises Malraux's style, and
exactly on the grounds that (far from being "free" of the world it treats)
it is a splendidly contrived equivalent of its own setting—that the syn-
tactical disjointedness, the jerky cadences, the rapid transitions, and the
startling juxtapositions in Malraux's novels serve as a precise enactment
of the discordant realities they describe. Malraux's best novels, this critic
says without any detectable trace of irony, are "beautiful, disconnected
and truly *disordered.*" Mme. Magny, in short, endorses Malraux's effort
to commit what American criticism sometimes calls the fallacy of imita-
tive form: the fallacy of trying to render a disordered world by a dis-
orderly book. Gaëtan Picon appears to agree with Mme. Magny; he tells
us, "Of all the novels, *L'Espoir* is the one that vibrates most with discordant voices (and perhaps for that reason it is the greatest)." But Picon
is satisfied that one can locate the source of harmony in Malraux's novels
—in a virile fraternity, as we might say, of ideas and attitudes. Although
Malraux "never stops dramatizing inimical truths," and though his is
unmistakably "a universe of debate," nonetheless "all those enemies are
brothers," because all of them "unite in the one who animates their
dialogues," in the creative consciousness and the narrative voice of André
Malraux.

In this view (which approximates Hartman's), what provides whole-
ness and harmony in Malraux's writings is not so much the arrangement
of the incidents or the patterns of characters and relations between characters, and even less the control and shaping power of some dominant
idea.[3] It is rather a style, a presence, what Henry James would call a
tone: some quality of artistic expression, however we name it, that works
against and away from the images of chaos and defeat that the novels
otherwise contain. Such, certainly, has been Malraux's increasingly dedicated purpose. "The way to express the unusual, the terrible, the inhuman," he has said, talking about Goya, "is not to represent carefully
an actual or imaginary spectacle but to invent a script capable of representing these things without being forced to submit to their elements."
Nor was this any casual matter. For Malraux, everything—his own literary achievement, his view of the human condition and of the possibility

---

[3] "Malraux has little esteem for ideas. He would tend to say that they serve to
obstruct or to betray the moment of decision, and to be mere adornments to those
sham dialogues between beings or groups who have nothing to say to each other"
(Emmanuel Mounier, *L'Espoir des désespérés*). This is a challenging statement, partly
true and partly defensible, but eventually misleading. Victor Brombert, who quotes
the first of the two sentences, offers a subtle and necessary corrective of the argument.

of human freedom—hangs on the capacity of inventing that "script." This is, finally, the grand "truth" that emerges from the debate at Altenburg. *Les Noyers de l'Altenburg* is probably the best place to test any claim one would wish to make about Malraux as a novelist. For my part, I can only hope that Malraux's reputation will not stand or fall on *L'Espoir*, which, despite some uncommonly fine individual episodes, strikes me as a showy and ultimately rather tiresome performance, in which the style is held captive by the subject; though the reader is invited to consider the high estimates cogently argued in this volume. *La Condition Humaine* has, of course, been Malraux's most widely admired novel, and it is no doubt his major contribution to the history of literature in his generation; beyond that, and beginning with the title, it is so impressive and enduring a challenge to its own content that it is likely to endure long after that revolutionary content has ceased to agitate the minds of readers. But the work of Malraux's which best fulfills the requirements of art—in Malraux's terms or anyone else's—seems to me to be *Les Noyers de l'Altenburg;* and in the essays that follow, it is in fact this novel that receives the greatest attention.

The accomplishment of *Les Noyers* is the more astonishing, since it consists of only the first third of a novel called *La Lutte avec l'Ange,* ("The Struggle with the Angel") the remainder (which Malraux may yet rewrite) having been destroyed by the German Gestapo during the war. (Another mystery is that the book has still not appeared in this country twenty years after it came out in French.) I have suggested elsewhere certain reasons, in part extraliterary, for the special significance of *Les Noyers:* mainly the handsome way it crystallizes and gives final shape to themes—action and art, history and vision, involvement and transcendence—and human figures that between them, in my judgment, define the age of fiction represented by Silone, Camus, Faulkner, and others.

Les Noyers throws light backwards on Malraux's career, illuminating the early exchange with Trotsky and clarifying the precarious and continuing combination in Malraux of the adventurer and the artist, the minister of state and the art historian. It does so because it is constructed in such a way as to throw light forward and backward on itself. It is a work of art, which has at its center Malraux's most forthright statement about the nature and function of art as the means of escaping the human condition, as man's greatest resource for achieving freedom from history. It is presumably no longer possible for anyone to suppose, as some of the novel's first readers did, that when Möllberg asserts the utter discontinuity between human cultures he speaks for Malraux: or anyhow, that he is the whole voice of Malraux; for, like the other characters, Möllberg is a part of Malraux and one way of looking at the history Malraux had lived through. But a much larger part of Malraux is bespoken in the midst of the Altenburg debate in the quiet voice of Vincent Berger,

saying what Malraux had tried to say to Trotsky before he had himself
quite grasped the principle:

> To me, our art seems to be a rectification of the world, a means of escaping
> from man's estate. The chief confusion, I think, is due to our belief—and
> in the theories propounded of Greek tragedy, it's strikingly clear—that
> representing fatality is the same as submitting to it. But it's not, it's almost
> to dominate it. The mere fact of being able to represent it, conceive it,
> release it from real fate, from the merciless divine scale, reduces it to the
> human scale. Fundamentally, our art is a humanization of the world.

What Berger says (and what, later, Malraux would say in reference to
Goya) is precisely what the novel illustrates and enacts. The real answer
to the despair of Möllberg lies in the novel he inhabits: in the movement
and texture, the composition and tone of *Les Noyers* itself. The novel
is the final confirmation of its own stated conviction.

In the light of that conviction, Malraux's subsequent and voluminous
art studies are so little surprising as to be altogether inevitable. *La Psychologie de l'Art* and *Les Voix du Silence* (*The Voices of Silence*) are
vast, discursive demonstrations of the theory about the relation between
art and man's estate of which *Les Noyers* was the great fictional presentation. This is what, for us, lends a strangely moving accent to Maurice
Blanchot's discussion of Malraux's "museum" as standing for "the end
of history." The American reader will notice in Blanchot's expert account
certain parallels between Malraux's views and those espoused in Anglo-
American critical theory, parallels that help clarify the idea of art as
escaping from history. There is, for example, something like T. S.
Eliot's notion about the literary tradition, and the way every new masterpiece subtly reorders the body of past literature. More striking yet is the
parallel with Northrop Frye's *Anatomy of Criticism* and its concept
(spelled out more emphatically than it had been by Eliot) of the self-
contained nature of literature, the sense in which the *literary*—or, more
broadly in Malraux, the artistic—element of the art work exists outside
of time, and belongs to the timeless trans-historical order of art itself.
But it is not easy to find any sort of parallel to the sheer passion (reflected
in Blanchot) with which Malraux has proclaimed and elaborated these
principles. It is the passion born from the encounters with history—those
of Malraux's life and those of his fiction—and its form is the passionate
conviction that, while history has to be reckoned with, has to be entered
and participated in and investigated, it also has to be transcended; for
when all is said and done, the truth is not in it. The knowledge provided by the "museum," says Blanchot, "is historical, it is the knowledge
of histories, and of a series of histories that we accept"; but "at the same
time, it is not historical, it does not concern itself with the objective truth

of history . . . and this is the knowledge we accept and even prefer."
We prefer it, according to Malraux, because the knowledge discoverable
in the world of art forms (the museum without walls) is a definition of
man as free, heroic, creative, and purposeful. Art restores the definition
that had been questioned and shattered by history: restores it and gives
it an unassailable permanence. "To save one through the other—[Mal-
raux] was unable to resist this great temptation."

The Strangled Revolution

by Leon Trotsky

Unfortunately, I read *The Conquerors*[1] some two years after its publication. The book is devoted to the Chinese revolution, which is the most significant subject of the last five years. Everything—its dense and beautiful style, the keen eye of the artist, the original and daring observations—contributes to making this a novel of exceptional importance. If I speak of it at this time, it is not because the novel is filled with talent, though this is not a negligible fact, but because it is a most valuable source of political lessons. Do they stem from Malraux? No, they emerge from the story itself, unbeknown to the author, and testify against him, which does honor both to the observer and to the artist in him, but not to the revolutionary. However, we are justified in appreciating Malraux from this point of view: neither in his own name, nor, and above all, in the name of Garine his second self, is the author stingy with his judgments on the revolution.

The book is called a novel. What in fact we have before us is a fictionalized chronicle of the Chinese revolution during its first period, the Canton period. The chronicle is incomplete. It is in some cases deficient in its grasp of the social reality. By contrast, the reader sees not only luminous episodes of the revolution, but also clearly delineated silhouettes that engrave themselves in one's memory like social symbols.

By little touches of color, in the manner of the *pointillistes,* Malraux paints an unforgettable picture of the general strike, not, of course, as seen from below, as it is carried on, but as seen from above—the European colony is without luncheon, it suffocates from heat: the Chinese have stopped work in the kitchens and have ceased operating the ventilators. This is not by way of reproach to the author. The foreign artist could doubtlessly not have handled his themes otherwise. But another criticism can be made that is indeed important: the book lacks a natural affinity between the author, in spite of all he knows and understands, and his heroine, the Revolution.

"The Strangled Revolution," by Leon Trotsky. (Translated from the French by Beth Archer.) This first appeared as "La Révolution Etranglée" in *Nouvelle Revue Française*, No. 211 (April 1, 1931). Reprinted by permission of the Trotsky estate.

[1] *Les Conquérants* appeared in the *Nouvelle Revue Française* in the March-June 1928 issues.

The author's truly profound sympathy for insurrectionist China is undebatable. But it is corrupted by excesses of individualism and of esthetic caprice. In reading the book with sustained attention, one sometimes feels resentful when, from the tone of the writing, one perceives a note of patronizing irony toward these barbarians capable of enthusiasm. That China is backward, that certain of her political manifestations seem primitive, are not factors one asks be overlooked. But there should be a true perspective that puts everything in its proper place. The Chinese events that provide the backdrop for Malraux's novel are incomparably more significant for the future destiny of human culture than the vain and pathetic blustering of European parliaments and the mountains of literary products from stagnating civilizations. Malraux appears to be somewhat timid about recognizing this.

In the novel are pages, beautiful through their intensity, that demonstrate how revolutionary hate is born of imprisonment, ignorance, slavery, and how it tempers like steel. These pages might well have figured in the Anthology of Revolution had Malraux approached the masses with more freedom and daring, and had he not introduced into his story a little note of snobbish superiority, seeming to make excuses for his passing alliance with the insurrection of the Chinese people, perhaps as much to himself as to the academic mandarins in France and to the peddlers of intellectual opium.

Borodine is the representative of the Komintern and has the function of advisor to the Canton government. Garine, the author's favorite, is responsible for propaganda. All work is carried on within the framework of the Kuomintang. Borodine, Garine, the Russian "General" Gallen, the Frenchman Gérard, the German Klein, constitute a singular revolutionary bureaucracy that raises itself above the insurgents and carries on its own "revolutionary politics" instead of guiding the politics of the revolution.

The local organizations of the Kuomintang are thus defined: "A gathering of a few fanatics, seemingly courageous, a few rich people who seek consideration or security, many students and coolies. . . ." Not only do the bourgeois join each organization but they take over completely. The Communists are merged with the Kuomintang. The workers and peasants are persuaded not to do anything that might offend those friends come over from the bourgeoisie. "Such are the organizations that we control (only partially, do not be misled). . . ." An edifying admission! The bureaucracy of the Komintern tried to "control" the class struggle in China, just as the international banking system controls the economic life of underdeveloped countries. A revolution, however, cannot be commanded. One can only give political expression to its interior forces. One must know to which of these forces one will link one's destiny.

"The coolies are discovering that they exist, simply that they exist."

This shows keen insight on Malraux's part. But in order to know they exist, the coolies, industrial workers and peasants, must overthrow those who prevent them from existing. Foreign domination is indivisibly linked to the inner yoke. The coolies must not only drive out Baldwin and MacDonald, they must also overthrow the ruling class. One cannot be achieved without the other. Thus the awakening of a human personality among the masses of China—that outnumber by ten times the population of France—is at once rooted in the lava of social revolution. What a grandiose spectacle!

At this point Borodine comes on the scene and declares, "In this revolution the workers are obliged to do the work of coolies for the bourgeoisie." [2] The social enslavement from which the proletarian seeks to free himself he finds transposed in the sphere of politics. Who is responsible for this perfidious operation? The bureaucracy of the Komintern? In trying to "control" the Kuomintang it in fact aids the bourgeois, who seek "consideration and security," to enslave the coolies who wish to exist.

Borodine, who at all times remains in the background, is characterized in the novel as a man of "action," a "professional revolutionary," the incarnation of Bolshevism on Chinese soil. Nothing is more erroneous! Here is the political biography of Borodine: in 1903, at the age of 19, he emigrated to America; in 1918, he returned to Moscow where, thanks to his knowledge of English, "he worked in liaison with foreign groups"; he was arrested in Glasgow in 1922; later he was delegated in China as the representative of the Komintern. Having left Russia *before* the first revolution and returned *after* the third. Borodine appears as the accomplished representative of that bureaucracy of State and Party that acknowledged the revolution only *after* its victory. When it comes to young men, this may only be a matter of chronology. In the case of men of forty to fifty it is clearly a political characteristic. If Borodine brilliantly rejoined the victorious revolution in Russia, that in no way signifies that he was summoned to assure the victory of the revolution in China. Men of this type easily assimilate the manners and intonations of "professional revolutionaries." Many of them, because of their protective coloring, fool not only others but themselves as well. Most often, the unyielding audacity of the Bolshevik metamorphoses into the cynicism of the government official prepared for anything. Ah, to have a mandate from the Central Committee! That sacrosanct shield Borodine always carried in his pocket.

Garine is not an official, is more original than Borodine, and perhaps closer to the type of a true revolutionary. But he is lacking in the necessary background. A dilettante and temporarily at center stage, he gets hopelessly embroiled in the great events, and this is constantly evident. Referring to the slogans of the Chinese revolution, he pronounces him-

---

[2] Cf. letter by Chen Dou-siou: "La Lutte des Classes," *NRF*, No. 25-26, p. 676.

self in this way: ". . . democratic gibberish, rights of man, et cetera." This has a radical ring to it, but it is a fake radicalism. The slogans of democracy are execrable gibberish in the mouths of Poincaré, Herriot, Léon Blum—fleecers of France, jailers of Indochina, Algeria, and Morocco. But when the Chinese revolt in the name of the "rights of man," this is as unlike gibberish as the slogans of the French Revolution of 1789. In Hong Kong the Britannic vultures threatened at the time of the general strike to restore corporal punishment. "The rights of man and citizen" signified in Hong Kong the right for the Chinese not to be lashed by the British whip. To unmask the democratic decay of imperialism is to serve the revolution; to call gibberish the slogans of the insurrection of the oppressed is involuntarily to aid the imperialists.

A solid inoculation of Marxism might have protected the author from fatal mistakes of this nature. But Garine, on the whole, considers revolutionary doctrine to be "doctrinal rubbish." He is, as we see, one of those for whom the Revolution is only an "established state of affairs." Is this not remarkable? It is precisely because the Revolution is a "state of affairs"—that is, a stage in the development of a society conditioned by objective causes and subject to established laws—that a scientific mind can foresee the general direction of the process. Only through the study of the anatomy and physiology of society can one act on the current of events, basing oneself on scientific forecasts, not on dilettantist conjectures. The revolutionary who "disdains" revolutionary doctrine is worth no more than the healer who disdains the medical doctrine of which he is ignorant, or the engineer who rejects technology. The men who, without benefit of science, try to rectify the "state of affairs" known as sickness are called witch doctors or charlatans, and are prosecuted according to the law. Had there been a court to judge the charlatans of the Revolution, it is likely that Borodine, along with his Moscow inspirers, would have been severely condemned. Garine himself, I am afraid, would not have come off lightly.

Two figures in the novel oppose each other like the two poles of the national revolution: the venerable Cheng-dai, spiritual leader of the right wing of the Kuomintang, the saint and prophet of the bourgeoisie, and Hong, the young chief of the terrorists. Both of them are portrayed with great power. Cheng-dai incarnates ancient Chinese culture translated into the language of European culture. Under this refined cloak he "ennobles" the interests of all the ruling classes of China. Certainly, Cheng-dai desires national liberation, but he fears the masses more than the imperialists, he loathes the revolution more than the yoke weighing down the nation. If he marches at the forefront of the revolution it is only to abate it, to quell it, to extinguish it. He follows a policy of resistance on two fronts: against imperialism and against the revolution—the policy of Gandhi in India, and the policy that in different periods and differing forms the bourgeoisie followed in all longitudes and all latitudes. Passive resistance derives from the tendency of the bourgeoisie to channel the movement of the masses and to confiscate it.

When Garine says that Cheng-dai's influence is above politics, one can only shrug one's shoulders. The veiled politics of the "righteous," in China and in India, express in a sublime and abstractly moralistic form the conservative interests of the propertied classes. Cheng-dai's personal disinterest in no way conflicts with his political function: exploiters need the "righteous" just as church hierarchy needs saints.

Who gravitates around Cheng-dai? The novel replies with admirable precision. A world of "old mandarins, smugglers of opium and photographs, scholars who became bicycle dealers, lawyers of the Paris law school, intellectuals of all kinds." Behind them is grouped a solid bourgeoisie, allied with England and arming General Tang against the revolution. In anticipation of victory, Tang prepares to make Cheng-dai the head of the government. Both of them nevertheless continue to belong to the Kuomintang, administrated by Borodine and Garine.

When Tang attacks the city with his armies and sets out to slaughter the revolutionaries beginning with Borodine and Garine, his party comrades, they (with the help of Hong) mobilize and arm the unemployed. But after the victory over Tang, the chiefs try to change nothing of the previous situation. They cannot break their double tie with Cheng-dai because they have no confidence in the workers, coolies and revolutionary masses. They are themselves contaminated by the prejudice of Cheng-dai, whose chosen weapon they are.

In order not to rebuff the bourgeoisie, they have to oppose Hong. Who is he, and where does he come from?—"From misery." He is one of those who start a revolution, not join one when it is victorious. Having decided to kill the British governor of Hong Kong, Hong is concerned over one thing only: "When I have been condemned to death, it will be necessary to tell the young men to imitate me." Hong must be given a clear program: to arouse the workers, organize them, arm them, and set them against Cheng-dai as their enemy. But the Kuomintang bureaucracy seeks the friendship of Cheng-dai, rejects Hong and thus incenses him. Hong kills bankers and merchants, the very ones who "support the Kuomintang." Hong kills missionaries, ". . . those who teach men to endure misery must be punished, priests, Christians, or anyone else. . . ." If Hong cannot find his right way it is the fault of Borodine and Garine who have placed the revolution in the tow of bankers and merchants. Hong reflects the masses who are already awake but who have not yet rubbed their eyes or stretched their limbs. He tries with the revolver and knife to act *for* the masses, paralyzed by the Komintern agents. This, without adornment, is the truth of the Chinese revolution.

Nevertheless, the Canton government "wavers while trying not to fall from Garine and Borodine, who control the unions and the police, into the hands of Cheng-dai, who controls nothing but exists none the less." We have an almost complete picture of the diumvirate. The representatives of the Komintern have on their side the unions of Canton, the police, the cadets of the Wampoa Military Academy, the sympathy of the masses, and the aid of the Soviet Union. Cheng-dai has "moral authority," which is the prestige of the propertied classes. Cheng-dai's friends are part of an impotent government, benevolently supported by conciliators. Is this not the regime of the February revolution, the system of Kerensky and his troupe, with the sole difference that the role of the Mensheviks is played by pseudo-Bolsheviks! Borodine suspects nothing because he is disguised as a Bolshevik and takes his costume seriously.

The master plan of Garine and Borodine is to prohibit all Chinese and foreign ships making for port in Canton from stopping in Hong Kong. These men who take themselves for realistic revolutionaries hope, through this commercial blockade, to break the English hold on southern China. On the other hand, they in no way see fit, at the very outset, to overthrow the bourgeois government of Canton, which is only waiting for the moment to hand the revolution over to England. No, Borodine and Garine each day, hat in hand, knock at the door of the "government" asking that the revolutionary decree be promulgated. One of their comrades reminds Garine that in fact this government is a phantom. Garine remains unruffled. "Phantom or not," he replies, "so long as it runs—we need it." This is how the Pope needs relics that he himself fabricates out of wax and cotton. What lurks behind this policy that weakens and vilifies the revolution? The esteem of a revolutionary from the lower middle classes for a bourgeois of solid conservatism. So it is that the reddest of French extremists is always ready to fall to his knees before Poincaré.

Perhaps the masses of Canton are not yet ready to overthrow the government of the bourgeoisie? Out of this whole climate comes the conviction that without the opposition of the Komintern the phantom government would long ago have been overthrown under the pressure of the masses. Let us admit that the Cantonese working class is still too weak to establish its own power. What, generally speaking, is the weak point of the masses? Their training to submit to exploiters. In that case, the first duty of revolutionaries is to help the workers liberate themselves from their servile mentality. In spite of this, the work accomplished by the bureaucracy of the Komintern was diametrically opposed. It inculcated the masses with the notion of the necessity of submitting to the bourgeoisie and declared that the enemies of the bourgeoisie were its own.

Not to oppose Cheng-dai! But if Cheng-dai withdraws nevertheless, which is inevitable, that does not mean that Garine and Borodine are freed of their benevolent serfdom vis-à-vis the bourgeoisie. They will merely have chosen as the new gimmick of their hocus-pocus Chiang Kai-shek, scion of the same class and younger brother of Cheng-dai. Head of the Wampoa Military Academy, founded by the Bolsheviks, Chiang Kai-shek does not limit himself to passive opposition. He is willing to resort to blood—not in the plebian manner, in the manner of the masses, but in the military manner, and only within the limits that would permit the bourgeoisie to maintain unlimited power over the army. Borodine and Garine, in arming their enemies, disarm and reject their friends. And so begins the catastrophe.

Are we not, however, underestimating the influence on events of the revolutionary bureaucracy? No. It proved to be stronger than it thought, if not for good then for ill. The coolies who are only beginning to exist politically have need of bold direction. Hong needs a bold program. The revolution needs the energies of millions of men who are waking up. But Borodine and his bureaucrats need Cheng-dai and Chiang Kai-shek. They stifle Hong and prevent the worker from raising his head. Within a few months they will stifle the agrarian insurrection to avoid rebuffing the whole bourgeois brass of the army. Their power lies in their representing the Russian October Revolution, Bolshevism, international Communism. Having usurped the authority, the flag, and the subsidies of the greatest of revolutions, bureaucracy barred the way to another revolution that also had all the chances of becoming great.

The dialogue between Borodine and Hong is the most frightful indictment against Borodine and his Moscow inspirers. Hong, as always, is in search of decisive action. He demands the punishment of the most notable bourgeois. Borodine makes this singular reply: "One must not touch those who pay." "The revolution is not that simple," says Garine in turn. "The revolution means paying an army," Borodine cuttingly answers. These aphorisms contain all the elements of the noose that strangled the Chinese revolution. Borodine safeguarded the bourgeoisie who, in recompense, financed the "revolution." The money went to Chiang Kai-shek's army. Chiang Kai-shek's army exterminated the proletariat and liquidated the revolution. Was this really foreseeable? The bourgeoisie willingly pays only that army that protects it from the people. The army of the revolution does not wait for favors; it demands payment. This is called the dictatorship of the revolution. Hong successfully intervenes at workers' meetings and blasts the "Russians," devastators of the revolution. Hong's methods do not attain the goal either, but he is right, not Borodine. "Did the leaders of the Tai-Ping have Russian counselors? Or the leaders of the Boxers?" Had the Chinese revolution of 1924-1927 been left to itself, it might not have achieved victory immediately, but it would not have suffered humiliating capitulation and would have educated ranks of revolutionaries. Between the diumvirate of Canton and the one in Petrograd there is this tragic difference: in China, Bolshevism did not really exist. Under the name of Trotskyism it was declared counterrevolutionary doctrine and was persecuted by every method of calumny and repression. Where Kerensky did not succeed during the July revolution, Stalin in China succeeded ten years later.

Borodine and "all the Bolsheviks of his generation," attests Garine, "were marked by their fight with anarchists." This remark is essential to the author in order to prepare the reader for the battle between Borodine and Hong's partisans. Historically, this is false. Anarchy was unable to rear its head in Russia, not because the Bolsheviks successfully struggled against it, but because it had earlier dug its own grave. If anarchy does not remain within the four walls of intellectual cafes or editorial offices, but penetrates more deeply, it incarnates the psychology of despair among the masses, and represents the political punishment of the duperies of democracy and the betrayal of opportunism. The daring of Bolshevism in posing revolutionary problems and teaching their solutions left no room for the development of anarchy in Russia. However, even if Malraux's historic investigation is not precise, his story by compensation admirably shows how the political opportunism of Stalin-Borodine paved the way for anarchist terrorism in China.

Encouraged by the logic of this policy, Borodine agrees to outlaw the terrorists. The true revolutionaries, pushed aside from the path of the enterprise by the crimes of the Moscow leaders, now under the benediction of the Komintern, are declared outlaws by the bourgeoisie of Canton. They reply with acts of terrorism against the pseudo-revolutionaries who protect the paying upper classes. Borodine and Garine seize the terrorists and exterminate them, no longer to protect the bourgeoisie, but their own heads. This is how a policy of conciliation inevitably degenerates to the lowest level of felony.

The book is entitled *The Conquerors*. In the mind of the author, this double-edged title, concerning a revolution that takes the guise of imperialism, refers to Russian Bolsheviks, or more precisely, to a certain portion of them. The Conquerors? The Chinese masses arose for a revolutionary insurrection under the undeniable influence of the October *coup d'état* as their example, and of Bolshevism as their banner. But the "Conquerors" conquered nothing. On the contrary, they handed everything over to the enemy. If the Russian revolution produced the Chinese revolution, then the Russian epigones stifled it. Malraux does not make these deductions. He does not even seem to consider them. They only merge the more sharply from the depths of this remarkable novel.

Reply to Trotsky

by André Malraux

"A solid inoculation of Marxism might have protected Garine and the author from fatal mistakes." Let us note first of all that Borodine (who is a Marxist) and the bureau placed by the Third International in charge of Asian affairs (it too Marxist) commit these same mistakes. But before discussing the role of nonfictional participants in China's upheaval, let us first consider those things in Trotsky's critique that stem from the fictional aspects of the novel.

First the tone. When Trotsky, after having given a somewhat incomplete biography of Borodine, says "this man is not a professional revolutionary," he is right in comparison with Trotsky himself. But Borodine is a professional revolutionary compared to Garine and those of his entourage. An organizer of three insurrectional movements (in England, Spain, and China), and an official of the Communist International is, for the French reader, a professional revolutionary. Trotsky's secondary objections are all derived from this difference in viewpoint, and from his taking this novel "in which I have not been stingy with my judgments on the revolution" to be an affidavit. It is not my judgments that are found in *The Conquerors,* but the judgments of independent individuals, and above all (even where Garine is concerned) at particular moments, When I speak of "democratic gibberish" and "doctrinal rubbish," it is not the doctrine I am attacking, but the idiotic manner in which it was understood and revealed by these given characters. It seems to me that Trotsky, when judging certain aspects of Sun Yat-sen's *written* doctrine, uses harsher language than I do. I do not call gibberish the struggle against hunger and corporal punishment (the bare feet of those who died of hunger extending like a starched fringe on all sides of immense tarpaulins gave one ideas on the subject that are not likely to change). What I said is that suffering often had to be horrible to be recognized amid the claptrap of electoral meetings. At the beginning of 1925, to those who were dying of hunger one spoke of the right to vote, not the right to eat. Certainly, this book is first of all an accusation against the human

"Reply to Trotsky," by André Malraux. (Translated from the French by Beth Archer.) This first appeared as "Réponse à Trotsky" in *Nouvelle Revue Française,* No. 211 (April 1, 1931). Reprinted by permission of André Malraux.

condition. However, when Trotsky adds that there is no affinity between the author and the Revolution, that "the political teachings emerge from the book unbeknown to [me]," I am afraid he knows little about artistic creation. Revolutions do not make themselves, but neither do novels. This book is not a "fictionalized chronicle" of the Chinese revolution, because the main stress is placed on the relationship between individual and collective action, not on collective action alone. The documentation of *The Conquerors* is amenable to Trotsky's arguments, but only the documentation. He thinks that Garine is wrong; but Stalin thinks that he, Trotsky, is wrong. When, in his *My Life,* one reads the poignant account of his downfall, one forgets he is a Marxist, and perhaps he too forgets it. This novel is dominated by a *novelistic* vision. A talent for observation means nothing here; so complex an upheaval can be made understandable only by selecting. Since Trotsky grants my characters the quality of social symbols, we can now discuss the essential.

It would be absurd to contest the value of Marxism as a revolutionary doctrine. But a Marxist act is only possible as a function of class consciousness. As long as the masses believe it is more important to save their souls than to be happy and free, as long as they believe—as in China—that all life is provisional and prepares for a better life in which violence is forever removed, class consciousness remains secondary. It must be awakened, then developed; hence, Hong must be utilized.

But since the victory of the mercenary army marching on Canton will suppress any teaching, any organization of the proletariat, any revolutionary formation, it is first necessary to be victorious. Hence, utilize Cheng-dai.

"Wait a moment!" says the Marxist. "We are not making a revolution for the sake of revolution, but for the proletariat. Above all, we must preserve this budding proletariat, which is almost in the process of becoming. Otherwise our revolution makes no sense." How to place in the hands of a small Chinese proletariat, badly organized, barely aware of itself, a power that it is unable to take by itself; how to find that powerful bond between the workers and other classes (in Russia it was the demand for land)? How to discover the greatest need of the masses? For six years the International has given this question successive answers. In 1925 a widespread passion greatly simplified the problem—the hatred of England. The struggle against Hong Kong begins.

It is not primarily to "break England's hold over southern China" that the blockade is intended. With Hong Kong eliminated, the British Crown would find other courses of action. It is primarily for the Communists to show their efficacy. They strike at the head, and Hong Kong is the head because all China looks toward it. Borodine and Garine therefore have need of weapons. These weapons either they receive from the International which orders cooperation with the Kuomintang—with Cheng-dai—or they buy them. If they buy them, it is either with the money provided by the International's oil or with money from the Kuomintang. What can Borodine do except collaborate with the Kuomintang? I thought I had made clear, in *The Conquerors,* Borodine's dependence, on the one hand, on the Kuomintang, and on the other, on the International.

I fully understand that Trotsky's true adversary is precisely the International. He is less opposed to Garine than to Borodine, and less to Borodine than to Stalin. As a novelist, I take Canton as it appeared to me. The strength of the International in China, in 1925, was within very precise limits—namely, war. The Komintern did not have access to the Military Academy established by volunteers from the great families, directed by Chiang Kai-shek, and which fired on Gallen during a parade. As to the sympathy of the masses, the Komintern had it only when drumming up war. If the International chooses to talk about soviets rather than cannons, these men will follow Cheng-dai.[1] Gandhi, after all, has more influence on the masses of India than comrade Roy.

And so one has to play for time, convince the masses by showing them proof of where their true interests lie: the International agrees to dissolve the Chinese Communist Party in the Kuomintang.

And Trotsky asseverates: "You have Hong shot and you place yourselves in the hands of Cheng-dai, whose chosen weapon you are." He forgets that if Garine is Cheng-dai's chosen weapon, it is in order to have him killed, and Borodine knows that if he passes the decree against the terrorists, one of the consequences will be precisely the death of Cheng-dai. As to Hong, he represents not the proletariat but anarchy; he has never been a worker. Working at first in collaboration with the Bolsheviks, he later attacks them and accepts only his own orders. He must be convinced? Hong is not capable of being convinced. He does not care a fig for the future of the proletariat; the proletariat interests him only in its heroism. He too is Chinese and believes in justice—as does Cheng-dai—but not in the same kind. His aim is ethical, not political, and it is hopeless. I know what is captivating about this figure, its resolution and its savage purity. But I cannot forget that when Lenin and Trotsky came across Hongs they had the Cheka take care of relations with them.

The International knows it has to work fast. Its agreement with the Kuomintang, from one victory to another, is very reminiscent of stories of the starving who burn themselves in order to stay awake, for fear of being killed as soon as sleep falls upon them. Will the International

---

[1] The comparison that Trotsky makes between the Mensheviks and the Kuomintang is fascinating; but the Mensheviks waged an unpopular war while the Cantonese waged an enthusiastically supported one. (A revolution in France might have been *attempted* at the beginning of 1918. In August, 1914, the attempt would have been hopeless.)

manage in time to create a class consciousness and a program that will
allow it to stamp out the right wing of the Kuomintang, or on the contrary, will the right wing become sufficiently strong to destroy the International? That this is what Trotsky calls adventurism is quite certain
(adventurism that will soon be encountered, and in still more complicated
form, in India, and Indochina, where 800 million men are involved).
But what can the revolutionary do who refuses to participate in this
adventurism? "What is essential," says Trotsky, "is not to mix ranks or
banners."

Could the International maintain autonomous organizations? I think
it did not accept with a light heart, no matter what it said, the fusion of
the Chinese Communist Party with the Kuomintang. The catastrophe
that emerged from this union is known everywhere through detailed reports of its difficulties. There was no choice. I said that the objective of
the International was to give the proletariat, as quickly as possible, the
class consciousness it needed to attempt a seizure of power; the most
vigorous obstacle to class consciousness at that time was social consciousness. Every militant Chinese belonged to one of those innumerable
societies, so-called secret societies, whose history is the history of China
since 1911. The Kuomintang was the most powerful among them. All
other things being equal, the Kuomintang is more like our order of
Masons than our reactionary party. Before the fusion, Communist doctrine was the doctrine of a burgeoning society; immediately after, it
became the doctrine of the society with the largest membership. Of the
fifty million workers to be reached only two million were taken in by
the factories, and one and a half million consisted of women and children.
Preparation in theory was infinitesimal and excessively oral. Not a single
book on the subject. (We are still far from 1927, when a gigantic publishing enterprise follows behind the "Army of Steel.") Skilled workers,
particularly mechanics—one of the most powerful of the Cantonese
unions—still adhered to the *right* wing of the Kuomintang. Because of
its nature of rival society, the Kuomintang would not have tolerated that
the Communist Party be considered responsible for the victories; it would
not have allowed the Communists to make use of the enormous propaganda machine that it eventually handed over to them piece by piece,
in exchange for those victories. Refusal of the fusion would immediately
have unleashed fighting. The Communists were beaten when they had
their own army; they would surely have been defeated when they were
still without one. The contest in Canton would have been what it was
in Shanghai: cadets against union militia, and Chiang Kai-shek would
subsequently not even have had to fight the Red army. Let us go even
farther. The power once seized ("If we had had one chance in four to
last a year," says Borodine today, "we would have tried it"), the Kuomintang would reasonably have blocked Canton, which would have been
emptied out by sheer unemployment, as occurred later in Hankow.

By saying "party first," Trotsky defends a revolutionary principle whose value and supremacy one cannot deny. But perhaps one should distinguish, in the theory behind this principle, between two elements: on the one hand, discussion of a state of fact—the fusion, the union with Cheng-dai. I think that the Chinese Communist Party, at that moment, had only that choice or disappearance; disappearance that it might in fact have preferred on the assumption that it would only be temporary. (It might have become a clandestine party, but the slow strangulation of the Peking Communists by Chiang Tso-ling proves that we are not in a country of liberalism.) On the other hand, there was the possibility of a discussion of principle; for the International does not so much say: "constraint"; it rather says: "conciliation and forethought."

It is, I think, this second element that Trotsky holds dear, for its value is lasting. I can only admire the heroic—in the most realistic sense of the word—role that Trotsky demands of the proletariat. But I must confront him with the facts and point out that the stronger the Cheka (the Kuomintang controlled propaganda, not the secret police) from Hankow on, the more possible a solution. In bestowing on my characters the honor of considering them symbols, Trotsky takes them out of time; my defense is to put them back in.

André Malraux

by Edmund Wilson

Nobody on our side of the Atlantic has yet written anything, so far as I know, about André Malraux, the French novelist; and, though I have read only two of his half-dozen books and am unable to deal with his work in any thoroughgoing fashion, I want to bring this fascinating and profitable writer to the attention of American readers. If the recent apotheosis of André Gide has been tending to discourage you with French literature, you will be glad to see the French genius cropping up again in a field where you would least expect it. A fault of much French writing lately has been that it has all seemed to be steeped in the atmosphere of the literary world of Paris, with its smug and self-conscious dependence on the French literary tradition. But M. André Malraux turns up a long way from Paris, and he nowhere—at any rate, in either of the books I have read—pays his pious respects to Racine.

M. Malraux first visited the orient at the age of twenty-three as head of an archeological expedition to Indochina; but he presently dropped the cultural problems of ancient Cambodia for the political problems of the present. The orient that Malraux writes about is not the orient of *Madame Butterfly*. He published in 1928 a novel called *Les Conquérants*, which dealt with the events of the Chinese revolution in 1925. The reader who picked up this book was dazzled by an unhoped-for searchlight into a region which had previously seemed distant and dim. Here was a picture, based evidently on intimate knowledge, of the conflict of forces in modern China, with every figure, oriental or European, thrown into brilliant relief, every Chinese water-front or street—junks and steamers, pagodas, bars and banks—made distinctly and solidly visible. And here was something even more remarkable—something one had not yet found in contemporary fiction to the same degree: the psychological atmosphere of stress, with its own peculiar passions and moralities, its tense and sustained attitudes, which is coming to be felt throughout the world. A translation of *Les Conquérants* (*The Conquerors*)—made, I am told,

"André Malraux." From *The Shores of Light* (New York: Farrar, Straus and Co., Inc., 1952), by Edmund Wilson. Copyright 1952 by Edmund Wilson. (The article also appeared in the *New Republic*, August 9, 1933.) Reprinted by permission of Edmund Wilson.

at Aldous Huxley's suggestion—has been brought out in England, but seems to have had no success at all. I do not know whether the odious role that is played in the book by the British has had anything to do with this. The novel has done no better here. Harcourt, Brace brought over sheets and sold only eight hundred copies. Yet I urge American and English publishers—especially now that reviewers are beginning to take Jules Romains as solemnly as he takes himself—to consider bringing out a translation of Malraux's new and even more important novel, *La Condition Humaine*.

I have spoken of Malraux's achievement in conveying the sense of strain produced by the antagonisms of modern society. The publication of *Les Conquérants* was followed, in *La Nouvelle Revue Française*, by a controversy between Malraux and Trotsky. (Trotsky's two papers are included in his *Problems of the Chinese Revolution*.) It was Trotsky's complaint that Malraux, though he had chosen a revolutionist for hero, had "introduced into his observations a small note of blasé superiority, seeming to excuse himself for his transient contact with the insurrection of the Chinese people, as much perhaps to himself as to the academic mandarins in France and the traffickers in spiritual opium." This is putting it a little too strongly; but it is true that Malraux's hero, Garine, has a certain alloy of old-fashioned romanticism. There are moments when he gives the impression of being simply another René or Manfred, somber, tortured, terrifying, a solitary savage rebel, seeking in the revolution what René had sought in the American forests, grasping at his bureau of propaganda with the same sort of desperation that Byron had brought to Greece. Part Swiss and part Russian, formerly an anarchist, Garine hates the bourgeoisie without real fellow-feeling for the masses:

> "I don't love humanity. I don't love even the poor, the people—those, in fact, for whom I am fighting." "But you like them better than the others." . . . "I like them better, but only because they're beaten. Yes: on the whole, they have more feeling, more humanity, than the others—they have the virtues of the beaten. What's absolutely certain, however, is that I have nothing but hatred and disgust for the bourgeoisie from which I come. But as for the others, I know very well that they'd become quite abject as soon as we'd conquered together. We have our struggle in common—that's clear, at any rate."

His dominant passion, he admits, is for power, and in the final scenes of the story, worn out with his work and dying of malaria and dysentery, he declares in his delirium that he now regrets having chosen to serve the Communists instead of England, since it is England that commands the real power. Yet in spite of his doubt and his egoism, he sticks by the revolution and is receiving, on the final page, the dispatches that bring the news of victory. Trotsky has expressed the opinion that what Garine needed was "a good inoculation of Marxism." Malraux retorted to this that there was something of Garine in Trotsky—pointing out that when you read in Trotsky's autobiography "the moving account of his fall, you forget that he is a Marxist, and perhaps he forgets it himself." He also protested that *Les Conquérants* was not—what Trotsky had called it— a "novelized chronicle" of the Chinese revolution. "The principal emphasis," he says, "is on the relation between individuals and a collective action, not on the collective action alone." "The book," he explains, "is first of all a presentation of the human situation (*une accusation de la condition humaine*)."

André Malraux's new novel has this phrase for its title, *La Condition Humaine,* and it develops in a more explicit way the ideas implicit in *Les Conquérants. La Condition Humaine* is a much more ambitious and a more remarkable book than *Les Conquérants.* In the latter, Garine pretty well holds the spotlight, and there is an "I" who plays the role of Dr. Watson, deeply agitated by his hero's every utterance and standing by, indefatigably wide-eyed, while Garine receives portentous telegrams. He also plays the role of Conrad's Marlow. He is, in fact, our old friend the fictional observer who, from a more or less conventional point of view, looks on at a mystery or a moral problem. In this new book, however, the novelist gets rid of his European observer and, meeting Trotsky's challenge, attacks the revolution directly. Dealing with cultures the most diverse, moral systems the most irreconcilable, he establishes a position outside them which enables him to dispense with the formulas alike of the "academic mandarins" and of the orthodox Communists. I do not know of any modern book which dramatizes so successfully such varied national and social types. Beside it, even E. M. Forster's admirable *A Passage to India* appears a little provincial; you even—what rarely happens nowadays to the reader of a French novel—forget that author is French. You see juxtaposed the old Buddhist China and its half-Europeanized children; the vaporing imagination of ruined aristocratic Europe and the single-minded will to money of the European business king; the American Calvinist missionary unwittingly building the character of the young Chinese terrorist; and—growing up under all the rest like the elm that splits the pavement—the new world of the revolutionary Marxist which is reorienting all the moralities. Nor is this handled in the manner of the journalist, as Paul Morand might have done it. The personalities of Malraux's characters are organically created and thoroughly explored. We not only witness their acts and see them in relation to the forces of the social-political scene: we share their most intimate sensations.

The handling of this huge and complicated subject must have given the author a good deal of trouble. He evidently sat down like an engineer to the problem of designing a structure that would meet a new set of conditions; and an occasional clumsiness of mechanics appears. The device of presenting in dramatic scenes the exposition of political events, to which we owe Garine and his eternal dispatches, here appears as a series of conversations so exhaustive and so perfectly to the point in their function of political analysis as—in spite of the author's efforts to particularize the characters—occasionally to lack plausibility. And we are sometimes thrown off the track when a thesis that deals with psychology comes butting into a paragraph devoted to explaining the "objective conditions" or when a description that had seemed as external as a colored picture postcard of Shanghai takes a sudden subjective turn.

Yet, on the whole, the author has met these problems with amazing originality and skill. He has a genius for effects of contrast. The opening of *La Condition Humaine,* which follows the activities of a Communist group—a Chinese, a half-breed Jap, a Belgian, and a Russian—the night before the insurrection, is a masterly dramatization. The initial inability of Tchen to bring himself to murder the man from whom he must steal the orders for the guns and his immediate realization afterwards of his terrorist's vocation; Baron Clappique's romances in the night club and his subsequent revelation of his ignoble trade; the confession of Kyo's wife that, on the eve of the insurrection, she has been unfaithful to him, and its repercussions on revolutionary solidarity; Tchen's report of what he has done and felt to his Buddhist-sociologist master, Gisors, and Gisors' prompt liquidation of his own anxiety and horror in an opium dream, in which the ripples from a boat on a lake full of water-lilies spread out to sweep all horror and anxiety into the purity and peace of the Divine—followed immediately by the spectacle of the real boat putting out in the Shanghai harbor to steal the guns for the insurrection: each one of these shocks is a flash that illuminates the conflicts and anomalies of the tense international city.

I have spoken of Malraux's success in avoiding conventional formulas. Where, however, is his own center? What is his frame of reference? What he wants to show us, he says, is the human situation. What is his view of the human situation? What every human being wants, he makes his philosopher Gisors explain, is not the object of his ambition itself, but to escape from the conditions of life, to give oneself the illusion of being God. Gisors attains this through opium; Tchen through assassination— an act in which he immolates himself, is the destroyed as well as the destroyer; Ferral, the French businessman, tries to reach it through his sexual relations, in which he imagines himself in the roles of both possessed and possessor; even the rickety Baron Clappique finds it at the gambling table, where he identifies himself with the roulette ball, the master of both gain and loss; Kyo, the Japanese, rises above life when, for the sake of the revolution, he commits hara-kiri with cyanide; and Katov, the Russian Communist, gives his cyanide to brother Communists whose morale is weaker than his, when they have all been condemned to be burnt in the furnace of a locomotive. Tchen, Malraux lets us know, has saved his soul; Kyo has saved his, and more nobly; and Katov most nobly of all, because he can only fulfill himself by sacrificing himself to others. There is, then, something else in the book besides the mere theme of escape from the human situation. The events described in *La Condition Humaine,* which occurred in 1927, must still have been going on while *Les Conquérants* was being written. At the end of the earlier novel, the Chinese revolution—there presented as the work of Garine as well as of Chiang Kai-shek—is assumed to be already victorious; in the later, the Communists fail, sold out by Chiang Kai-shek to the interests of Western capital and paralyzed by the faulty policy of the Comintern itself. Malraux seems, in line with Trotsky's advice, to have made some progress in Marxism. His interpretation of recent events seems now essentially Marxist—though he never, as I have said, slips into the facile formulas; and though the criticism his characters make of the line of the Comintern is more or less that of Trotsky, he maintains in relation to Trotsky, too, an attitude of independence. Marxism, Gisors observes, is not a doctrine but a will; and it is simply that, in Malraux's world, the only men he respects are animated by the Marxist will. *La Condition Humaine* ends with Gisors, who has lost his son Kyo, sinking back into the culture of the East and lighting up the opium pipe, while May, Kyo's widow, sets out for Moscow.

August 9, 1933

M. Malraux, on reading this article, wrote me the following letter:

Le 2 oct. [1933]
Monsieur—Je trouve à mon retour à Paris l'article que vous voulez bien me consacrer.

Comme je vous réponds en suivant cet article permettez-moi d'abord quelques précisions. Je n'ai publié, en plus des livres que vous avez lus, qu'un livre et une plaquette (que je vous envoie)—le reste est très court et sans importance. D'autre part, mon père n'etait pas fonctionnaire en Indochine.[1] Je suis allé en Asie à 23 ans, comme chargé de mission archéologique. J'ai alors abandonné l'archéologie, organisé le mouvement Jeune-Annam, puis suis devenu commissaire du Kuomintang en Indochine et enfin à Canton.

Il y a du vrai dans ce que dit Trotsky de Garine, et dans ce que vous en dites vous-même. Peut-être faudrait-il pourtant tenir compte d'une certaine objectivité. Que ce personnage soit marxiste, certes non. Peut-être a-t-il tort, mais c'était ainsi. Il y avait à Canton en 1927 (ce fut très différent en 1927) singulièrement plus d'aventuriers révolutionnaires que de marxistes. Et lorsque Borodine discutait avec Sun-Yat-Sen, il n'était jamais question de lutte de classes.—Je ne voudrais pas faire de cela un argument, mais une nuance. Car il est fort vrai que le rôle joué dans mes livres par l'objectivité

---

[1] This corrects an erroneous statement that I had made in the original version of my article. [E. W.]

n'est pas de premier plan, et que *Les Conquérants* sont un roman "Expressioniste" comme, toutes proportions gardées, *Wuthering Heights* ou les *Karamazoff.*

Vous dites très justement que *La Condition humaine* développe certaines idées implicites dans *Les Conquérants.* Et aussi que le livre est meilleur (à la verité, du moins, c'est le seul que j'aime). Ma construction, en effet, ne pourrait rejoindre celle d'un écrivain comme Morand: ses types reposent sur l'observation ironique, le mien sur le besoin de traduire à travers des personnages un certain ordre de valeurs éthiques.

Ne voyez en ce semblant de discussion qu'un moyen de remercier plus longuement le premier critique, en Amérique, qui s'intéresse a ce que j'écris et croyez, je vous prie, Monsieur, à ma sympathie artistique, car je suis depuis longtemps l'effort de la *New Republic.*

André Malraux

Oct. 2

[Dear Sir,

On my return from Paris, I find the article which you were good enough to devote to me.

In replying to this article, let me first of all make a few corrections. In addition to the books you have read, I have published only one book and one pamphlet (which I am sending you)—everything else I have written is very brief and unimportant. Another point: my father was not a functionary in Indochina. I went to Asia when I was twenty-three, in charge of an archeological mission. Then I abandoned archeology, organized the Jeune-Annam movement, and later became a commissioner of the Kuomintang in Indochina and finally at Canton.

There is some truth in what Trotsky said about Garine, and in what you say about him yourself, but perhaps one ought to retain a certain objectivity. This person was certainly not a Marxist. Perhaps he was wrong, but that is the way it was. At Canton in 1927 (for it was very different then, in 1927), there were remarkably more revolutionary adventurers than there were Marxists. And when Borodine argued with Sun Yat-sen, there was never any question of the class struggle.—I don't want to make a debate about this, but only to suggest a nuance. For it is certainly true that the role played by objectivity in my books is not of the first rank and that *The Conquerors* is an "expressionist" novel: allowing for all necessary distinctions, like *Wuthering Heights* or *Karamazov.*

You are quite right to say that *Man's Fate* develops certain ideas implicit in *The Conquerors.* And also that this is a better book (at least, to tell the truth, it is the only one that I really like). My method of construction, indeed, could not possibly resemble that of a writer like Morand: his characters rest upon ironic observation, and mine on the need to translate a certain order of ethical values by means of human persons.

I hope you will realize that these remarks are only a means of thanking at greater length the first American critic who has interested himself in what I write; and please believe in my artistic fellow feelings, for I have been a follower of the *New Republic* for a long time.

André Malraux]

The Power and the Glory

by W. M. Frohock

". . . One of the secret and highest forms of the Power and the Glory of being a man."

—THE CREATIVE ACT, p. 216

For many readers the quintessence of Malraux is summed up in the scene at the beginning of *Man's Fate*. Tchen stands in the hotel room by the bed of the sleeping man he has been sent to murder and debates with himself whether to lift the mosquito netting or to drive his blade through the material into the receptive flesh. This is an act of irreparable violence; we are in the presence of death; the atmosphere is unbearably tense; the motive of the murder is political and yet the motives of the murderer transcend politics; politics has committed an intellectual to a career of action (or possibly vice versa); the action fails to satisfy either the demands of his intellect or those of his emotions; and we are trying to understand the psychology of the killer and fathom the great loneliness which overwhelms him as it will overwhelm so many other characters in the story. The action is full of despair, anguish, loneliness, violence, and sudden death. We are plunged into a dynamic situation; events already in motion here on the first page are of such import that a hundred pages later we shall still be struggling to catch up.

Tchen tenterait-il de lever la moustiquaire? Frapperait-il au travers? L'angoisse lui tordait l'estomac; il connaissait sa propre fermeté, mais n'était capable en cet instant que d'y songer avec hébétude, fasciné par ce tas de mousseline blanche qui tombait du plafond sur un corps moins visible qu'une ombre, et d'où sortait seulement ce pied à demi incliné par le sommeil, vivant quand même—de la chair d'homme. La seule lumière venait du building voisin: un grand rectangle d'électricité pâle, coupé par les barreaux de la fenêtre dont l'un rayait le lit juste au-dessous du pied comme pour en accentuer le volume et la vie. Quatre ou cinq klaxons grincèrent à la fois. Découvert? Combattre, combattre des ennemis qui se défendent, des ennemis éveillés, quelle délivrance!

31

La vague de vacarme retomba: quelque embarras de voitures (il y avait encore des embarras de voitures, là-bas, dans le monde des hommes . . .). Il se retrouva en face de la grande tache molle de la mousseline et du rectangle de lumière, immobiles dans cette nuit où le temps n'existait plus. (P. 15.)

Should Tchen try to raise the netting? Or strike through it? Anxiety twisted his stomach. He knew his own determination, but could think of it now only through a daze, fascinated by the white shape of the muslin that fell from the ceiling over a body less visible than the shadow, out of which came a single foot, turned half-slantwise in sleep, but alive—human flesh. The only light came from the next building, a great rectangle of pale electric light, cut by the bars of the window, one of which cut a line across the bed just below the foot as if to accentuate its volume and life. Four or five auto horns screeched at once. Discovered? To fight, fight waking enemies who defend themselves, what a relief!

The wave of racket fell back: some traffic jam (there were still traffic jams off there, in the world of men . . .). He came to himself before the great soft white streak of the muslin and the rectangle of light, unmoving in this night when time did not exist.

The two questions state the immediate psychological problem and introduce a single visual element, the netting. The declarative sentence following goes from the physical effect of Tchen's nervous tension, through the reason for it, back to the object of his fascination, adds a topographical element (since the netting hangs from the ceiling the scene must be a room), moves Tchen's eye from the net to the body just barely visible under it, fastens his glance on the foot, and ends with a leap from the concrete physical detail to the abstract, almost metaphysical consideration of its qualities, life and humanity—thus returning from the exterior detail to the mind behind the eye. The next sentence first adds more topographical information (the room is in a city since there is a building close by), adds the visual image of the light falling on the bed, under which the foot of the sleeper stands out, and returns to the renewed consideration of the abstraction, life. Now comes the sudden impingement of the world outside the drama, the racket of the auto horns, followed by the question asked by the alerted consciousness, now aware of something outside its own preoccupations; the question is followed in its turn again by the reversion of the consciousness to its own problem —of which the hesitation about the mosquito bar is only a symptom— of inflicting death. After this the consciousness turns once more to the exterior and identifies the cause of the commotion, and then twists back to contemplate its own condition in the realization that there are now two worlds, distinct from each other, which it must simultaneously inhabit. And the final sentence returns Tchen to the scene in the room but ends in another abstraction: the suspension of time.

Thus the style involves a constant shuttling of the consciousness between the mind and the world outside, frequently within the confines of the same sentence. Exposition—the actual furnishing of the scene—and the establishment of Tchen's mental state are accomplished in alternate touches, with the alternations taking place so rapidly that they seem simultaneous to the reader, much as the successive stills in a movie create the illusion of motion. Malraux has now dropped the dramatic present tense of *The Conquerors,* trusting the rapidity of the images and the immense tension of Tchen's nerves to give the illusion of immediacy.

Meanwhile, as the passage progresses, a picture emerges which is essentially baroque: the contrast of the deep shadow with the harsh highlight on the bed matches the equally violent contrast between the inherent potential violence of Tchen's act and his complete physical quiescence. But the picture becomes completely visible only late in the passage, through the presentation of one detail at a time, and the order in which the detail is arranged in itself adds to the significance of the picture. For the man on the bed possesses a paper, with which the revolutionists can obtain the arms they need to set off the revolt of Shanghai. The paper must be obtained secretly; it must not be missed; there must be no outcry. The weapon must be the silent knife. Tchen must kill by stealth, take the paper, return to Headquarters, and set off a chain of momentous events. But the reader at this point does not know who Tchen is, or why he is here, or where "here" may be, or the identity of the man on the bed. Malraux thus opens his story with a picture which shows one human figure identified only by name, another who is nameless, an act of decisive violence, and a more detailed presentation of the torture of the figure to whom the performance is entrusted. By a curious paradox, a method which at least in part consists of exploiting only the most immediately relevant, specific, and above all concrete detail achieves a great deal of generality. The creature on the bed, thanks to the completely dominant detail of the highlighted foot, has but one characteristic, the fact that he is alive. Presently this life will be extinguished, and the important fact will be not that this unknown has died but that a life has been taken—to have the full meaning that the passage confers upon it, the verb "kill" must have no object. Thus the movement of feeling in the passage, as opposed to the movement of the style between alternate visual images and mental states, here goes from concrete statement toward metaphysics.

For Malraux is dealing with his favorite and perhaps only subject, "one man and his destiny." We are already in the presence of the great themes of *Man's Fate.* "A man," Kyo Gisors will remark later in the story, "resembles his suffering" (p. 48). The causes of Tchen's suffering will be double: a fascination with death such that he will eventually die by his own choice, for the relief of his own *Angst,* and in circumstances such that he is practically a suicide; at the same time the experience of having killed which will shut him away in that private world he is discovering in this passage, as he stands with knife in hand, preparing to strike. Meanwhile, the paragraph also introduces the fundamental problem of the relation of the individual revolutionist to the revolutionary action in which, as an individual, he expects satisfactions entirely distinct from the ends of the revolution itself—thus joining at the start of *Man's Fate* the presiding theme of *The Royal Way* with the presiding theme of *The Conquerors*. These themes are already visible as the story opens. In its first twenty pages, Malraux's investigation of man's destiny is thus well under way.

Primarily, *Man's Fate* is a sequence of events. Tchen kills his man and gets the paper, goes back to party Headquarters; Kyo takes the paper to the go-between who can arrange to get the Communist raiders aboard the steamer lying in the harbor laden with arms; holding up the crew, loading the launch with arms, and distributing them case by case to the headquarters of the neighborhood groups is a matter of a few hours. And events follow each other at this rate throughout the novel. But action itself is not all—the shortness of time forces the events into a special pattern, and in the pattern itself, the rhythm of the events, we see the outlines of tragedy. And recognition of the tragic nature of the pattern and rhythm is further impressed upon us by the great episode of Katov's death—Malraux's habitual contradiction of the logic of the events themselves. Meanwhile, there are other important figures on the edges of the tragic action, who have their own lives and their own suffering: Tchen the terrorist, Clappique the mythomaniac, Ferral the man in search of power, Kyo's old father Gisors, and Hemmelrich the phonograph merchant. Malraux's exploration of the human lot is no longer concerned with a single representative individual but with a number. And yet, finally, it is the central tragedy of the novel which reveals the full meaning of these other lives: and to the tragedy, and the figures of Kyo and Katov, one must at length return for the final summing up.

All of these aspects of the novel must concern us: the action, its compression in time, the resulting pattern and rhythm, the tragic emotion which emerges from them, the effect of Katov's death, the plights of the ancillary characters and *their* significance, and their relation to the central tragedy.

After Tchen has murdered the sleeper and made off with the precious paper, events move rapidly through a night crowded with action. From Headquarters, after Tchen's return, Kyo Gisors and Katov set off together, the first to find Baron Clappique, who will negotiate for the delivery of the arms, and the second to check on preparations for the insurrection. Kyo finds his man entertaining two trollops in a night club called the Black Cat and sends him off on the errand, then returns to his father's house to await word of Clappique's success. He spends some time talking with his father about Clappique's curious mentality, and is plunged into bitterness by learning from his wife, May, that during the afternoon she has been unfaithful to him. Clappique now returns to report gaily that all is well and Kyo goes out to dispatch Katov with the raiding party who will take the arms off the *S.S. Shantung* by force. As he leaves, Tchen arrives to talk with old Gisors about the psychic aspects of murder. After this conversation we pick up the raiders, board the *Shantung,* hijack the arms, and finish distributing them to the local insurrection groups, who even now are preparing their attack.

The next morning, Ferral is busy buying off Chiang Kai-shek. We learn his background and history, hear him interview the head of the European police about countermeasures against the strike, then go out with him in his car; toward noon we see him surrounded by the crowd that has poured into the streets with the start of the general strike, his car stopped and the chauffeur deserting him.

The scene shifts. We are with Tchen in the first violent fighting. The action is the bloodiest in the book. And all over Shanghai similar fights are going on. By the end of the afternoon, the insurrection clearly has the upper hand.

Again the scene shifts back to Ferral's office, where he negotiates further with a Chinese colonel to bribe Chiang. Ferral promises the decisive fifty million. Then afterward, he joins his mistress, Valérie, and we witness a curious erotic episode involving a light switch.

Another change of scene and we pick up Kyo, Katov, and Tchen as they wait for Chiang's artillery to come and finish off the government's armored train. They have heard of the order to turn over their arms to Chiang. At this point, Tchen proposes the murder of the renegade general. Without arms, the Communists will be completely at Chiang's mercy.

Now there is a five-day break for Kyo and Tchen to go to Hankow. They interview Vologuine, the delegate from the Moscow International, and also talk to Kyo's old friend Possoz. The answer is categorical: it is not expedient for the party to support the Shanghai insurrectionists. The latter are free, at most, to work out their own salvation when and as they can. Tchen departs for Shanghai determined to kill Chiang, and Kyo follows him, choosing the forlorn hope of organizing some sort of local resistance in preference to seeking his own safety.

There is a break of another two weeks before we open on Clappique learning from the policeman Chpilewski that his part in getting the arms has been discovered and that he will do well to be out of Shanghai in forty-eight hours. Learning also that the police want Kyo, Clappique starts for Gisors' house to pass the word.

From him we pick up Tchen, striding along the street in European clothes with a bomb in his brief case. He meets the old clergyman who brought him up and they walk together for a way discussing Tchen's anxieties. Then Tchen posts his two confederates and himself takes up a

stand in an antique shop in the street where Chiang's car must pass. Unfortunately the dealer, seeing a sale lost when Tchen starts for the door,
seizes Tchen's arm and by the time Tchen has freed himself the car has
disappeared. The confederates also miss their chance. They now retire
to Hemmelrich's phonograph shop, where the latter has to refuse them
shelter because of the danger to his wife and child. Tchen reveals a new
plan to his colleagues: he will throw himself, with the bomb, under
Chiang's car.

We return to Clappique, who is at Gisors' house on a double errand:
to warn Kyo and to borrow the money to ship out of Shanghai. He buys
a few water colors for Ferral from Kyo's uncle, the Japanese painter
Kama, and they discuss, briefly, the difference between Eastern and Western art. Kyo refuses to leave Shanghai and promises to meet Clappique
between eleven and eleven-thirty at the Black Cat club with some money.
We learn that now, much too late, word has come from Hankow for the
insurrection to keep its arms. As Kyo leaves the house May asks to come
with him; he first refuses because of the danger, then relents and allows
her to share it.

We switch back to Hemmelrich's shop and Katov. Both men know
that a showdown has come. Hemmelrich berates Katov violently because
he, Hemmelrich, is not free to join the others in their last stand.

We switch to Ferral, going to join his mistress. He discovers that she
has played him a trick: another man is also waiting for her; she has gone
off with still another admirer, leaving each of the disappointed men a
note saying that the other will explain. Ferral buys out a pet shop and
releases the birds and animals in her room. Then, in a bar, he meets old
Gisors, who has come out to gather what news he can, and they have a
quiet conversation in which the old man tells him what is meant by *la
condition humaine*. Still enraged by the way Valérie has humiliated him,
Ferral goes away completely exasperated, picks up a courtesan, and, to
relieve his own anguish, purposely humiliates her.

Tchen is now waiting with his bomb. Chiang's auto approaches. Tchen
throws himself beneath the wheels. In a moment he recovers consciousness, horribly mangled, and has just strength enough to put the barrel
of his pistol in his mouth and pull the trigger. He never knows that
Chiang was not in the car.

A few minutes later we are in the Black Cat with Clappique, who has
learned that all the party headquarters are now surrounded by police. A
bit early for his rendezvous with Kyo, he goes upstairs and loses himself
in a game of roulette. When he comes out the hour of meeting is long
past and he wanders off to find a prostitute.

Thus unwarned, Kyo and May leave the Black Cat. Near Headquarters they are caught by the police. May is left unconscious on the side-
walk. Kyo is taken off to jail.

Now we pick up Hemmelrich, who has come back to his shop at midnight to find it wrecked by a bomb and his wife and child killed. Free at last to act as he wants, he goes off to join Katov and the others in the last fight against the Nationalists.

Again we rejoin Clappique, who has just met Gisors. Gisors asks him to go to König, the chief of Chiang's police, to plead for Kyo. Gisors goes but gets a bitter refusal.

Following this we move to party Headquarters. The Communists have exhausted their ammunition and are being wiped out. Katov is wounded and made prisoner. Hemmelrich slips out the back way, kills an enemy almost with his bare hands, and escapes to freedom.

From here we go to the prison where Kyo is confined with the political prisoners. A guard beats him when he protests the maltreatment of a madman, but Kyo succeeds with a few dollars in bribing him to stop. Kyo is taken to König, who offers him freedom if he will inform on his fellows. Kyo refuses and is returned to prison.

Now we follow Clappique again. With no money and nearly insane, with fear, he disguises himself as a sailor carrying a set of new brooms, goes aboard a steamer, and makes good his escape. Ferral leaves for Europe by the same ship.

We return to Kyo, who is in the recreation shed of a school where the prisoners are gathered for execution. With him are Hemmelrich's partner Lou, Tchen's confederate Souen, and others. By ones and twos the men are taken out to be shot, or, if important personages in the insurrection, burned alive. Kyo takes the cyanide he has been carrying. Katov gives his pellet to two comrades whose nerve has failed them and accepts death by fire for himself.

Fade out, now, to the next day at Gisors' house. The old man and May have recovered Kyo's body. Gisors, temporarily as it turns out, has given up smoking opium.

Next, after a break of some months, Ferral is in Paris pleading with a group of bankers and the finance minister for help to keep his great enterprise afloat. Various piddling objections are raised. Ferral is helpless. We do not know definitely that aid is refused, but we see clearly that he has become an absurd suppliant, absurdly frustrated.

The last scene is in Kobe, where Gisors is now living with Kama the painter. May invites him to go with her to Moscow, where she can go on with medicine and where there is a teaching job for him. He has no heart for the trip and prefers to stay here with his opium. We learn from May that Hemmelrich is happy, working in a generator plant under the Five-Year Plan, and that Pei, Tchen's other confederate, is there as a fellow-traveling revolutionary writer. Then in farewell she tells the old man that she has almost ceased to weep.

Certainly Malraux's account, thus summarized, is the account of a defeat. Taken at greater length, however, it is something else. The difference is precisely the difference between prose and poetry—especially Malraux's poetry. And what makes the difference is, first, the way the action is compressed in time and, second, the pattern and rhythm resulting from the compression.

At half after midnight of March 21 Tchen kills his man. At one he is back in the phonograph shop. At two Kyo is in the Black Cat looking for Clappique. In the next two hours Clappique does his errand and reports; Gisors has his conversation with Kyo; Kyo learns of May's infidelity. At four he leaves and Tchen arrives. At four-thirty the raiders put out to the *Shantung*. At eleven the same morning, after a break of no more than five hours, we join Ferral. By one we are with Tchen and in the thick of the fighting. At five Ferral is interviewing the Chinese colonel and we know both that the insurrection has won its first battle and that the rest will not be so easy. This is the end of the first rush of action, and there is a break of about six hours before we follow Ferral to the bedroom of his mistress. And here we pass into the next day; at four in the morning Kyo, Tchen, and Katov are watching the last gasp of the armored train and already have the bad news from Chiang. The entire first segment of the action, comprising Parts One and Two of the novel, occupies twenty-eight hours, in twelve of which nothing happens.

For the interlude at Hankow, no time, but merely the date, is indicated.

But back in Shanghai, on April 11, events acquire momentum again and Malraux returns to his detailed timetable. At twelve-thirty after noon Clappique has his talk with Chpilewski. Tchen's walk with the clergyman Smithson and his subsequent, bobbled attempt on Chiang, start at one. At three Clappique visits Gisors and Kyo to borrow money and warn the latter of developments. The conversation between Katov and the bitter Hemmelrich comes a quarter-hour later. At six Ferral discovers that he has been baited by Valérie. Tchen dives under the auto at, or shortly after, ten-fifteen. An hour later, Clappique is upstairs at the Black Cat. At eleven-thirty Kyo and May tire of waiting and are caught by the police. At midnight Hemmelrich finds his shop wrecked. At one-thirty in the morning Clappique meets Gisors and they go off to appeal to König. At five the Communist Headquarters is overrun and Hemmelrich makes his escape.

Now there is another break. At ten in the morning, when Kyo confronts König, he has already been beaten by the guard "some hours" earlier. After the interview there is another break until four, when Clappique makes good his stowing away on the steamer. At six we return to the school to witness the deaths of Katov and Kyo.

Thus the second segment of intense action is over in eighteen hours, and even so is slowed considerably by the breaks in the last day. The rest of the events, like the Hankow part, are vaguely labeled, "The next day," "Paris—July," "Kobe—Spring."

Such is the timetable of the novel. Rhythm and pattern are implicit in it. First there is the burst of frenetic action of the opening insurrection, full of rush and tension. Then the slow, unhurried, ominous trip to Hankow and back. Next the renewed rush in which the insurrection is crushed. And finally comes the part where again time is unimportant and where nothing really occurs, where reader and characters alike *learn* something rather than *witness* something.

The first burst of action, from the murder in the hotel to the success of the insurrection, presents itself as an apparently successful effort toward achieving the first purpose of the protagonists. They seem on the point of victory. But with the receipt of the order from Chiang to give up the arms, it begins to dawn on us, as well as on the characters, that the purpose toward which the action has progressed is not the true purpose at all, that this victory is not a victory, and that the situation of these people is very different from what it has up to now appeared to be. The suspicion deepens to conviction during the more or less timeless visit to Hankow where Tchen and Kyo learn that Moscow has abandoned them. And in the light of this new revelation we embark upon a second rush of action in which the victory turns inexorably into defeat and the central characters come, each according to the rule of his private nature, to catastrophe.

At this point the rhythm again changes. After the capture of Kyo and the reduction of the last Communist forces under Katov the pace again slackens. Between dawn and dark of this day there are only three episodes: Kyo's facing his captors, Clappique's abject departure, and the scene of execution at the school. We are allowed time to contemplate Kyo, who at Hankow determined to return and face what was in store for him, now accepting his fate with the quiet gesture of taking poison, and Katov accepting a last cup of suffering for the sake of two comrades. We are invited to dwell upon the greatness of two human beings who comport themselves so in defeat that out of the defeat rises a kind of victory—a victory whose lineaments are clearer for the contrast with the abjection of Clappique.

The closing events of the story, after the death of Kyo, may even seem to be something like the final lament which, in Sophocles, seems designed to soothe the spectator and send him out of the theater somberly happy to be a man. In any event, we can surely identify the arrangement and design of what happens in *Man's Fate* as tragic.[1] Malraux's account of what took place at Shanghai is the account of a victory.

---

[1] Bert M.-P. Leefmans, in an unpublished essay, "Malraux and Tragedy: the Structure of *La Condition Humaine*," finds that this novel follows very closely the pattern of tragedy outlined by Francis Fergusson in his *Idea of the Theater*. Fergusson, in turn, builds upon Kenneth Burke's statement of the tragic rhythm which makes the protagonist move "from Passion, through Purpose, to Perception." I am heavily indebted to Mr. Leefmans, and less directly so to his predecessors.

The effect of victory is greatly enhanced by the quality of the picture which Malraux manages to juxtapose to the obvious and inescapable logic of events, and which reduces the logic to relative unimportance. Discursively, what happens to Kyo and Katov demonstrates that revolution is something for the prudent to avoid, just as the *Oedipus* demonstrates that the prudent will not find it good to kill one's father or sleep with one's mother. But at this point, in both tragic poem and tragic novel, discursive logic has to yield to the sheer magnificence of poetry.

Katov's gesture is both an act performed in the name of human dignity and a proof of human solidarity. After Kyo's death he has felt a horrible loneliness: ". . . alone, alone between the body of his dead friend and of his two frightened companions, alone between this wall and that whistle lost in the night." But a man can be stronger than his feeling of solitude. He gives the man next to him the cyanide and presently submerges in a new anguish when the man drops the pellet. Then, when they find it, he is in a paroxysm lest the poison have decomposed and lost its virtue. He holds the man's hand tightly while they wait for the cyanide to work. The man dies, and Katov once more feels abandoned. But then the guards come and find the bodies.

"Isolate the six nearest prisoners."
"No need," replied Katov, "I'm the one that gave them the cyanide."
The officer hesitated:
"And what about yourself?"
"There was just enough for two," Katov answered with deep joy. (P. 288.)

But *Man's Fate* uses a canvas broader than the canvas of tragedy and broader than Katov and Kyo can occupy by themselves; it involves other destinies than theirs; it has intentions additional to the tragic ones. Tchen, Ferral, and Clappique take turns absorbing the attention of the reader. In a sense they are secondary characters—that is, their roles are subordinate in the development of the story as a piece of fiction. But with respect to the exposition of the book's essential subject they loom large and one hesitates to affirm that they are any less important than Katov and Kyo. If Malraux had chosen to continue writing fictions on the scale of *The Conquerors* and *The Royal Way,* each of their destinies could easily have been made the matter of a separate novel.

Tchen's act of killing establishes his essential status in the world and condemns him to a special kind of anguish. The falling knife sets off his old latent obsession with death, and renews his feelings of fundamental isolation. In the midst of life, death will come to seem the safest, most final refuge and the abode of peace. From a shadow in a room he changes to a type, the Terrorist, and from type to man, and as he does so he comes to accept both his obsession with death and his estrangement. By the time he leaves the hotel and is on his way back to the party council at the phonograph shop he is taking a certain solace in the fact that he has killed. "There was a world of murder and he was staying in it as if in a warm place" (p. 21). We see him still more clearly when his problem becomes one of living simultaneously in two worlds. Among his companions he manages a social gesture, asking for and eating a handful of candy from Katov's bag; and the gesture reveals the anguished man.

But even his old teacher, Gisors, is unable to help him. After their interview, later on the night of the murder, the old man knows that the death of the young one is now inevitable. "Capable of victory, but not of living in victory, on what could he call except on death" (p. 63). He sees Tchen's predicament as not greatly different from the plight of the Conqueror type: once more it is the predicament of the man equal to conquest but not equal to enjoying its fruits. For Gisors, Tchen is a man who has thrown himself into terrorism as if into a prison from which he cannot emerge alive. He has always known that this adolescent can never live by an idea unless the idea is translated immediately into act. The feeling of estrangement antedates Tchen's first murder. Revolution has given this solitude a sense and meaning, but only temporarily. Murder has given it another, also temporary.

Tchen's counterpart in *The Conquerors,* the terrorist Hong, is motivated by a hatred which is the product of the human wretchedness he has lived in. His behavior is explicable in almost completely material terms. Tchen is more complicated. Beneath the disposition to murder lies the predisposition, the twist of the urge to destruction, Thanatos, gradually dominating the personality and condemning it at last. If from one angle Tchen's suffering seems metaphysical in nature, in that it reflects the suffering of a man condemned as all men are, to live in isolation, it is also something buried in his subconscious. We merely see Hong. We see *into* the tortured Tchen.

His solitude hangs heavy on him, even in battle. And when he is one of a chain of men on the roof of the police station—the top man holding the chimney and the bottom one hanging over the eaves whence he can toss his grenades through the window into the room below—even here where every man is dependent on every other and none is stronger than the weakest, Tchen is still alone. "In spite of the closeness of death, in spite of the fraternal weight tugging at his arms, he was not one with them" (p. 101).

The order for the insurgents to turn over their arms makes Tchen's fate certain. Learning at Hankow that the order is irrevocable, he announces his revolt against the party discipline: he will take upon himself the murder of Chiang Kai-shek. (Now the opportunism of the Communist bureaucrats becomes clear. They will not approve and back Tchen, but they will not prevent him; if he fails the failure will be his own, but if he succeeds . . . .) The failure of the first attempt is bitterly ironical. But the irony disappears when he reaches his new decision, to throw himself

under the car with the bomb. Everything now becomes simple. He attains
the euphoria of complete certitude.

Since Hankow, Kyo has known that this is how Tchen will end. Tchen
has tried to explain the attraction of terrorism:

> "I want a stronger word than joy. There isn't any. Even in Chinese.
> A . . . total peace. A sort of . . . what do you say? Of . . . I don't know.
> There's only one thing deeper. Further from man, nearer . . . Are you
> familiar with opium?"
> "Hardly at all."
> "Then it's going to be hard to explain. Nearer what you might call
> ecstasy. Yes. But thick. Deep. Not light. An ecstasy toward . . . downward."
> "And it's an idea that gives you that?"
> "Yes: my own death." (P. 142.)

And he dies with the feeling of complete possession of himself, in total,
absolute knowledge. For an hour and more before his death he has felt
nothing of the old weight that hung upon him.

Much can be made, if one reads *Man's Fate* as a sort of political par-
able, of the fact that Tchen does not kill Chiang. It is even possible to
treat his death, as Mr. E. B. Burgum[2] does, as retribution for having rejected the discipline of the party. And certainly Malraux is haunted by
the political problem of the man who wants to be a revolutionist but
cannot abide the discipline, whose particular destiny it is that he must
take direct action. Hong, Garine, Tchen, and Hernandez (in *Man's
Hope*) end in revolt, and one way to read *Man's Hope* is to take it
as the account of the conflict between the individualists whose ideal is
being something and the Communists, whose ideal is *doing*. But as a final
reading of Tchen's story, this purely political one seems inadequate.

Tchen's motives are only superficially political. When he kills the man
at the hotel he forgets why he is killing him, and when he dashes himself
under Chiang's empty car, there is no shadow of feeling in his heart that
thanks to his sacrifice the revolution may now succeed. He is at last burst-
ing the gates of his prison, destroying his solitude, freeing himself from
the bonds of man's predicament. Dostoevsky speaks somewhere of how
man is the only animal bent upon his own destruction. For Tchen, at
least, self-destruction is man's fate, and like Kyo and Katov he ends by
accepting his fatality.

Tchen is so interesting in himself that he threatens the unity of the

---

[2] In *The Novel and the World's Dilemma,* of which the chapter on Malraux gives
an extreme example of the not uncommon habit of reducing Malraux's novels to
mere political fables. The author assumes that Malraux is an orthodox Marxist,
engaged in dealing out rewards and punishments to his characters according to their
observance of the party line. Signs of Marxist orthodoxy in Malraux's work are, as a
matter of fact, extremely rare—as is also any evidence of direct knowledge of Marx's
writings.

book as a whole; the reader becomes so absorbed in him as almost to forget the main plot. The same is even truer of Clappique. When Kyo first sees him at the Black Cat, Clappique is entertaining a brace of de luxe prostitutes with a wonderful account of his maternal grandfather's life, loves, and fantastic burial—upright on his horse like Attila. One girl is too drunk to listen, the other too dull to follow, but Clappique hardly needs a listener. He is his own audience. One part of his personality listens while the other performs, lost in its role. The more fantastic the role the better. His voice changes with the needs of the story. He assumes character after character, entirely different with the girls from what he is with the waiter or with Kyo when Kyo finally gets his attention. His narrative is accompanied by a wealth of gesture, some of it as strongly pantomimic as the gestures of Rameau's nephew.

Le baron pelotait la Philippine, mais il continuait de parler au visage mince, tout en yeux, de la Russe:
— ... le malheur, chère amie, c'est qu'il n'y a plus de fantaisie. De temps en temps,
l'index pointé:
«... un ministre européen envoie à sa femme un pp'etit colis postal, elle l'ouvre—pas un mot ...
l'index sur la bouche:
«... c'est la tête de son amant. On en parle encore trois ans après!
Eploré:
«Lamentable, chère amie, l-lamentable! Regardez-moi! Vous voyez ma tête? Voila où mènent vingt ans de fantaisie héréditaire. Ça ressemble à la syphilis. —Pas un mot!
Plein d'autorité:
«Garçon! du champagne pour ces deux dames, et pour moi ...
de nouveau confidentiel:
«... un pp'etit Martini ...
sévère:
«trrès sec.» (P. 34.)

The Baron was fondling the Filipino girl, but went on talking to the thin-faced, wide-eyed Russian one.
"It's a sad thing, my dear, but there's no fantasy any more. From time to time . . ." (He points his finger.)
"A European cabinet minister mails his wife a l-little parcel. She opens it . . . Not a word . . .
(The finger goes to his mouth.)
"It's her lover's head. Three years after, people are still talking of it!
(On the verge of tears.)
"Lamentable, my dear, l-lamentable. Look at me. You see my face? That's what twenty years of congenital fantasy gets you. It's like syphilis . . . Not a word . . .
(All authority.)
"Waiter! Champagne for the ladies, and, for me . . .

(secretively again.)
"A l-little Martini . . .
(Sternly.)
"Very dry."

One suspects this scene of being carefully, almost lovingly, worked over, just as one suspects that Clappique was copied from life.[3] From the start, although his part in the action is minor, he is treated as a major character.

When at length he pays his check, he pockets only ten dollars of the change from a hundred-dollar bill and hands the rest to the Russian girl. Here at last is something she can understand; she rises to take him upstairs. He refuses. He would prefer it to be some other night, preferably when he has no money. For the moment, his mythomania has given him all the satisfaction he needs and its attractions have proved stronger than those of sex.

But Clappique is not merely a mythomaniac; he is also a buffoon. The two things need not go hand in hand: in *The Royal Way* we had the word of the ship's captain that there is a necessary element of mythomania in every adventurer. Clappique is a mythomaniac who is *also* a buffoon. There is very small doubt that the personage of Clappique invites Malraux not only because mythomania is one form of man's condition, but also because the buffoonery offers possibilities for the shaping of the novel itself, through "comic relief," of course—the at once funny and extremely horrid behavior of the Gravediggers' scene—but even more through the possibilities of contrast. Between the scene where Kyo rejects König's proposal, in the name of human dignity, and the scene where the protagonists die, Malraux sandwiches the episode of Clappique's last day. Insane with fear, and hounded by his mythomaniac reveries, the Baron finally disguises himself and sneaks aboard the steamer. The effect is to raise the tone of the master scene of the whole novel.

Clappique is the creation of a writer who has learned much from Dostoevsky. His ability to drop into a role is very reminiscent of the accomplishment Fyodor Karamazov demonstrates in the scene at Zossima's cell. His inability *not* to tell a lie makes him sound like old General Epanchin

---

[3] In general I have avoided discussing the possible prototypes of Malraux's characters, partly because I am persuaded that the question of who sat for what portrait is rarely more significant in literature than it is in painting, and partly because such discussions might involve libeling living persons who are entitled to privacy. The case of Clappique is in point. Literary gossip makes him a composite of two actual people, one the husband of a close friend of Mme. Clara Malraux, the other a traveling companion of one of Malraux's journeys. The fact, if it is a fact, adds less to our understanding of Clappique than does the consideration that to these models should be added Malraux himself, at least to the extent that the mythomaniac character has an inevitable interest for any novelist whose fictions closely parallel, and rectify imaginatively, his own experiences.

in *The Idiot.* (Malraux refers frequently to both these books, incidentally, in later writings.) Clappique also has the facility of getting out of touch with reality that we marvel at in the hero of *Notes from Underground* when the latter harangues the prostitute in the name of morality. And doubtless Malraux's reading of Dostoevsky was as influential in the formation of Clappique as any direct observation of characters he may have met in his travels. But Clappique remains quite different from Dostoevsky's buffoons even so: he is much better bred; there is small evidence that he takes direct pleasure in self-laceration; he is not so colossally capable of limitless self-abasement; the roles in which his imagination casts him are not an escape from a social situation—an intolerable feeling of inferiority in the presence of others. His mythomania is a denial of life, old Gisors tells us. Like opium, action, eroticism, or the creation of empires, it lifts, temporarily, the weight of human servitude. Clappique is absent from the story from the completion of his errand in Part One to the beginning of Part Four, but from the latter point he commands a constantly increasing share of Malraux's attention. We watch him in the bar with Chpilewski, learning that his jig is up; we meet him again at Gisors' house where he warns Kyo a first time and also wangles a loan; we pick him up again at the Black Cat and follow him up to the roulette table where he fritters away both his money and Kyo's life.

In the earlier episodes we watch him as he appears to some other character, but in these later scenes the point of view shifts so that we can look out from inside him and see the world as he sees it. Alternate gains and losses pin him to the table. He does not forget the passage of time and the plight of Kyo: his inability to move his left hand, which he holds in such a position that the face of his wrist watch is always turned down, betrays a determination to deny time, not an unawareness of it. He manages to confuse reality and unreality, and to relegate Kyo to the realm of the unreal; reality is here in front of him, this brightly lighted table, this agile, demonic little ball. Momentarily he contrives to reconcile the two personalities within himself: the Clappique who, like Tchen, wants to be destroyed and the Clappique almost frantically eager to live. The roulette ball becomes alive and seems so capable of liberating him from his own anguish that he wants to go on winning, not for the money but so that he will never have to stop playing. One part of him—the part that is the actor in his eternal charade—even identifies itself with the ball. And so he lets Kyo get away unwarned.

Now, Kyo's fate has already been decided, long before this evening, back in Hankow, and by Kyo himself. Clappique's feckless conduct is decisive only in that it determines the time and the manner in which that decision to continue the fight in Shanghai results in Kyo's undoing. Clappique is under the spotlight here no more because of his effect on the other characters than because his conduct is, itself, of great human significance. He has, for the moment, found a refuge from life. For the next few hours he will do his utmost to stay in the refuge, until at last life, with its anguish, crowds in upon him again. He comes out of the gaming house and goes off to find a prostitute with whom to continue his feverish make-believe. After this encounter, he tells her, without believing it himself, he is going to commit suicide. Actually he is going on into ever thickening guilt and fear.

There is potent testimony that, in writing the novel, Malraux became so fascinated with his Clappique that the latter threatened to run away with the story. In *Marianne,* December 13, 1933, there appeared a Malraux item entitled, "Un chapitre inédit de la Condition humaine." The page is ornamented with photographs of two naked women, one clearly Oriental and smoking what is probably opium. The accompanying legend runs: "Dans l'hôtel des sensations inédites." An editorial note offers supplementary information:

> This chapter, lifted out of the final version of the work, was placed between the scene where Clappique, fascinated by the game, allows Kyo to be captured and the one where he joins the latter's father, Gisors. The text was taken out, not at all because of the kind of scene it contains, but because it gave too great an importance to the secondary character of Clappique. When the chapter begins, Clappique, exhausted by his night of gambling during which he has betrayed his friend, by the fascination that he has just discovered in the pleasure of losing, uses his last remaining strength to escape and gets back to his hotel in a state of chaotic frenzy.[4]

The material not included in the final text turns out to be what the presentation in *Marianne* suggests. Clappique is lured by a nude woman into her darkened room, where, in the midst of the erotic episode, he discovers that he is performing for the benefit of a group of *voyeurs* hidden in the darkness. The plot departs from scatological folklore only in that Clappique, whose anxiety state has been so intense all that night, connects his audience with Chiang Kai-shek and the Kuomintang, feels himself in vague but great danger, bolts for the door but finds it locked, manages finally to reach and twist the key, and emerges in such disarray as to provoke the mirth of a passing *boy*.

Why did Malraux suppress the episode?—The theme of eroticism, already copiously exploited in the scenes between Ferral and Valérie, had possibly become an esthetic problem. Moreover, the tone of an episode in which Clappique appears with no more dignity than the victim of a particularly lurid farce, may provide too much contrast with the serious tone of the episodes that precede and follow it. But it is also evident that as a fictional character Clappique is becoming an embarrassment. The

⁴ For further details see "Note for a Malraux Bibliography," *Modern Language Notes,* LXV (June, 1950), 392-95. I have to thank my colleague Jean-Albert Bédé for assistance in preparing the article.

momentum of the story is forcing events toward their conclusion. The destinies of May, Kyo, Gisors, Katov, Ferral, and a number of others have yet to be dealt with. This consideration calls for the curbing of Clappique. Actually, the suppressed episode, if left in the book, would have raised hob with the time table. He leaves the gaming house at one o'clock. The narrative requires him to be joined by Gisors by half after one or shortly thereafter. If the chapter printed in *Marianne* had not been taken out of the book, simple arithmetic reveals that Clappique would have been placed in the necessity of having had carnal knowledge of three different women in three different places in little more than half an hour. Malraux suppressed the episode so that Clappique would not run away with the story.

Like the protagonists of the main, tragic, story, Clappique has his little moment of seeming victory, there at the gaming table where for a short time he succeeds, or almost succeeds, in denying life. But at the end he simply crawls away. His victory is turned into defeat, just as the defeat of Kyo and Katov has been turned into victory.

Like Clappique, Ferral seems to grow as the novel progresses, after a beginning where he seems to be no more than the official bad man. In the economy of the novel he seems the least necessary of the characters. Two of his four big scenes—those which he shares with Valérie Serge —are certainly marginal and could easily be omitted without affecting the course of the action. As the representative of foreign, imperialistic capitalism busy at an office telephone, energetically organizing the reaction, squeezing money out of the Chinese conservatives, directing the efforts of the police, and arranging to bribe Chiang Kai-shek, he sets in motion the forces that eventually crush the insurrection; he is interesting less as a human being than as a source of harm. He is the Antagonist, necessarily an unsympathetic figure.

But just as *Man's Fate* is not just a novel about an insurrection, so Ferral is not merely a convenient substitute for the devil. When he appears in his new role of unassuaged lover, he is far less antipathetic, much less the mere tycoon industriously defending the fortune he has built. The Consortium is the expression of human drives which identify him with the earlier heroes of Malraux. Socially he is on the other side of the barricades, but in other respects he is in the same predicament as they. The Consortium expresses his lust for power, and is his means of "leaving a scar on the map." Money is less important to him than his ability to impose his will on other people. The geography has changed and we have come out of the jungle, but this exploiter is still recognizably the same type as Perken, the man who, though not walled off in an inaccessible hinterland, is still one who would be king. Further, he has the same anarchic temperament as Garine, like him has no use for law except such law as he can turn to his own ends, like him has attached himself to a "great action" (his Consortium is comparable to Mitsubishi and Standard Oil), and like him has committed himself to these things in order to satisfy his own personal and private needs.

Critics who look everywhere in Malraux's novels for portraits of the Adventurer should give Ferral more attention. Much more clearly than either Kyo or Tchen, he is cut to the adventurer pattern; he is a member of a prominent middle-class family; a brilliant career as an intellectual is already behind him (like Vincent Berger in *Les Noyers de l'Altenburg* he is an ex-professor); after a try at politics, he has now placed himself where such types are happiest, in a situation where a man is what he does. In Ferral we once more have Malraux's version of the *Übermensch,* though an *Übermensch* in a sack suit who frequents the best hotels.

It is in a hotel that his full identity is revealed—he is incapable of assuagement, a *grand inassouvi*. Merely to possess a beautiful woman does not satisfy him. He must share her private experience. And so while the sporadic gunfire in the background marks the agony of the armored train, Ferral denies Valérie the privacy of darkness. She protests and turns off the light. He turns it on again. She capitulates. But like the victories of men who escape man's fate through opium or through mythomania, this one also is illusory.

For when the insurrection has been put down and its leaders are on the eve of their final passion, Valérie not only makes a fool of Ferral, but says in the letter she leaves him that she has done it to show him that she does not accept his domination. After he has loosed the birds and animals in her room, he has his moment of conversation with Gisors in the bar and then goes off to find a courtesan and take her home with him. Such women are not mere trollops. They are trained in social accomplishments, and custom dictates that they entertain their clients. This one offers to sing for Ferral. "No," he replies brutally, "take off your clothes." The affront to her dignity is fully intentional. Ferral is finding relief from his frustration. The only consolation for the blow he has taken from Valérie is to humiliate some other human being, even the most defenseless. A few hours earlier than Kyo and Katov, he has found *his* victory changed to defeat, thus recapitulating the experience pattern so common in the book, just as did Clappique. And like Clappique, Ferral will have no moment of reconciliation with fate.

Ferral is certainly not a winning character, but the fact that the novel does not drop him at this point attests Malraux's persistent interest in him. The scene where Ferral reappears, in Paris, actually reveals nothing explicit about the Consortium Ferral is there to defend. What is revealed very clearly indeed is that whether he retains the nominal chairmanship of the Consortium or not, Ferral is no longer dominant; he is at the mercy of a group of sedentary nonentities who sit sucking on caramels as they listen to his arguments. Given Ferral's temperament and the drives which have determined his career, this situation is the embodiment of the Absurd. To have this character end in complete absurdity was clearly important to Malraux, for to risk an eighteen-page return to the fortunes of Ferral, just after the passage on the death of Katov, was to make a heavy wager: if it failed it could easily dull the intense tragic emotion of the finest pages in the novel.

Where Ferral is a victim of his inner urge to dominate, old Gisors—Kyo's father—is a victim of his own apathy. He is also superbly intelligent, and endowed with that understanding of life that Malraux tends to attribute to those who, like Gisors, are lifelong students of art. Possibly we should take him merely as an example of the human type whose action is inhibited by the unrestrained play of the intelligence. But this reading seems inadequate, after all. Gisors is also a father, and the specific source of his anguish is his fatherhood. He loves Kyo so deeply that he is tortured by the separation caused by Kyo's commitment to a life of action in which the father cannot participate. This kind of human relationship is something new for Malraux. The recent death of his own father, for whom Malraux seems to have had both great affection and intellectual respect, may have turned his attention to the latent poignancy of a father's feelings about his son. At the same time, he had been intimately friendly with Bernard Groethuysen, who was old enough to have been his father and who appears to have combined Gisors' magnificent gift of understanding with an innate ineptitude and distaste for action very like his. And in addition, Malraux was writing his book just before the birth of his daughter Florence, his first child, and we know from Gide's *Journal* [5] that Malraux feared paternity as a deterrent to action.

Gisors is thus wise as a father should be wise. In addition to his own special wretchedness he knows all the other forms of anguish. Much of our understanding of Tchen, Kyo, Ferral, and Clappique derives from our knowing what they look like to him. But this man whose teaching at the University of Peking helped form a revolutionary generation is powerless against his own paralysis. The physician cannot save himself. He owes his famous serenity to opium.

For a moment after Kyo's death he gives up his pipe and pellets and accepts the fullness of his suffering. But at Kobe he is smoking again and with the help of opium has fallen back into apathy. He no longer feels the burden of life and the awareness of death which, we now learn, have always plagued him, but he has joined those like Clappique and Tchen, those who have tried to escape man's fate by denying life. In the end, nothing is real to him but the vanity of everything. His presence and his

[5] Entry for September 4, 1936. Gide learns that Malraux, momentarily in Paris between battles, feels, remarkably freer to lead a life of action since his separation from his family.

mood dominate the last pages of the book and quite outweigh the happiness—which we do not see but only hear about—of the people who have escaped to Moscow.

Gisors' escape from his anguish has at least the merit of harming no one but himself. A type like König, on the other hand, finds relief only in inflicting pain. Like Tchen, he is psychically condemned to shed blood. Like Ferral, he is driven by the need to humiliate. He is happy, he tells Clappique, only when killing. It seems that years ago he was serving in Seminoff's White army and was taken prisoner by the Reds. They beat him unconscious, and while he was unconscious tore the insignia off his shoulders and replaced it with red stars fastened by nails driven deep into the flesh. In his pain he wept like a woman. The traumata of his experience are indelible. He takes a perverted pleasure in recalling the details of his humiliation, and heats his fury with it each time he has an opportunity to torture or to execute. For Malraux, some such experience is necessary to explain the otherwise inexplicable mentality of the Policeman, not merely in Asia but everywhere; not merely the jailer who serves the enemy but (witness Nicolaïeff in *The Conquerors* with his smiling statement that there is no courage that will survive a ten-minute private conference with an experienced interrogator) the policeman who is one's own ally. The police mentality, we shall learn in *Days of Wrath,* is everywhere alike; the work requires a special human type. Such men exist to preside over prisons and the prison is so completely assimilated to the idea of humiliation that as Malraux's novels follow each other the prison achieves the status of a symbol: Garine leaves Europe to escape a prison sentence after the absurdity of his trial; Kyo's ultimate ordeal of humiliation—from which he emerges victorious—comes when he is whipped on the hands by his Chinese jailer; for Kassner in *Days of Wrath* the time of his imprisonment is another name for the Days of Scorn; in *Man's Hope* the liberated proletariat is equated, in a striking medical metaphor, with men newly released from jails; the great novelists listed by the debaters at the Altenburg Priory, Defoe, Dostoevsky, Cervantes, are all men who have served time. (One can only speculate as to the relation between the persistence of the symbol in the novels and the fact of Malraux's early, and absurd, detention in Indochina.) For a König the need to humiliate is so powerful that it unseats the normal need of the individual: he has been a year without going to bed with his wife. Clappique, who has come to him to plead for Kyo's life, immediately senses the hopelessness of his errand; he recognizes in König one of those men whose anguish can be assuaged, *like his own,* only by a sweeping, universal negation of the world. The difference is that Clappique's instrument of negation is his mythomania.

Meanwhile, humiliation is also at issue in the case of the wretched little Hemmelrich, the complete victim of circumstance. Hemmelrich's humiliation does not come out of one horrible incident, as does König's.

His whole life has been a traumatic experience. He has never been able to earn a living that would let him respect himself. The source of his present misery is that now that the opportunity offers to strike back at his anonymous humiliators, he is not free to do so. He has married a Chinese woman out of pity for someone even more wretched than he. She is ill. Their child has mastoiditis. For him to take an active part in the revolution is to expose them; he has to begrudge the use of his little shop, and deny it entirely to Tchen when Tchen needs a refuge. He does not even have the dignity of being free to die as he likes. Every call to volunteer for a dangerous mission renews his anguish, and the torture is so great that in anger he lashes out at the only man who really understands him. Then at last a bomb relieves him of his responsibilities and he leaves the mangled bodies of his wife and child to run to Communist headquarters and share in the ultimate battle. It is one of the unexplained ironies of *Man's Fate* that Hemmelrich should be one of the few characters to emerge not only unscathed but happy, learning for the first time in Russia that human labor can be a sign of dignity as well as one of humiliation.

Man's Fate is clearly intended to do what tempted Malraux when he was writing *The Conquerors*—to surround his protagonists by a number of other characters who illustrate the variety of forms man's destiny can take. The later novel not only brings to life the population of *The Conquerors* and *The Royal Way*; it even adds types like Hemmelrich to their number. To do so, Malraux has had to find a new technique. He has adopted a shifting point of view.

Limiting the point of view by the use of a central intelligence had cramped Malraux considerably in the first two novels. In *The Royal Way* he had been forced to discard it occasionally because there were essential things in the story that Claude Vannec could not possibly know. In *The Conquerors*, where he expended an inordinate effort to put the whole narrative in the mouth of one character, his method inhibited his exploring many areas which obviously interested him, for the relentless focus upon Garine made investigation of the other characters look digressive. The limitation of point of view had advantages, most particularly the advantage of heightening the dramatic intensity of the novels, but it also implied the neglect of many other tempting dramatic possibilities.

In *Man's Fate* the reader sees the reputedly "secondary" characters as clearly as he sees Kyo and Katov, and perhaps understands them better, precisely because of this change in optics. Of Hong, Rensky, and Rebecci —and much of the time Perken and Garine—we saw only the exteriors, and fathomed their conduct only as some intermediary character between us and them fathomed it; in the case of Hong, we did not get even that close, since the narrating character saw him only once and reported most of Hong's activity as it was reported to him, at second remove. But now the reader sees the world, from time to time, as Tchen, Clappique, and Ferral see it. Sharing their vision does much to erase the difference between primary and secondary character.

The method permits an extremely useful variation in emphasis. While we are seeing the action with Tchen, for example, Clappique and Ferral are minor people. We are admitted to Clappique's mind only in the second half of the story, *after* we have already watched him through the puzzled eyes of Kyo and the somewhat amused ones of Gisors. And we begin seeing as Ferral sees, only when he appears as the unassuaged erotic, the humiliated man bent on vengeance, the man who has staked all on an enterprise that has come to a dead end. The change in optics as the story progresses may mean merely that Malraux's interest in these characters increased as he went along. But it occurs at those places where we become aware that these people, as well as the protagonist, mirror the universal fate of man. We no longer feel them to be minor figures. The change naturally enlists not only the interest of the reader but also his sympathy. It is infinitely harder to remain aloof and not identify oneself somewhat with a character, however unpleasant, when one sees the world as he sees it. The identification and resultant sympathy does much to persuade us that the condition of these individuals, even though they may need the psychiatrist more than we, is part and parcel of our own.

The new technique makes Malraux give up one signal advantage. Since there is no longer a surrogate for the author whose opinions are privileged, critics have tended to take the utterance of any character, so long as it suits their book, to be the utterance of Malraux himself. For an author like Malraux, whose books are combed for political opinions, the disadvantage is doubtless considerable, but it is certainly outweighed by the *literary* advantages of the method. For it permits him to probe his characters more deeply, and not only this but to show them from various angles, as they appear to various fellow characters, thus rounding them and obviating the danger, grave in the early novels, of creating personae rather than men. When necessary, he assumes the omniscient and omnipresent author. Like Flaubert's "God in creation," he is everywhere present and never visible. Or hardly ever: he makes in cold fact a number of interventions, but they are always unostentatious and subdued in tone; one is hardly aware of them. Most of the time the action is presented from the point of view of the character best placed to see it; more rarely, for lack of an available character, it is seen as it would be seen by a well-informed but rather uninvolved bystander. The reader's credulity is not strained and the presence of so many important characters is rendered possible.

Meanwhile, in adopting the broader canvas and the ramified action, so that the reader's interest would extend to a half-dozen characters at once, Malraux has assumed the burden of keeping the reader aware of the continuity of the action and the structural relations between episodes. The care he has expended in this respect is evident. He links various separated episodes by repetition of detail whose significance bridges the gaps between: Ferral in Valérie's room hears the drumfire of the armored train which is the government's last resource and which Kyo, Katov, and Tchen will shortly watch expire. And when Kyo needs money to bribe the prison guard who beats the madman, he has ready in his pocket the money which he would have handed Clappique the night before if Clappique had kept the rendezvous. Such details are not forced upon the reader, but are present by the dozen to testify to Malraux's awareness of the complexity of his task.

The intention behind Malraux's technique, then, is to permit him to juxtapose a number of individual human destinies with the destinies of the heroes of his central tragedy. So the meaning of the novel must be looked for in the relation of these ancillary stories to the main one—not in the main story alone, not in the ancillary stories alone, but in all together. Too exclusive interrogation of the ancillary gives . . . chaos. Too exclusive attention to the fate of Kyo and Katov gives back an answer too simplistic, because too exclusively political.

For, politically, *Man's Fate* is a very ambiguous book. Official Communist critics have been right, from their point of view, in approaching it warily; for them it is tainted by an individualism such as Trotsky had already denounced in *The Conquerors,* and this individualism is one which no few readers, including the brilliant and non-Communist Sartre,[6] have felt to be extremely middle class. To be sure, since in the end Kyo and Katov enjoy a human dignity and a feeling of fraternity which is denied to the other characters, revolution appears to be at least an instrumental good. But beyond this? Kyo and Katov may not be identifiable with the "Conqueror" type, like Garine (who would like to find in revolution a Good-in-itself); but they are no more imaginable as "curés de la révolution," the custodians of progress who take over when the fighting has finished; their place in the classless society of the Marxist future is hard to see. And much of the pathos of the book emerges from the inevitable conflict between the legitimate interests of the individual and those of the grand revolutionary enterprise.

Considering what happens to the protagonists, the revolution looks like a very immoral thing; Kyo and Katov die because of no fatal defect in their characters, but because the International lets them down, because it is more expedient for brave men to die than for the International to come into open conflict with Chiang Kai-shek. They die, moreover, as a result of bureaucratic fecklessness and incompetence, for the order they have asked for, authorizing them to keep or hide their arms, is finally

---

[6] In "Etude," published as preface to Roger Stéphane, *Portrait de l'aventurier.*

issued too late to be anything but an additional irony. Thus, if we are to
be guided by the most emotionally compelling part of the story, we may
conclude that the situation of Kyo and Katov in the revolution merely
illustrates another of the various blind alleys which make up man's lot.
For if revolution is the only acceptable form of human activity, it is one
that leads straight to disaster. One participates at the cost of one's eventual
destruction. In fact, if the book were first and foremost a political fable,
and if its import were to be judged by the fates of its principals, it could
easily be understood to condemn revolution.

But in the last section of the book we learn that Pei, Tchen's second
in the attack on Chiang, is happy in Russia, writing propaganda. Hemmelrich, we know, is there also. In fact, all those "who could escape"
from Shanghai are back in revolutionary work. May is on her way back
to Moscow, because to take up her medicine there is the best way to
"avenge" Kyo. As she sits there in Kobe, waiting to leave, she thinks:
"The Revolution had just been through a terrible malady, but it had
not died" (p. 308). Does she mean, by "malady," the failure of the
Shanghai insurrection, or is she thinking of a weakness nearer the heart,
at Moscow? In any case, she takes satisfaction from the thought and is
willing to continue her part in the struggle.

Why not dismiss the ambiguity by insisting upon a distinction? There
is Revolution, with a capital letter, and opposed to it there is the specific
revolution, owned and operated by a group of men in Moscow. Why not
say that Revolution in general is good, but that the Communist revolution
kills those who serve it, is fallible, opportunistic, sooner an evil than a
good? There is a hint of such a distinction in Pei's remark that while he
is glad to be a revolutionary writer, he will never be a "pure" Communist. Possibly it is also suggested in the contrast between May's desire
to avenge Kyo and her lack of enthusiasm for the return to Moscow. But
the real reason for not making such a distinction is that Malraux's novel
does not make it, and to insist upon it would be to insist upon clearing
away an ambiguity which the novelist prefers to maintain.

The dialectic of the novel is too complicated to permit such simplifica-
tions. The pages in which we see men made happy by the revolution are
in an obscure position. They occur where there is no dramatic tension.
They convey information from off stage; what we *see* in these same pages
is a saddened young woman, about to try to make what she can of a life
from which the animating force, her love for Kyo, has been removed, talking with a pathetic old man. His suffering is what dominates these last
pages.

Légers, très élevés, les nuages passaient au-dessus des pins sombres et se
résorbaient peu à peu dans le ciel; et il lui sembla qu'un de leurs groupes,
celui-là précisément, exprimaient les hommes qu'il avait connus et aimés,
et qui étaient morts. L'humanité était épaisse et lourde, lourde de chair, de

sang, de souffrance, éternellement collée à elle-même comme tout ce qui meurt; mais même le sang, même la chair, même la douleur, même la mort se résorbaient là-haut dans la lumière comme la musique dans la nuit silencieuse: il pensa à celle de Kama, et la douleur humaine lui sembla monter et se perdre comme le chant même de la terre; sur la délivrance frémissante et cachée en lui comme son coeur, la douleur possédée refermait lentement ses bras inhumains. (P. 313.)

Light and very high the clouds went by above the dark pines and were absorbed again into the sky; and it seemed to him that one of their groups —that very one—expressed the men he had known and loved, and who were dead. Humanity was thick and heavy, heavy with flesh, with blood; with suffering, eternally clinging to itself, like everything that dies: but even blood, even flesh, even suffering, even death was reabsorbed up there in the light like music absorbed by the night's silence: he thought of Kama's music, and human sorrow seemed to rise and be lost like the song of the earth itself; over his relief, trembling and hidden inside him like his heart, once more sorrow slowly closed its inhuman arms.

The slowness and insistence of the rhythm is inescapable. So is the effect of repeating the important words: *lourde, même, sang, mort, résorbait, douleur.* The enumerations, slowed down and emphasized by the repetitions of *même,* in the parallel constructions, form something like a procession. This passage is of course an extreme example, but an extreme example of the feeling which presides over the closing of the book, and the fact that we learn in the same pages that for some men the revolution is proving beneficent is dwarfed by the unhappiness of the old man.

This is one of the many places in Malraux's work where the discursive logic is overwhelmed by the picture. We may be in doubt about the political argument; there can be no doubt about what has happened to Gisors. Nothing is real now but his suffering, and since life is nothing but vanity, the suffering is meaningless and irremediable. Gisors is conquered by the Absurd.

The Absurd is mentioned explicitly only once in *Man's Fate* and then, curiously enough, by Katov, who never appears at all worried by such metaphysical considerations. No character is directly motivated, as Garine is, by the consciousness of the vanity of what he does. But negatively the old worry about the Absurd is still with us. And since, in Malraux's earlier novels, man's fate was defined in terms of the Absurd, we do well—having abandoned the political interpretation as incomplete and unclear—to re-examine what happens to the other characters in *Man's Fate.*

During that last moment of calm before the catastrophe, in the bar where Ferral joins him after releasing the animals and birds in Valérie's room, Gisors tries to put into words that will mean something to Ferral the essence of the human predicament. ". . . Man does not merely want to govern. He wants to constrain other men to his will, as you say. To be more than human in a human world; not just powerful—all-powerful. The chimera called the will to power is just an intellectual justification. It's the will to Godhead; every man dreams of being a God. . . . A god can possess but can't conquer. . . . The dream of a god would be to become man but keep all his power. The dream of man is to become god but keep his personality. . . ." (P. 213.)

Gisors is talking to a man who has just defined intelligence as "the means of making other people obey," and is picking up the words Ferral has used. Clearly he means that the "will to constrain" is only a symptom. But wanting to be a god, or to be at once man and god, applies to every character in the book, for to be a god in this sense implies at once the enjoyment of the benefits of being human and the escape from all the servitudes which are the badges of the human condition. *Man's Fate* could conceivably have been called *Of Human Bondage*. Out of the gulf which separates what we are from what imagination makes us want to be flows the anguish that plagues us.

The badge of this generally shared condition is man's loneliness. Each of the characters in turn suffers from solitude. Malraux freights this suffering with significance by multiplying symbols: Kyo's phonograph record, the whistles which shrill throughout the early parts of the book to remind the characters (particularly Tchen) of the world from which they are cut off, and the armored train which Mme. Magny makes a presiding symbol of the novel and of Malraux's work as a whole. On the morning of the second day of the insurrection, when Kyo, Katov, and Tchen watch the train expire, there comes a new burst of firing. The officers, helpless at their telephones, have passed the word to fire at will; as death approaches, the attempt to maintain communication is useless. Each man is on his own in his last hour. The approach of Chiang Kai-shek's army becomes audible. "Behind each turret, each man in the train heard the sound as if it were the voice of death itself" (p. 124). The symbol will turn up twice in later novels (the planes of the Spanish Republicans, the tank in *Les Noyers*) but will be less explicit in meaning and even ambivalent, since these later armored vehicles are also scenes of fraternity. But for *Man's Fate* one may easily accept the reading of Mme. Magny.

But not in all the extension she gives it. It is true that when the revolt of Shanghai expires, each of the central characters is overwhelmed by a feeling of essential separation from the rest of mankind. But it is also true that, in two of them at least, the feeling proves weaker than a feeling of essential human fraternity. Kyo and Katov come the nearest to finding, if not escape from, at least a way of transcending, man's fate.

In the crucial scene where König offers Kyo the opportunity to betray his friends and then threatens him with torture for refusing, Kyo defines his own motives with luminous clarity. "I think that Communism will make dignity possible for those I am fighting for. What is opposed to it, anyhow, is what keeps them from having any—unless they have a wisdom that's as rare among them as among others; perhaps they would have to have even more, because they are poor and their labor separates them from their lives" (p. 269). König challenges impatiently: "What do you call dignity?" Kyo replies: "The opposite of humiliation."

Certain of Malraux's characteristic themes are compulsive drives that determine conduct. Human dignity does not belong among these, even though its opposite, humiliation, certainly does. Dignity is a moral value. It does not drive men to die; when they die for it they die by choice. In a purely negative way a concern for it underlay the conduct of Hong in *The Conquerors:* his hatred was directed at those who respect themselves and he could not imagine such people respecting themselves without scorning someone else. But he was less intent on relieving the burden of social injustice than on exterminating those who profit by it or even those who simply do not object to it.

Kyo sees the great problem to be one of turning human pack-animals into men. He has worked with the laborers on the docks, shared their life, speaks with authority of their predicament. At Hankow he is present when a group of seven dock workers is brought in, handcuffed, for having set upon the Red Guard and tried to make off with rations meant for the troops. Why did they do it?

"Before," says one of them, "we could eat."

"No," Kyo contradicts, "before we didn't eat. I know. I worked on the docks. And if we have to starve anyhow, we can at least do it so that we can be men" (p. 145).

Kyo and Katov are obviously something new among Malraux's heroes. Neither is a case of exacerbated individualism seeking in action (revolutionary or other) the relief of a private anguish. Kyo is protected from some forms of anguish by his sense of the heroic. He is subject like other men to the feeling of solitude (note that it is *before* he has learned of May's infidelity that he is so bothered by the phonograph recording) but his loneliness has been largely relieved by his love for his wife. What anguish Katov may have known belongs apparently to the past. As we see him in the novel, except at the end, where, after all, he has every right to feel for a moment that he has been abandoned, he seems even less concerned than Kyo about escapes. These certainly do not figure among his present motives. And possibly this is why, until the book comes to its climax, Kyo and Katov attract the reader's attention less than do Tchen, Ferral, and Clappique; they are both reasonably well adapted to the lives they have chosen and thoroughly devoted to the revolution. Consequently they are less picturesque as psychological cases.

Kyo's devotion to human dignity is what liberates him, in the last moments of his life, both from the feeling of solitude and from the "metallic realm" of the Absurd. Lying there in the school hall among all these men who are about to die, he realizes that his death, as much as his life, has meaning.

Partout où les hommes travaillent dans la peine, dans l'absurdité, dans
l'humiliation [note the repetition of the prepositional phrases, a rhetorical
device on which Malraux falls back almost invariably when he wants an
intense and solemn emotion], on pensait à des condamnés semblables, à
ceux-là comme les croyants prient; et, dans la ville, on commençait à aimer
ces mourants comme s'ils eussent été déjà morts ... Entre tout ce que cette
dernière nuit couvrait de la terre, ce lieu de râles était sans doute le plus
lourd d'amour viril. ... Il mourait, comme chacun de ces hommes couchés,
pour avoir donné un sens à sa vie. (P. 283.)

Everywhere where men worked in suffering, in absurdity, in humiliation,
they were thinking of condemned men like him—thinking as believers
would pray—and in the city they were beginning to love these dying as they
would the dead. . . . Out of everything that this last night covered on the
earth, this place of death was probably the richest in virile love. . . . He
was dying, like each of those lying there, for having given meaning to his
life.

For Kyo, death is not the final monstrous ignominy, the ultimate monstrous defeat. He can face it; dying is easy, he thinks at one moment, in
these circumstances. With death's horror he has also escaped the victory
of the Absurd and the torture of loneliness. The best commentary is to
put the passage above beside the dying words of Perken in *The Royal
Way:* "There is no death . . . There is just *me* . . . *me* . . . going to
die" (p. 178).
And what is true of the death of Kyo is even truer of the death of
Katov. Here is the latter's exit from the story:

«Les petits auront eu de la veine, pensa-t-il. Allons! supposons que je sois
mort dans un incendie.» Il commença à marcher. Le silence retomba, comme
une trappe, malgré les gémissements. Comme naguère sur le mur blanc, le
fanal projeta l'ombre maintenant très noire de Katov sur les grandes fenêtres
nocturnes; il marchait pesamment, d'une jambe sur l'autre, arrêté par ses
blessures; lorsque son balancement se rapprochait du fanal, la silhouette de
sa tête se perdait au plafond. Toute l'obscurité de la salle était vivante, et
le suivait du regard pas à pas. Le silence était devenu tel que le sol résonnait
chaque fois qu'il touchait lourdement du pied; toutes les têtes, battant de
haut en bas, suivaient le rythme de sa marche, avec amour, avec effroi, avec
résignation, comme si, malgré les mouvements semblables, chacun se fût
dévoilé en suivant ce départ cahotant. Tous restèrent la tête levée: la porte
se refermait. (P. 288.)

"The kids must have been lucky, he thought. Come on! Let's suppose I
died in a fire." He began to move. Silence fell again, like a trapdoor, in
spite of the moaning. As before, against the white wall, the spotlight projected Katov's shadow, now very black, against the great night-darkened
windows; he walked heavily, dragging his legs, slowed by his wounds: when
his swaying brought him up to the light, the shadow of his head was lost

against the ceiling. All the darkness of the room was alive, and eyes followed him step by step. The silence had become so complete that the ground echoed each step; every head, nodding up and down, took up the rhythm of his stride, with love, with fright, with resignation, as if, though all were doing the same thing, each had revealed himself as he followed that clumsy exit. Then the raised heads stopped; the door was closing behind him.

Here again the rhythm is slow, and solemn, although the slowness and solemnity are not so reinforced by rhetorical devices (there is only one instance of the repetition of the preposition: *avec amour, avec effroi, avec résignation*) as the passage about Gisors' despair. Its unevenness may be Malraux's instinctive response to Katov's heavy limp. A certain note of simplicity is set by the slightly vulgar *les petits,* the slangy *auront eu de la peine,* the familiar *allons,* and these are a further guaranty against the intrusion of unwelcome rhetoric. The next sentence, which shifts the point of view from Katov's mind to the observer's, is stripped of everything but fact. And then, in the silence, one watches not the figure of Katov but the black shadow of the man (once again Malraux's basically cinematographic imagination) climbing the dark window. We are not completely sure whether our attention is on the man or on the shadow, since the *il* of the following phrase cannot grammatically stand for *ombre,* but certainly one is as fully aware, in this sentence, of the shadow as of the flesh. In the next, with the phrase which begins *lorsque son balancement,* it is the shadow that one is most aware of, and the awareness confers upon the hero the stature of the shadow, greater than life size. Then the head is lopped off by the ceiling, in prefigurement of the imminent execution, and we become aware of the other men in the room who as they watch Katov's exit are living through what will shortly be the experience of each, so that the departing man represents to each of the others his own fate. And at the same time the reader realizes that he has himself been watching through the eyes of, sharing the experience of, identifying himself with, the condemned. But now one no longer sees Katov; one retires into one's own identity and watches the heads move slightly to the rhythm of Katov's limp, conscious of him *through* these persons from whom one is separated. Then there is the interpolated comment that in the unanimous movement each man reveals himself, the door closes, and Katov is gone.

This picture is what turns defeat into tragic victory and in a sense orients and orders all the values in the book. The destiny of the man whom the International has abandoned is so much more brilliant than the destinies of those who survive the insurrection that the political import of the novel pales before the more broadly human import. Revolution now seems to be not the subject but the setting in which the qualities and defects, the strengths and weaknesses of human character stand clearly out.

Just before the deaths of the heroes we watched Clappique sneak aboard the steamer in disguise. Shortly after, we move to Paris and see Ferral sit frustrate while a group of candy-chewing financiers decide whether or not they will let him go on being a great man. Then we pick up old Gisors, waiting in Kobe for death to end meaningless suffering From their destinies we know the power of the Absurd. But at the same time we have also seen Katov go out to die and we know that there in heres in man's fate, in spite of all the possibilities of defeat, the pos sibility of the power and glory of being a man.

The Return from Hell

by Geoffrey H. Hartman

Wer spricht von Siegen? Überstehen ist alles.

Rilke

Malraux's development, after *Man's Fate*, is illumined by a comment of his on Dostoevsky, Cervantes, and Defoe, writers separated as much in spirit as in nationality, whom he joins nevertheless in a surprising collocation. "All three," he remarks in the year of his next novel (after *Man's Fate*), *Le Temps du Mépris* (1935), "wrote of the counterpart of solitude, the reconquest of the world by a man who has returned from hell." The remark has a direct bearing on all his novels, but especially on the sequence beginning with *Le Temps du Mépris*. This novel (whose title is best translated *Days of Contempt*) tells the story of a militant Communist named Kassner who survives solitary confinement in a Nazi prison and returns home deeply marked by the experience. It is the first work in which the author depicts the survival of the hero as well as of his cause, and so departs from the purer tragic structure which exacted the death or disabling of a major character. The hero's "descent into hell" is now accompanied by a "return" to the world of men, a return susceptible of various interpretations but increasing in thematic importance.

For Malraux's earlier heroes there was no return. Their actions led simultaneously to self-awareness and self-estrangement. They paid every step toward consciousness with a step toward utter solitude, so that the fullness of the knowledge of man corresponded to the fullness of solitude, or death. Katov and Kyo do not become as gods, knowing good and evil, but as men, knowing death. The return of the hero means, in this light, an emancipation of the knowledge of Man from that of death or solitude. He attains a vision of mankind without suffering an irremediable experience of isolation.

Although the theme of the return is absent from Malraux's first novels, it is still deeply implicit in their form: they contain an Ishmael, a char-

"The Return from Hell." From *Malraux* by Geoffrey H. Hartman (New York: Hillary House Publishers, Ltd.; London: Bowes and Bowes, Ltd., 1960). Reprinted by permission of the publishers and Geoffrey H. Hartman.

acter who survives and whose function is to tell what he has witnessed. In both *The Conquerors* and *The Royal Way* we have such a witness, a younger man who watches an older man (the hero) die. The author, strictly speaking, does not need such a figure, since the convention of the novel gives the role of witness to him. What Malraux seems to represent through the separate person of the witness is a possible separation of the paths leading simultaneously to the knowledge of man and to death.

While the figure of the sustained first- or third-person witness disappears in *Man's Fate,* a new and important development is found. . . . The style itself intimates the author's freedom from the law to which his world remains subject, so that if the idea of Man remains inseparable from the idea of tragedy, the idea of the artist pairs with the idea of freedom. To discover the meaning of style, says Malraux in reference to Goya, is to understand that "the way to express the unusual, the terrible, the inhuman, is not to represent carefully an actual or imaginary spectacle but to invent a script capable of representing these things without being forced to submit to their elements." The implications of this concept are not worked out in their complexity until we come to *The Psychology of Art,* and even there are more eloquent than clear.

Man's Fate is also the first book explicitly to raise the question of the survivor. Malraux, instead of ending with the deaths of Kyo and Katov, adds a moving epilogue in which May, Kyo's wife, and Gisors, his father, argue about the function of the surviving revolutionary. What "return" to the world is possible for him? The answer of both is deeply wrong in so far as neither really proposes his return to the world of ordinary, peaceful action, but rather a calm rejection of life (Gisors) or a vengeful remembrance of the dead (May). The figure of the survivor remains ambivalent: we do not know whether he can return to daily life or whether his sense for it has been mortally injured.

In *Days of Contempt* the question of the survivor moves from epilogue to center. The plot of the story shows a dream-like repetition of the hero's first descent into "hell," the Nazi prison in which Kassner was confined. It possesses a power analogous to the subversive climate of China, the clandestine violence of the Cambodian jungle, and Tchen's white-walled room in which Man loses his sense of identity:

> Only a sly, submissive kind of sub-human creature grown utterly indifferent to time could adapt itself to the stone. Prison-Time, that black spider, swayed back and forth in their cells as horrible and fascinating as the Time of their comrades sentenced to death. . . . Something in him attempted to adapt itself, yet adaptation was, precisely, stupor. . . .

The prison does not threaten Kassner with clear, external forms of danger. It plunges him into the thought that he is irremediably separated from the world of men. The fear of being buried while conscious rouses him the temptation to forget his identity as a man, to adapt himself whatever frees him from consciousness. This *fascination du néant,* as Malraux calls it in a later novel, is man's deepest and most secret danger. The prison's literal purpose is to soften Kassner for interrogation by cutting his links with the outside world; its symbolic purpose to erase from him the very idea of Man.

This place where Man is estranged from himself is the scene of the most arduous *Cherchez l'Homme* ever described by Malraux. Kassner invokes every human memory in his possession against his crushing solitude. Where all imaginative defenses fail, a fellow prisoner's tapped code establishes a moment of real human communication and saves him from being decisively cut off—he is drawn back into the world of men and composes an imaginary speech to members of the party until his release. This occurs when an unknown person surrenders under his name, taking his place as he had taken that of a comrade.

Though Kassner survives he remains deeply unsure of his identity. The problem of identity plays, in fact, a crucial role in the entire plot. Kassner is saved from death when the Nazis cannot identify him. Later he is saved from prison by the unknown person taking his name. A pilot risks his life to fly him to Prague without knowing anything about him except that he is a party member. At Prague, finally, Kassner has the futile experience of wishing to locate his wife among a crowd of a thousand similar faces at a mass demonstration. Thus his life, when he comes up from hell, is simply an oblique repetition of that adventure. Even in the world of men he must continue to search for Man.

He succeeds in his search; but the more each experience strengthens his fraternal vision of man, the more it puts his personal identity in doubt. Kassner remains a shadow, not a person; an interchangeable part, not a unique existence; back home he must remind himself that his wife is alive, and she is afraid to be alive, knowing he will leave on other missions. The absence of descriptive detail, as well as the stripped nature of the plot, in which some have seen Malraux's poverty of imagination and others his power to create types, reflect Kassner's ambiguous position midway between *everyman* and what Heidegger calls *das man.*

His return is not, therefore, without its price. That curiously strict theme of compensation which, in the previous novels, demanded the death of the hero in exchange for his full understanding of the idea of Man persists in slightly modified form. Kassner's solitude is overcome only with a distinct loss in personal identity. The picture of an endless chain of substitution arises as one Communist sacrifices himself for the other. Kassner is delivered by "Kassner." Malraux already approached this view in depicting the Narrator-Garine, Claude-Perken type of relationship: the younger man absorbs the experience of the older and becomes, potentially, his redemptive double. If fate imposes anonymity, Man aspires to synonymity.

Hence human freedom is no more than to substitute one man f(
another, or one fatality for another. An ironical sequence, common (
all the novels, reaches every level of the plot. All of the hero's attemp(
to escape the grip of fate are still re-presentations of it, and this appli(
as much to his experience after returning to the upper world as to h
sufferings in the underworld. There is no victory once for all—a fa(
inscribed even on Kassner's hand, which is said to bear two life-line(
One was made by himself, ironically, with a razor, the other "had bee(
made not with the stroke of a razor but with patient and steadfast wil
what was man's freedom but the awareness and organization of h
fatalities?"

In *L'Espoir* (1937) both concepts of human power (that of the razo(
line and that of patient organization) are proved insufficient. The boo(
describes the attempt of the Spanish Republicans to transform their rav(
idealistic fervor into a force capable of fighting Franco, who commanc(
an army much superior in discipline and equipment. The novel may k
divided into two main parts, which correspond roughly to Malraux(
own (I, *Illusion Lyrique*, II, *Les Manzanares*), although the constructio(
is symphonic rather than linear, so that motifs cross and intermingle i
both parts. "Descent" and "Return" are not apparently separate mov(
ments as in *Days of Contempt*, but their lineaments remain.

The first part shows the heroic insufficiency of men who follow a razo(
straight line and sacrifice themselves without the possibility of retur(
The ideal of the noble warrior, who conquers by exemplary gestures i(
the nineteenth century revolutionary tradition, is purged in blood an(
defeat. People like Puig, the Anarchist, or Captain Hernandez, an arm(
officer of the old school, die voluntarily and too quickly, sacrificed (
their particular idea of the revolution rather than to its success. Th(
most ironic example of their inutility comes when Mercery, a Frenc(
miles gloriosus, dies in a grotesquely heroic moment dousing Fasci(
airplanes with a waterhose.

In the second part survival and victory, not heroism, are the mai(
theme. "Our humble task," says Garcia, the Loyalist's chief of Intell(
gence, "is to *organize* the apocalypse." During the process of organizatio(
the Communists, well trained in obedience, and faithful to party rath(
than to individual, inevitably replace the Anarchists as the core (
Republican resistance. The turning point of the war comes when Manue(
the only "pure" Communist among the central characters of the boo(
halts the rout of the Republicans, and refashions them by using a Con(
munist cadre. But it is also Manuel who, estranged from his men throug(
the responsibilities of command, understands in the very moment (
victory the price it exacts: "Every day I get to be less human. . . ."

Malraux, however, adds a postlude entitled "Hope." In it he augmen(
a tension that exists between the external signs of victory and the inn(

consciousness of the victors. The latter understand, as in Malraux's first novel, that Man is always both conqueror and conquered. In so far as he fights against others he also fights against himself, as if every life that is lost were a subtraction from the life of Man as a whole. The hope in his heroes which secretly goes *beyond* victory is that the triumph of one power will not mean the death of some other. Manuel, in the final pages of the novel, goes off to listen to Beethoven and to dream of the infinite possibilities in Man's life—not, perhaps, the most orthodox Communist meditation. With excited voices proclaiming the statistics of victory ("Kilometre 93! . . . 94! . . . 95! . . .") he thinks of something far removed from Kassner's razor-straight line. The sounds besieging him transcend, by their very diversity, the immediate, bloodfilled and monotonously intoned present

The artist's entire skill pits itself against what may be called the razor-concept of human destiny, but within a world which demands it, and is justified in its demand by the artist himself. It is hard to imagine a greater tension. Malraux would respect the single-minded will to action, yet portray the tragic dualism of agent and act which springs from it, and preserve (at least in his own artist consciousness) what Garcia calls "corpses," alternate voices and destinies rejected by the present. The result is a sustained structural counterpoint—so sustained, in fact, that *Man's Hope* is often as "paralysed" as any novel of Flaubert's. That ultra-human speed first expressed in *The Conquerors* resolves more curiously than ever into an ironic intervention of new obstacles or into the simultaneous presence of all powers, the moment of truth in which Manuel discovers the unpredictable possibilities of life, the moment of art and fairyland "in which those who are killed all come back to life." It is not a matter of chance that the world of art intrudes as theme and source of vision into many pages, because art alone stands beyond victory and defeat, preserving to human consciousness whatever is swept aside by the sharp decisions of the immediate historical present.

The most obvious way in which Malraux modifies the idea of an absolute victory is by his continual use of the *trompe l'œil* and "double-take." An occasional device in previous novels, it now assumes the proportions of a method and serves to express the eye's effort to achieve straight-line interpretations. But just as actions, in Malraux's world, must constantly be doubled or reaffirmed, so must this movement of the mind's eye. In one scene, for example, Manuel watches his tanks advance, and as he looks, their line assumes the form of a crescent so that they seem to be turning back—he realizes they belong to the enemy. A liaison car pulls up with an officer in it relaxed and snoring—what Manuel hears is a death-rattle. He can't see the officer's wound because it is in the back of his neck, *presumably* this one had turned. Manuel then takes his field-glasses and sees men running toward the Fascist tanks, which apparently do not fire, for no one falls. He refocuses his glasses—his men are going over to the enemy. While wondering why another of his companies is moving forward to certain death ("Couldn't their captain recognize Italian tanks?") this captain is carried up dead, a bullet in his back. Manuel realizes at last that these facts together spell internal treachery. The movement from an external to an internal form of menace is also characteristic, and repeats a sequence first found in *The Conquerors*. For Malraux's novels are, fundamentally, about civil war: Spanish against Spanish, Chinese against Chinese, man against himself. If so, it is absurd to think that Man can conquer himself without defeating himself, so that the dilemma of Western activism appears once again lighted by a glaring contradiction. *L'Espoir* inherits yet another device from *The Conquerors*, the "obstacle-course" plot in which things happen so quickly that as soon as one danger is overcome another like it stands in the way. So many inimical facts bombard reader and victim that suspense dies and the concept of victory is again put in doubt. A good example is Sembrano's experience. When bullets riddle his airplane, he asks the second pilot to catch hold of the controls, but the latter is grievously wounded. He then decides to use his weakened arm, but his arm has "disappeared" . . . After the airplane crashes, one of the crew reaches a telephone—the wires are cut; another finds a truck for the wounded—no gasoline; they drain off the airplane's gas—the truck's magneto has been sabotaged. . . . Thus Malraux's warriors always face a monster who will sprout two more for every head cut off.

All these inventions project external as internal danger, fatality as will, or the finite act as an infinite repetition. They may be grouped under the general term of "prolepsis," a well-known figure of thought which reverses temporal or spatial perspectives. An especially fine instance occurs when Hernandez watches the Fascist firing squad which will soon come to him:

> They leap perilously backward. The squad fires, but they are already in the ditch. How can they hope to get away? The prisoners laugh nervously.
> They won't have to get away. The prisoners have seen the leap first, but the squad fired before that. Nerves.

Nothing "beats" death: the apparent movement to evade one's fate is really its consummation. Malraux's irony does not have the prisoners or Hernandez as its target but a *metaphysical haste* which characterizes man in the face of the world, and of which the physiological reflex is a basic sign. The scene of Hernandez' execution is a fine extension of this irony, for the methodical shooting of the prisoners, three by three in a hot, pervasive atmosphere, evokes sentiments not of death but eternity.

Malraux, like Valéry in *Le Cimetière Marin*, questions that "holy impatience" which is deeply, inseparably human. The counterpoint structure of his novel establishes a rhythm very similar to Zeno's arrow, which vibrates, wings on, yet never moves. We have studied, in the main, features of style which are manneristic, but these point to a technique shaping the whole. Malraux perfects his usage of short narrative units which he juxtaposes neatly and elliptically by cinema methods of "fadeout" and "montage." Through this art of antitheses he finds for every fact a further fact that questions, compensates or opposes it, and again disturbs the notion of an absolute victory. The descent of the aviators, for example, the novel's most moving episode, and one in which the author uses repeated views of a procession winding slowly down a mountain, comes after the apocalypse of fraternity has been "organized," yet shows in the peasants, in the wounded and through the over-arching consciousness of Magnin a spontaneous fraternal passion which is ageless and beyond organization. Or when two airmen (Leclerc and Attignes) have successfully bombed a gasworks, causing a tremendous explosion of red-and-blue flame, they suddenly notice that their airplane, flying between two layers of cloud sealing them from the ground and the moon, glows with a ghastly blue phosphorescence: "The measure of all human gestures was lost: far from the instrument panel, the only visible light in the waste of air around them, that sense of well-being which follows on all combat was disappearing into this geological tranquillity, into the mystic union of moonlight and pale metal gleaming as precious stones have gleamed for countless ages on the extinct stars." The counterpoint of gaslight and moonlight, of human success and a moment of inhuman beauty that mocks it, is far too mechanical. But it shows Malraux intent on finding ironic doubles that throw completed acts against a timeless field.

In *Man's Hope* Malraux has achieved a novel which depicts the necessity and vanity of action by the same stylistic means. The idea of victory is put in doubt: every conquest demands its sacrifice, and the survival of man, as the return of the hero in the previous novel, depends on actions that involve a deep loss to his humanity. The idea of Man, however, is not put in doubt. It survives through the consciousness of the artist, that is to say of his surrogates, figures like Garcia, Manuel and Magnin. It is they who, in victory or defeat, revive what Coleridge called "the dread watchtower of man's absolute self." They see exactly what is gained and what is lost, yet do not despair at the Manichean nature of action. *Man's Hope* realizes a symbol aimed for but never achieved in *Days of Contempt*. There the journey downward, into hell or utter solitude, remains a separate movement from the return of the hero to the world of men. The *descent* of the wounded aviators, however, seen against "the deep gorges into which they now were plunging, as if into the bowels of the earth," and through the artist-consciousness of Magnin, is not a descent into hell but a triumphant communal return to life.

In *The Walnut Trees of Altenburg* we start, for the first time, with the fact of survival. The narrator is a prisoner of war who tells the story in his own person from Chartres Cathedral, converted by the Germans into a temporary prison camp. Not only is the novel (with the hero removed from the sphere of immediate action) reflective in structure and mood, but the Cathedral's permanence at once overshadows it. Vincent Berger, the hero, is a reincarnation of Magnin watching the wounded men and offering glimpses of their individual yet similar destinies, though all are now part of, or associated with, one family, the Bergers. He describes a sequence of descents into solitude, each accompanied by a return to the world of men, except that the grandfather of the family commits suicide shortly after his son's homecoming—a relic of the stricter pattern of substitution we find in the preceding novels. The narrator, a Berger of the third generation, is already at several removes from that strange and mysterious death, of which he learns through notes left by his father. It is with these, entitled "My Encounters with Man," that he compares his life and fashions the substance of his story.

The experiences of Berger *père* and *fils* are strikingly similar, a "prefiguration" mentioned by the narrator himself. Events replace and repeat one another as in *Days of Contempt* and suggest an eternal recurrence with subtle progressions. The important fact characterizing the life of all three Bergers is that they are solitaries. But the form of their solitude, and their means to overcome it, vary significantly. The grandfather, angry with the Catholic Church, remains within the community, worshipping Christ from the ground outside the Church building. The father is a T.E. Lawrence type of adventurer, who supports the Young Turk movement even in preference to his own national obligations. In the First World War, Alsace being a part of Germany, he participates in a poison-gas attack against the Russians, and later joins his soldiers, horrified at the inhumanity—"Man was not created to moulder," says one of them—in rescuing the victims. In the Second World War, Alsace once more a part of France, Vincent fights against the Germans—a fact which once again shows the essentially civil and internecine nature of war. But now neither solitude nor fraternal action can be shaped into forms of protest as in the case of his fathers. In the half-blind tank which carries Berger to the front, the tank crews are as isolated from each other as from their enemy. The only communication between Vincent (the guide) and Prado (the driver) is a piece of string which breaks at the critical point. The soldiers in that tank do not live in a world of men. War is no longer, even among fellow soldiers, a fraternal effort, but reduces all participants alike to an inhuman solitude.

A return of the Same, as if fated, seems to govern the lives of grandfather, father and son. "I am anxious to come to the point where writing, at last! will no longer be a mere change of hells," says Vincent, prefacing the last adventure he depicts. This episode, in which he and his companions fall into a tank trap, expect immediate death, then return to the world of men, is as fearful as the gas attack witnessed by his father. Both reveal a demonic parody of Man's power to impose his world on the world. The touch of the gas translates everything at once into a living death ("The form of the flowers was almost intact. Just what corpses are to the living . . ."), which is also the nature of the ground over which Berger's tank is rolling:

> Of the ancient accord between man and the earth nothing remains: these fields of wheat over which we roll and pitch in the darkness are no longer wheatfields but camouflage: it exists no more, this earth of harvests, there exists only an earth of traps, an earth of mines. . . .

There has been an irreversible advance beyond the grandfather's sphere of influence, which was one small community in France. The very earth itself seems now to depend on Man's power for good or for evil: he can make it assume either the form of his affliction or that of his love. The concern of the writer is not for one region or religion or even for the larger-scale conflict of various nations: it is the survival of Man on earth. The enemy, for Garine, Perken and others, was "Asia." The enemy for Möllberg, principal speaker at the Altenburg colloquium, who has spent his life preparing a truly Germanic book on "Civilization as Conquest and Destiny," is "Africa"—the terrible African wasteland before which the idea of Man pales and over which his manuscript lies scattered. But the enemy of Man for Vincent Berger is Man himself, not fate, gods, or earth.

This crisis is reflected in the very nature of Malraux's art. He has said that the writer defends himself against his obsession "not by expressing it, but by expressing something else with it, by bringing it back into the universe." This "repetition-compulsion," however, still relieves suffering by a transference of suffering, and does not draw man out of the vicious circle that defines him as the form of his affliction. It involves more and more of the universe until today Man's fate and that of the world are barely separable. Man conspires against himself in Malraux's novels because he *is* the world. The novelist's structural repetitions integrate an obsessive anguish into the world, yet each recurrence shows more intensely how treacherous is this identity of human and universal. "It seems," says Berger, "as if the tank were crawling of its own will toward a snare dug by itself, and as if the human species were beginning, this very night, their struggle with each other, beyond the human adventure. . . ."

Despite this crisis, the novel looks more firmly toward survival than any of the others. Here, where Berger replaces Berger, and the synonymity to which Man aspires in *Days of Contempt* is a natural rather than artificial thing, each alienation from the world of men results in the hero returning with a greater degree of consciousness. For the grand-father, as for Malraux's earliest heroes, there is no return: the fullness of his knowledge is also the moment of his death. Just before he takes his own life, he remarks that if he had another life he would choose to repeat his own. This strangely Nietzschean comment shows that his suicide is not an act of despair. The father experiences several moments of alienation and return, which give rise to many pages of reflections, not to one cryptic dictum. But the consciousness nearest to and yet most removed from death is that of Vincent, the artist. It can pass through hell without taking hell's form or that of forgetfulness. After escaping the deadly earth of traps and mines, Vincent looks at the land around him with innocent, fraternal eyes: "It seems to me suddenly as if man came from the depths of time only to invent a watering can." Behind these words is a feeling, rare in the work of Malraux, for a life in accord with nature, a deep respect for the slow, generative powers of an earth which has always outlasted man's self-destructive haste. But when Vincent adds, at the end of the novel, "I know now what those ancient myths mean which tell of people snatched from the dead," he expresses Malraux's belief that the idea of Man is more dependent on the evidence of the artist than on the evidence of history.

The first-person narrator of *The Conquerors* attempts to catch up with history by running after it as quickly as possible. The author parodies or transforms techniques of realistic narrative so that the journalist becomes an artist despite himself, and we are given, finally, an *ecce homo* rather than the history of a revolt. But the narrator of *The Walnut Trees* knows from the start that Man is his concern. The enemy, for him, is not an external menace, this or that nation, this or that historical event. After the fall of France, in the absence of clear and present danger, he still rescues from the void of his prison images of Man's resistance to the void. Explicitly an artist ("To write is here the only means of continuing to live"), he expresses Malraux's maturest thesis, that the idea of Man is involved with the power of art to remind us of it.

André Malraux: The Image of Man

by Joseph Frank

We know that we have not chosen to be born, that we will not choose to die. That we have not chosen our parents. That we can do nothing against time. That between each of us and universal life there is . . . a sort of gulf. When I say that each man experiences deep within himself the presence of destiny, I mean that he experiences—and almost always tragically, at least for certain moments—the world's indifference vis-à-vis himself.

These lines are from André Malraux's last novel, *The Walnut Trees of Altenburg* (1943), and they go 'a long way to explain why, of all the French writers famous before the Second World War, Malraux is one of the few to whom the younger generation still pays homage. Better than any other figure of his epoch, Malraux anticipated and crystallized the postwar Existentialist atmosphere that has become associated with the names of Sartre and Camus. Man's irremediable solitude: his absurd but unquenchable longing to triumph over time: his obligation to assume the burden of freedom by staking his life for his values: his defiance of death as an ultimate affirmation of "authentic" existence—all these Existentialist themes were given unforgettable artistic expression by Malraux long before they became fashionable intellectual catchwords or tedious artistic platitudes. Indeed, the genesis of French Existentialism as a full-fledged cultural movement probably owes more to Malraux than to Heidegger or Jaspers, Berdyaev or Chestov. For it was Malraux, through his novels, who shaped the sensibilities which then seized on doctrinal Existentialism as an ideological prop.

André Malraux has thus taken on the status of a prophetic precursor in contemporary French literature, and at the same time the essential contours of his own work have begun to stand out in much clearer relief. Up to the beginning of the Second World War, Malraux was the radiant symbol of the free liberal intellectual who had dedicated his life to the Communist Revolution and the struggle against Fascism; and the focus of critical interest in his novels was their political content.

But the Communists were never too happy about Malraux as an ally—
and with good reason. For Malraux's heroes were never simply engaged
in a battle against a particular social or economic injustice; they were
always somehow struggling against the limitations of life itself and the
humiliation of destiny. Communist critics were never loth to advise
Malraux to shed his "romanticism," i.e., his Pascalian awareness of *la
condition humaine;* but while this was unquestionably good advice for
a political commissar, it would have been death to Malraux the artist.
For what makes *Man's Fate* the greatest of all novels inspired by revolution, what gives it a poetic resonance invulnerable to changing political
fashions, is precisely that Malraux was able to experience the revolution
in terms of man's immemorial longing for communion in the face of
death.

But if Existentialism has now allowed us to see Malraux's work in a
juster perspective, it also carries with it a new danger of misunderstanding. This danger consists in reading into Malraux's work the fixities of
later doctrine, and overlooking the extent to which, from his very first
serious book in 1926 (*La Tentation de l'Occident*), Malraux has been
driven by the need to transcend the dilemmas of claustrophobic egoism
and the anguish of rootless liberty which Sartre has absolutized into
ontological categories of human existence. It was this need which originally impelled Malraux toward Communism, and, when the latter dis-
played its determination to mutilate the total "quality of man," has now
led him to search for a human communion in other realms of experience.
The latest French book on Malraux, Jean Delhomme's dizzyingly dialecti-
cal and impressively intelligent philosophical study, *Temps et Destin,*[1]
attempts to force Malraux's work into a system of categories derived from
Kierkegaard, Heidegger, and Sartre (with a dash of Bergson to boot);
but while such categories are applicable to isolated characters and moments in Malraux's novels, they are entirely misleading when used to
interpret Malraux's dominating artistic impulse as a whole. This is
particularly true for the latest phase of Malraux's evolution, which com-
prises *The Walnut Trees of Altenburg* and the great series of works on
art and esthetics which have continued to appear since the end of the
Second World War. For here if anywhere in contemporary literature is
a major effort to counterbalance Existentialism and restore some of its
former luster to the tarnished image of the species Man, or, as Malraux
himself puts it, "to make men conscious of the grandeur they ignore in
themselves."

I

André Malraux's *The Walnut Trees of Altenburg* was written in the
early years of the Second World War, during a period of enforced leisure

[1] Jeanne Delhomme, *Temps et Destin, essai sur André Malraux* (Gallimard, 1955).

after the fall of France. The manuscript, presumably after being smuggled out of the country, was published in Switzerland in 1943. The work as it stands is not the entire book that Malraux wrote at that time—it is only the first section of a three-part novel called *La Lutte avec l'Ange;* and this first section was somehow preserved (there are always these annoying little mysteries about the actual facts of Malraux's life) when the Gestapo destroyed the rest. If we are to believe the list of titles printed in Malraux's latest book, *La Metamorphose des Dieux*, Vol. I (1957), he is still engaged in writing a large novel under his original title. But as he remarks in his preface to *The Walnut Trees*, "a novel can hardly ever be rewritten," and "when this one appears in its final form, the form of the first part . . . will no doubt be radically changed." Malraux pretends, perhaps with a trifle too self-conscious a modesty, that his fragmentary work will accordingly "appeal only to the curiosity of bibliophiles" and to "connoisseurs of what might have been." Even in its present form, however, the first part of Malraux's unrecoverable novel is among the greatest works of mid-twentieth century literature; and it should be far better known than it is.[2]

The theme of *The Walnut Trees of Altenburg* is most closely related to its immediate predecessor in Malraux's array of novels: *Man's Hope* (1937). This magnificent but greatly underestimated book, which bodies forth the very form and pressure of its time as no other comparable creation, has suffered severely from having been written about an historical event—the Spanish Civil War—that is still capable of fanning the smoldering fires of old political feuds. Even so apparently impartial a critic as W. H. Frohock has taken for granted that the book was originally intended as a piece of Loyalist propaganda; and has then gone on to argue, with unimpeachable consistency, that all the obviously nonpropagandistic aspects of the book are simply inadvertent "contradictions."[3]

Nothing, however, could be farther from the truth. The whole purpose of *Man's Hope* is to portray the tragic dialectic between means and ends inherent in all organized political violence—and even when such violence is a necessary and legitimate self-defense of liberty, justice, and human dignity. Nowhere before in Malraux's pages have we met such impassioned defenders of a "quality of man" which transcends the realm of politics and even the realm of action altogether—both the action of Malraux's early anarchist-adventurers like Perken and Garine, and the self-sacrificing action of dedicated Communists like Kyo, Gisors, and Katov in *Man's Fate*. "Man engages only a small part of himself in an action," says old Alvear the art-historian; "and the more the action claims

---

[2] I have the translation published in Great Britain (John Lehman, 1952) as a basis for some of my quotations, with appropriate corrections.

[3] See Frohock's useful study, *André Malraux and the Tragic Imagination* (Stanford University Press, 1952), pp. 104-125.

to be total, the smaller is the part of man engaged." These lines never cease to haunt the book amid all the exaltations of combat, and to make an appeal for a larger and more elemental human community than one based on the brutal necessities of war.

It is this larger theme of the "quality of man," a quality that transcends the ideological and flows into "the human," which now forms the pulsating heart of Malraux's artistic universe. Malraux, to be sure, does not abandon the world of violence, combat, and sudden death which has become his hallmark as a creative artist, and which is the only world, apparently, in which his imagination can flame into life. *The Walnut Trees of Altenburg* includes not one war but two, and throws in a Turkish revolution along with some guerrilla fighting in the desert for good measure. But while war still serves as a catalyst for the values that Malraux wishes to express, these values are no longer linked with the triumph or defeat of any cause—whether that of an individual assertion of the will-to-power, or a collective attempt to escape from the humiliation of oppression—as their necessary condition. On the contrary, the frenzy and furor of combat is only the somber foil against which the sudden illuminations of the human flash forth with the piercing radiance of a Caravaggio.

II

The Walnut Trees of Altenburg is composed in the form of a triptych, with two small side panels framing and enclosing the main central episode of the novel. This central episode consists of a series of staccato scenes set in the period from the beginning of the present century up to the First World War. The framing scenes, on the other hand, both take place in the late Spring of 1940, just at the moment of the defeat of France in the second great world conflict. The narrator is an Alsatian serving with the French Army, and he has the same name (Berger) that Malraux himself was later to use in the Resistance. Like Malraux he was also serving in the tank corps before being captured, and we learn as well that in civilian life he had been a writer. These biographical analogies are obvious, but far too much time has been spent speculating on their possible implications.

Much more important is to grasp the feelings of the narrator (whose full name is never given) as he becomes aware of the disorganized and bewildered mass of French prisoners clustered together in a temporary prison camp in and around the cathedral of Chartres. For as his companions gradually dissolve back into a state of primitive confrontation with elemental necessity, as they lose all the appanage of their acquired culture, he is overcome by the feeling that he is at last being confronted with the essence of mankind. "As a writer, by what have I been obsessed these last ten years, if not by mankind? Here I am face to face with the primeval stuff."

The intuition about mankind conveyed in these opening pages is of crucial importance for understanding the remainder of the text; and we must attend to it more closely than has usually been done. What does the narrator see and what does he feel? A good many pages of the first section are taken up with an account of the dogged determination of the prisoners to write to their wives and families—even when it becomes clear that the Germans are simply allowing the letters to blow away in the wind. Awkwardly and laboriously, in stiff, unemotional phrases, the soldiers continue to bridge the distance between themselves and those they love; they instinctively struggle to keep open a road to the future in their hearts. And by a skillful and unobtrusive use of imagery (the enclosure is called a "Roman-camp stockade," the hastily erected lean-to is a "Babylonian hovel," the men begin to look like "Peruvian mummies" and to acquire "Gothic faces"), Malraux projects a fresco of human endurance—which is also the endurance of the human—stretching backward into the dark abyss of time. The narrator feels himself catching a glimpse of prehistory, learning both of man's "age-old familiarity with misfortune," as well as his "equally age-old ingenuity, his secret faith in endurance, however crammed with catastrophes, the same faith perhaps as the cave-men used to have in the face of famine."

This new vision of man that the narrator acquires is also accompanied by a re-vision of his previous view. "I thought I knew more than my education had taught me" notes the narrator, "because I had encountered the militant mobs of a political or religious faith." Is this not Malraux himself alluding to his own earlier infatuation with the ideological? But now he knows "that an intellectual is not only a man to whom books are necessary, he is any man whose reasoning, however elementary it may be, affects and directs his life." From this point of view the "militant mobs" of the past, stirred into action by one ideology or another, were all composed of "intellectuals"—and this is not the level on which the essence of mankind can be discovered. The men around him, observes the narrator, "have been living from day to day for thousands of years." The human is deeper than a mass ideology, certainly deeper than the isolated individual; and the narrator recalls the words of his father, Vincent Berger: "It is not by any amount of scratching at the individual that one finally comes down to mankind."

The entire middle section of *The Walnut Trees* is taken up with the life of Vincent Berger himself, whose fragmentary notes on his "encounters with mankind" are now conveyed by his son. "He was not much older than myself" writes the narrator, "when he began to feel the impact of that human mystery which now obsesses me, and which makes me begin, perhaps, to understand him." For the figure of Vincent Berger, Malraux has obviously drawn on his studies of T. E. Lawrence (though Berger fights on the side of the Turks instead of against them), and like both Lawrence and Malraux himself he is a fervent admirer of Nietzsche. A professor at the University of Constantinople, where his first course of lectures was on Nietzsche and the "philosophy of action," Vincent Berger becomes head of the propaganda department of the German Embassy in Turkey. As an Alsatian before the First World War he was of course of German nationality; but he quickly involves himself in the Young Turk revolutionary movement to such an extent that his own country begins to doubt his patriotism. And, after becoming the right-hand man of Enver Pasha, he is sent by the latter to pave the way for a new Turkish Empire embracing "the union of all Turks throughout Central Asia from Adrianople to the Chinese oases on the Silk Trade Route."

Vincent Berger's mission is a failure because the Ottoman nationalism on which Enver Pasha counted does not exist. Central Asia is sunk in a somnolence from which nothing can awaken it; and amid a dusty desolation in which nothing human seemed to survive, Vincent Berger begins to dream of the Occident. "Oh for the green of Europe! Trains whistling in the night, the rattle and clatter of late cabs. . . ." Finally, after almost being beaten to death by a madman—he cannot fight back because madmen are sacred to Islam—he throws up his mission and returns to Europe. This has been his first encounter with mankind, and, although he has now become a legendary figure in the popular European press, it leaves him profoundly dissatisfied. Despite Berger's report, Enver Pasha refuses to surrender his dream of a Turkish Blood Alliance; and Vincent Berger learns that political ambition is more apt to hide than to reveal the truth about men. But as he discovers shortly, on returning among intellectuals obsessed by *le culte du moi,* his experience of action had also taught him a more positive lesson. "For six years my father had had to do too much commanding and convincing" writes the narrator, "not to understand that man begins with 'the other.' "

And when Vincent Berger returns to Europe, this first result of his encounters with mankind is considerably enriched and deepened by a crucial revelation. For a dawning sense of illumination occurs in consequence of two events which, as so often in Malraux, suddenly confront a character with the existential question of the nature and value of human life. One such event is the landing in Europe itself, when the mingled familiarity and strangeness of the Occident, after the blank immensities of Asia, shock the returning traveller into a realization of the infinite *possibilities* of human life. Significantly, Malraux compares this shock to that undergone by a man who has just committed murder. "This evening he [Vincent Berger] felt released . . . with a poignant liberty indistinguishable from license." The other event is the suicide of Vincent's father five days after his landing and just two days after a conversation in which Dietrich Berger had said: "Well, you know, *whatever happens,* if I had to live another life again, I should want none other than Dietrich Berger's."

Both these events pierce through the thin film of the quotidian, the horizontal surface on which most of human life is spent, and disclose the vertical depths of the contingency of human existence and the anguish of human liberty. This anguish of liberty is a familiar phenomenon to all readers of Malraux—it possesses Malraux's adventurers, as well as the terrorist Tchen in *Man's Fate*—and always, in the past, it had resulted in a release that was equivalent to a condemnation. The answer to this anguish had always been a paroxysm of the will-to-power: a convulsive attempt of human liberty, freed of all attachments, to prove its own autonomy by an impossible duel with the power of inhuman fatality. But the release that now occurs in Vincent Berger is of an entirely different order:

> The human adventure, the world. And all of it, like his father's fulfilled destiny, could have been other than it was. He felt himself gradually possessed by an unknown sensation, as he had once been at night in the highlands of Asia by the presence of the sacred, while around him the velvet wings of the little desert owls fluttered in silence. It was the same agonizing sense of freedom, only far more pronounced, that he had felt that evening at Marseilles watching the shadows glide in the faint odor of cigarettes and absinthe—when Europe had seemed so unfamiliar, when he had watched it as if, liberated from time, he would have watched an hour of the distant past slip slowly by with all its strange retinue. In the same way, he now felt the whole of his life becoming strange; and suddenly he felt delivered— mysteriously a stranger to the earth and astonished by it, as he had been by that street where the people of his rediscovered race slid by in the greenish twilight . . .

The experience of the contingency of existence thus leads Vincent Berger to an intuition of "the sacred." But the category of the religious —as we have learned from Kierkegaard, and as we could have learned even earlier from Job—transcends the category of the social or ethical; and in this sense Perken, Garine, and Tchen had also been initiated into the mystery of "the sacred." But the sacred is no longer the equivalent of the demonic (also a religious category); nor is it, as in Asia, a sense of the nothingness of man before the awfulness of the infinite (the desert is monotheistic, as Renan remarked in a once-famous phrase). Rather, "the sacred" is now for Malraux an intuition of the infinite mystery of human liberty, of a world and a life which "could have been other than it was" and which, in being what it is, testifies to the existence of a human essence that endures and persists underneath the equally infinite vicissitudes of time and history. Vincent Berger's "agonizing sense of freedom" is, as it were, only the coming-to-consciousness of the freedom which exists as an inchoate but irreducible and immortal possibility at the center of human life itself. And this is the intuition of "the sacred" in man that Vincent Berger defends in the famous colloquy at the old abbey at Altenburg.

III

This debate is certainly one of the most brilliant scenes of its kind in contemporary fiction. Nothing is more difficult than to dramatize serious intellectual discussion successfully: and Malraux does so with an aphoristic intensity and an emotional vibrancy that can only be matched in the very best pages of Thomas Mann. Indeed, Malraux's formulations are so striking and so luminous that they have provided an irresistible temptation for critics to overstress their importance. W. H. Frohock has maintained, in a view which is generally accepted, that Vincent Berger is "rationally" defeated by the Spenglerian arguments of the ethnologist Möllberg; and that at the end of this sequence he can only fall back on an "irrational" vision of the walnut trees of Altenburg to establish his faith in an essence of man.[4] But such an interpretation is inadmissible for a number of reasons. For one thing, Malraux is too well acquainted with Spengler, who prided himself precisely on his "intuitive" view of history, to identify Spengler's position with any kind of "rationalism." For another, it is perfectly clear in the novel that Möllberg's views spring from the same existential level as Vincent Berger's but reflect a temperament and an outlook that leads to despair instead of to a grave and sober exaltation. And on this level, the refutation of Möllberg already has been given both in the opening pages of the book and in Vincent Berger's intuition of "the sacred."

"Is there something given on which we can base the notion of man?" This is the issue at stake in the great debate as it is formulated by Vincent's uncle, Walter Berger, the famous intellectual impresario who orchestrates the colloquies at Altenburg. The first answer proposed is that man's essence can be founded on the creation of "culture," that is, on great works of art, the gift of individual genius to mankind, which free us "from the bonds of space, time and death." This "subtly banal" view, however, is rejected by Edmé Thirard, who sounds a good deal like the great literary critic Albert Thibaudet and whose words receive the silent approval of Vincent Berger. "Culture," Thirard asserts, "doesn't teach us about man, it merely teaches us about the cultured man, in proportion to the degree of his culture." The religion of culture, in other words, isolates culture from the roots of life and fails to make contact with "the commonplace human misery . . . in hospitals, in maternity wards, and in the rooms of the dying."

The next answer suggested is that we can get at the essence of man

---

⁴ Frohock, *op. cit.*, p. 132.

by psychology, that is, by "scratching at the individual" in search of his "secrets." Vincent Berger's experience of "the other" has already implicitly rejected this answer according to the artistic logic of the novel; and now, intervening directly in the argument, he attacks the emphasis on psychology as Occidental cultural chauvinism, a consequence of the influence of Christianity on the Western psyche. "It's our old struggle against the Devil . . . which makes us confuse our knowledge of man with our knowledge of his secrets." The mystery of man is precisely that no "secrets" can ever explain his inviolable freedom. And when Thirard remarks that our "knowledge" of man is always dubious because "we can hardly ever foresee the really important actions of those nearest to us," the figure of Dietrich Berger rises before Vincent's eyes as a vital confirmation of this assertion. This is the manner in which, underneath the glittering swordplay of ratiocination, Malraux constantly appeals to the deeper level of experience portrayed elsewhere in the book; and unless we situate the ideas in this framework, we can hardly understand either the underlying movement of the discussion or the nature of its resolution.

In place of man as the creator of "culture," or as the repository of "secrets" which, once brought to light, would eliminate the mystery of freedom, Vincent Berger proposes another image of man: as eternally engaged in a struggle with destiny, as eternally striving—and succeeding —in transforming fate into freedom. Here again art is invoked as evidence just as in the thesis about "culture"; but it is very important to grasp Malraux's distinction (not, it must be admitted, made very clearly) between the two. Art is no longer a miraculous gift of individual genius to mankind which *creates* a freedom from destiny; now it is only a symbol that *expresses* man's collective and eternal struggle to transcend the conditions of his servitude:

> To me [Vincent Berger says] our art seems to be a rectification of the world, a means of escaping from man's estate. The chief confusion, I think, is due to our belief—and in the theories propounded of Greek tragedy, it's strikingly clear—that representing fatality is the same as submitting to it. But it's not, it's almost to dominate it. The mere fact of being able to represent it, conceive it, release it from real fate, from the merciless divine scale, reduces it to the human scale. Fundamentally, our art is a humanization of the world.

It is this "humanization of the world"—a humanization that stems from the assertion of human liberty in the face of destiny—that Vincent Berger has already felt in his intuition of "the sacred"; and the validity of this intuition is denied by Möllberg in the speech that follows.

Möllberg's presence in the book is far from being merely that of a disembodied voice grinding out a string of irrefutable arguments; and perhaps if critics had paid a bit more attention to his human contours, they would have been able to place his arguments in a juster perspective. In any case, it is certainly not accidental that when Vincent Berger enters Möllberg's room (in a scene preceding the debate), he finds it filled with grotesque little figurines—imaginary gargoyles with animal traits incongruously scrambled together, all looking curiously like their creator and all with an "air of gripping sadness, like Goya's monsters which seem to remember they were once human." Möllberg has been molding these figurines for many years; and Malraux obviously wishes to feel him as a sensibility haunted by the infinite malleability of nature, and by the extent to which man is merely another element in the eternal flux. Moreover, when he is asked, at the end of the debate, what "concept" drove him to the conclusions he presents, he snaps back angrily: "Not a concept. Africa!" Upon which follows an hallucinatory parade of images: "The succession without end of days under the dusty firmament of Libya or the heavy, grey sky of the Congo, the tracks of invisible animals converging toward the water-holes, the migration of famished dogs under the empty sky, the hour when all thought becomes weariness, the gloomy thrust of giant trees in prehistoric boredom. . . ."

This should be enough to show that Möllberg's views are no more "rational" than Vincent Berger's intuition of "the sacred"; and what resounds in the background of Möllberg's impressive speech is the thwarted bitterness of his defeat by "Africa," that is, by a nature so savage and so terrible that it has confirmed his latent fear of nature's ultimate triumph over man.[5] Projected on the plane of ideas, and buttressed with an impressive amount of ethnological evidence, this fear amounts to the Spenglerian thesis that every culture-cycle is an airtight and self-enclosed whole imprisoned in its own assumptions. There is no possibility of communication between cultures, hence no escape from the determinism of fate (in the form of the isolated mental structure of each culture), and no essence of man based on the continuity of his struggle against destiny. Directly addressing himself to Vincent Berger, Möllberg affirms: "Men are, perhaps, more thoroughly defined and classified by their form of fatalism than by anything else." The mental structure of our own civilization is dominated by the idea of history, and even more fundamentally by the discovery of "time." Time is the fatality of modern man, and, while earlier cultures had believed in some sort of eternal value impervious to time, we make no exception to the inexorable iron grip of fatality on all of human life.

Now it is simply not true, as has been asserted over and over again,

---

[5] See also the following comment of the narrator while Möllberg is speaking: "Discussion and logic, the books in serried ranks on the shelves, were fighting for their rights against the voice of the dark continents." Möllberg is the voice of "the dark continents," not of "rationalism"; the very conception of reason is meaningless unless we believe in man as somehow superior to nature.

that Möllberg crushes all his interlocutors into a speechless mutism by the power of his arguments; the fact is that he is forced to concede a very important point to Thirard. For Möllberg's whole position hinges on the identification of man with what he "thinks," i.e., with being what has been called an "intellectual" in the opening pages. Malraux thus expects the attentive reader to know that Möllberg's argument is humanly fallacious from the very start; and he brings out this point in Thirard's question. Even if an Egyptian high priest and a Catholic cardinal exist in different psychic realms, Thirard asks, would not an Egyptian laborer and an Alsatian one have something in common? Möllberg cannot deny the pertinence of this thrust; and here is where the issue is joined. Möllberg is speaking:

"The less men partake of their civilization, the more they resemble each other. I agree! But the less they partake of it, the more they fade away. The permanence of man can be conceived, but it's a permanence in nothingness."
"Or in the fundamental?"
It was my father [Vincent Berger] who put the question. *The point at issue was no longer the history of man, but the nature of each present; everyone felt himself at stake.* [Italics added]

The debate has now become a reflection, in the last analysis, of the nature of the individual participants; what is at stake is *their* quality as men. And Möllberg's position is a perfect illustration of the arrogance of the intellectual who has not learned, like Vincent Berger, that man begins with "the other," and who, equating "humanity" only with his own sub-species, contemptuously relegates everyone else to the realm of "nothingness," i.e., animality. The reverse side of this arrogance is the susceptibility to despair, the self-hatred and *Schadenfreude* (the German word is appropriate) that impels Möllberg to say "with sardonic self-satisfaction" that "there's no better way of concentrating on man than looking at an ant-hill." Erich Heller has pertinently written that "Spengler's history is untrue because the mind which has conceived it is, despite its learning and seeming subtlety, a crude and wicked mind. The image of man which lurks behind Spengler's vast historical canvas is perverted. . . . For Spengler has no idea of the true stature of the problem of human freedom. Therefore his historical vision is lacking in depth as well as in love, pity and pathos." [6] Malraux is saying nothing else in his portrait of Möllberg, though with a nuance of sympathy for his character that Heller finds it impossible to muster for Spengler himself.

During the discussion with Möllberg, the latter exemplifies the nothingness of nonintellectual man by pointing to some statues on the wall

[6] See Erich Heller, "Oswald Spengler and the Predicament of the Historical Imagination," *The Disinherited Mind* (Meridian Books, 1959) , p. 193.

carved from the walnut trees surrounding the abbey of Altenburg. These, he asserts, are either statues—the product of a specific cultural tradition —or they are nothing, mere logs of wood; there is no "fundamental walnut" intermediate between the two, just as there is no "fundamental man" intermediate between intellectual or ideological man and the brute. Trees also take on symbolic value in another context, for Möllberg explains earlier to Vincent Berger that the pages of his proposed (and now abandoned) book demonstrating civilization as a conquest by man "are hanging from the lower branches of various types of trees from the Sahara to Zanzibar. Right. In accordance with tradition, the victorious carry off the spoils of the defeated." With these words as well as Möllberg's reference to the statues still in his mind, Vincent Berger strolls across the fields of Altenburg after the debate and looks at the rows of carefully cultivated walnut trees receding in the distance and framing the cathedral of Strasbourg in their perspective.

"Between the statues and the logs there were the trees" he thinks, "and their design which was as mysterious as life itself." The walnut trees of course figure forth the reality of "fundamental man" (neither intellectually self-conscious nor mere blank nothingness); and the human effort embodied in their cultivation is no doubt intended to contrast with the wilderness that broke Möllberg's spirit. Nonetheless, although the meaning of Malraux's symbolism is clear enough, one cannot help feeling a certain disharmony in the prominence given the tree-metaphor by Malraux's title. It is true that the sight of the trees evokes an impression of "will and metamorphosis without end" in Vincent Berger's consciousness; but trees are still only a part of nature, and the use of this symbol clashes with Malraux's central thematic focus on *Man's* freedom and creativity.[7]

IV

Vincent Berger's defense of man's eternal capacity to "humanize" the world, to transcend the circumstances in which the fatality of history may imprison him, is the spiritual climax of the middle section of the novel. And the remainder of the action of this section, which ends with Berger's death by poison gas, is a magnificent projection of this capacity in one of the most moving scenes of the contemporary novel.

[7] To make matters worse, Malraux unfortunately stresses the insignificance of man's endeavors at this point compared to the spectacle of the trees: "And that spire [i.e., of the cathedral] rising like the prayers of the maimed, and all the human patience and the human labor that were the waves of vineyards descending to the river, were only an evening background to the immemorial upsurge of the living wood, for the two thick clumps that wrested the strength from the earth itself to spread in their branches." One has the uneasy feeling that at this point Malraux's imagery swept him away and caused him to lose control of his theme.

After the outbreak of the First World War, Vincent Berger is assigned to German Intelligence on the Eastern Front; and he is detailed to look after a scientist who has invented a new poison gas which is ready to be tested in combat. Malraux again punctures the pretentions of the species "intellectual" by sketching the innocently obtuse inhumanity of the scientist with merciless *brio*. By contrast, the naïve and childish chatter of the ordinary German soldiers, waiting in the trenches before the attack, is dense with the warmth of an all-pervasive humanity. The most absurd legends, myths, and suggestions flash out like Roman candles as the voices sound in the enveloping darkness; but all of them bear the unmistakable stamp of man. One soldier ferociously advocates that all the enemy be castrated, but then adds this reflection: "It's not humanitarian, perhaps, but that way we'd finish them once and for all, and without killing anyone." Stories of adultery and lust end in the laconic comments: "But he let it go on, because of the kid"; or: "So the chap, instead of appearing in court, he went home, and then he hung himself." Exactly as his son was to do twenty-five years later, Vincent Berger senses that he is at last coming close to "the fundamental" in man. "Listening in this live darkness, my father was conscious for the first time of the people of Germany. Or perhaps just of people: men." And what men really are, or what they can become in certain privileged moments, is gloriously shown in the "human apocalypse" unleashed by the gas attack. For when the Germans reach the Russian trenches, pushing their way through fields turned by the gas into an eerie universal putrefaction, the sight of the Russians in the terrible convulsions of strangulation releases an instinctive combination of anguish and fraternity that cannot be denied. Instead of advancing, the German soldiers return to their own lines and hospital units, bearing the bodies of men who have become their brothers. Not so much out of pity, as out of an impulse far deeper that seemed to arise from a need for *self*-protection against the spirit of evil: each Russian soldier was a talisman. Vincent Berger, abandoning his duty like the rest, meets his end in this fulfillment of his faith.

The power and majesty of this scene are so great that all writers on Malraux (including myself, in an earlier article)[8] have unanimously taken it as the key figuration of the novel's major theme: the fraternity of the human. My opinion now, however, is that such a reading unduly narrows the scope of Malraux's range, and that "fraternity" is only one manifestation of his theme rather than its entire substance. This substance is embodied essentially in Vincent Berger's intuition of "the sacred," the "humanization of the world" that arises out of man's liberty to oppose destiny; and this "humanization" can disclose itself not only in the upsurge of fraternity but also in art—or in the contemplation of the hum-

---

[8] See *The New Republic*, August 30, 1954.

blest work of human hands and the lowliest of human creatures. This is why Malraux, in the final section of the book, returns to the narrator —Vincent Berger's son—to bring us back to the present and give us a final epiphany of his true theme in its full extent.

This last scene centers on a French tank attack in which the narrator takes part, presumably in the series of battles leading to the French defeat. After being bogged down in a tank trap all night, and expecting the pinpointed artillery to zero in on them at any moment, the narrator's crew finally manage to disengage themselves and they stop in an evacuated village at dawn. Still harrowed by his night of terror, the narrator feels the simplest signs of life to be a miracle, an apparition: "The world might have been as simple as the sky or the sea. And at the sight of the shapes in front of me, which are only the shapes of an abandoned, condemned village—I feel in the presence of an unaccountable gift—an apparition. All this might never have been, might never have been as it is! . . . There are other worlds, the world of crystals, of oceanic depths. . . ." The wonder of the human world being as it is overwhelms Vincent Berger's son, as it had overwhelmed his father on the night of his landing at Marseilles.

But the greatest miracle of all is man himself, in the guise of an old peasant couple too enfeebled to have gone on with the rest. The narrator looks at the wife:

> Harmonized with the cosmos like a stone. . . . Yet she smiles, a slow, pensive smile; beyond the football-field with its solitary goalposts, beyond the tank turrets gleaming in the dew like the bushes camouflaging them, she seems to be viewing death at a distance and even—oh, mysterious blink, sharp shadow at the corner of the eyelids!—even with irony. . . . Let the mystery of man reappear from that enigmatic smile, and the resurrection of the earth becomes nothing more than a trembling backdrop.

That the earth should not be as simple as the sky and the sea, but everywhere bear the imprint of man; that an old peasant woman should be capable of looking with a smile in the face of death—this is the miracle of the human that Vincent Berger had felt in his intuition of "the sacred," and which now shines forth again, as from a Biblical illustration of Rembrandt's, in the débris of a war-torn village. "I can scarcely remember what fear is like" writes the narrator finally; "what I carry within me is the discovery of a simple, sacred secret."

No writer in modern literature can compete with Malraux—at least with the Malraux of this final scene—in evoking so poignantly what Wordsworth called "the still, sad music of humanity." And this music, despite its stillness and sadness, never ceases to sound in Malraux's novel above the roar of battle and the tumultuous march of the centuries. Malraux manages to wrest an affirmation of an absolute value in man out of the very teeth of the experience which—for example, in Sartre's *La Nausée*—had led to Antoine Roquentin's frightening vision of man's absorption into the world of brute materiality. The disclosure of the contingency of existence had led Sartre to portray man himself as a futile excrescence on the blank surface of things; and despite the role that liberty plays in Sartre's philosophy, he has not yet succeeded (it is dubious whether he ever will succeed) in transcending the hopelessness of *La Nausée* by any equally powerful artistic expression. Indeed, one wonders whether Malraux's *The Walnut Trees of Altenburg*, consciously or otherwise, might not have been intended to meet the challenge of the vision of man proposed in *La Nausée* (which after all appeared in 1938, and which Malraux very probably would have read).

However that may be, there is no doubt that Malraux has managed, by the sheer force of his artistic genius, to extend the bounds of Existentialism in an extremely significant fashion. Even when Extentialism is determinedly atheist, as in Heidegger or Jean-Paul Sartre, the movement as a whole has drawn its image of man from the tortured cogitations of Kierkegaard; and that means from a Christianity which emphasizes the fallen nature of man and all the dark and gloomy aspects of human existence. Malraux, on the other hand, might be said to have created—paradoxical as it may sound—an Existentialism of the Enlightenment. For in reading *The Walnut Trees of Altenburg,* one thinks of Kant rather than of Kierkegaard—not to be sure the Kant of *The Critique of Pure Reason,* but the Kant who, in *The Critique of Judgment,* defined the "dynamic-sublime" as man's consciousness of the final inability of the power of nature, however menacing it might be, to force him to surrender his humanity. Malraux's image of man is therefore "sublime" in the strict meaning given that term by the greatest mind of the Enlightenment. Perhaps in no period of modern culture has such an image of man been more necessary or seemed less possible; and that Malraux can still make us believe in its viability is surely a remarkable tribute to his quality both as an artist and as a man.

Malraux, Möllberg, and Frobenius

by Armand Hoog

All those who are somewhat acquainted with André Malraux know that they know nothing of his private life, or little. About his adolescence, his formative years, his schooling, there is not a single precise detail. Only one journalist, an American woman, was able to gather a few biographic elements. It is none the less certain, and to a greater degree than one imagines, that Malraux's work is full of allusions, disguises, and keys. For example, among the Parisian journalists there are some who still remember the real character whom Malraux described in *La Condition Humaine* under the name of the colorful Baron Clappique, the clown "Toto" of Shanghai bars. This was René Guetta, the clown "Toto" of Paris bars, a reporter for the paper *Marianne,* known for his love of very dry Martinis, his "p'petits argents" and "rentrez sous terre." Guetta is dead but his gloomy image lives on as one of the keys to Malraux's sarcasm.

Of all his novels, one in particular offers the reader a flavor of the actual that is stronger than the memories of revolution, adventure and war scattered throughout his other writings. In this sense, *Les Noyers de l'Altenburg* is the most mystifying, the most fascinating of Malraux's books. At every page one seems to hit on a secret order of references. This is the only story, outside of *Les Conquérants,* told in the first person. (But there is a considerable difference between these two tales. The one who says "I" in *Les Conquérants* is only a spectator. The narrator of Altenburg is a participant, the son, in fact, of Vincent Berger whose intellectual experience provides the background of the novel.) This is also the only novel in which Malraux recounts the story of a family. Far be it from me, however, to suggest an absolute identification of the novel with the author. But it is nevertheless possible to note certain relationships. The name Berger—this is the name Malraux used during the Resistance; in 1944, he was "Colonel Berger" of the Brigade d'Alsace-Lorraine. In addition, Vincent Berger's father, like Malraux's father and perhaps even his grandfather, kills himself in the novel. Most important, it should be noted, is that *Les Noyers de l'Altenburg* is the only novel of Malraux that is *not based on current events* but goes much deeper, back to childhood and recollections of the clan. This contrast becomes striking if one estimates to what extent Malraux usually required an event to stimulate his imagination—Malraux, the only *photographic* genius of the French novel. Date by date, book by book, his work seemed for some time to be merely the commentary of just-completed action. *Les Conquérants,* appearing in 1928, evoked the Canton rebellion of 1926. *La Voie Royale,* in 1930, was the barely disguised archeological adventure of Malraux's mission to Cambodia a few years earlier. The material of *La Condition Humaine* (1933) was still drawn from the events of 1926. *Le Temps du Mépris* (1935) and *L'Espoir* (1937) followed almost immediately—within two years—the events described in them: the Nazi revolution and the Spanish Civil War. It may well be the first time that a great French writer so closely juxtaposed his fiction with contemporary history. For even if Balzac depicted the Restoration, it was after the July revolution, and the best of Proust concerns the period of MacMahon and the Dreyfus affair.[1]

But in *Les Noyers de l'Altenburg,* written in 1940 and 1941, Malraux refers back to events of thirty years earlier, previous to the First World War, that war which divided the history of the modern world. Agadir, German Alsace, the Balkan Wars, pre-Kemal Turkey. Ancient events, fabulous events, antediluvian events concealed behind the mists of Old Europe. And only the deluge itself can account for this return, however transmuted, to the saga of the family. At the time of the Balkan Wars, in 1912, André Malraux was just 11 years old. What is said in *Les Noyers* about the wars, as seen through the eyes of the father, has something of the naïve quality of the tuppence-colored that betrays childhood memories, whether they are interpreted as stories read or accounts heard in childhood.[2] No other work of Malraux conveys so much of the pervasive presence of childhood, as though finally, in this key work, half-confidences united constantly with the central themes of his entire work.

In fact, *Les Noyers de l'Altenburg,* at times a difficult, obscure and even equivocal novel, becomes remarkably clear if one does not try to discover in it some *new* aspect of Malraux's personality, but rather seeks its most *permanent* characteristics. I shall never forget the outburst of surprise, concern, and bafflment that accompanied the publication, in 1947, of the *Musée Imaginaire* and the first Parisian edition of *Les Noyers.* More than one critic marveled, however admiringly, that such an excel-

---

[1] *Le Feu* by Barbusse is no more than a reportage although in parts highly admirable. But it is no longer read. Neither 6 February, 1934 nor the Second World War has yet inspired any great French novels.

[2] And other such anecdotes that come straight out of family mythology. Like the image of Walter Berger, as a child around 1850 or 1860, explaining "what he will do later" at the Académie Française (NA, p. 37). Throughout this article, all references are to the Skira edition of Malraux's works. Text references have been abbreviated to the first letters of the novel's titles.

lent novelist should turn into an art historian.[3] Can it be, they exclaimed, that Malraux is not only a man of action but an art lover as well? It did not escape their attention that the core of *Les Noyers* lies in the pages relating the "symposium" held under the towering gothic arches of Altenburg. But the intention of this symposium was misinterpreted.

A German ethnologist, Möllberg, who had explored in Africa, the Sahara, and Egypt, expounds his views on the diversity of cultures during this colloquy. "Does the concept of man have any meaning?" he asks, and replies negatively. Could Möllberg be Malraux by any chance? There are some who hasten to say yes. Has not Malraux betrayed the revolutionary universalism that he professed in *La Condition Humaine* and *Le Temps du Mépris?* Has not Malraux just joined ranks with General de Gaulle in a reactionary venture, the *Rassemblement du Peuple Français?* Are not Möllberg's words in *Les Noyers* the very ones that Malraux pronounced at the Sorbonne in 1946? "The problem of today is to find out whether, on this ancient soil of Europe, *man is dead or not.*" [4] And if Möllberg believes in man's death, that is, in the destruction of universalism, is this not a proof that Malraux, after a complicated ideological and political evolution, has espoused Fascist ideas? One can find this reasoning developed in twenty critical articles that appeared at the time. A good example of this malevolent conclusion is furnished by Pierre Debray's study, published in the special issue of *Esprit* devoted to Malraux during the fall of 1948. The author of *Les Noyers de l'Altenburg,* writes Debray icily, "has consummated the rupture of man's unity."

I find this critical thesis absurd. Absurd and indefensible. I said so at the time, when there was perhaps more merit in saying so than today. And I am scarcely more convinced by the idea that Malraux had undergone serious ideological evolution. (Political, surely. Still, the Malraux of 1930-1933 was in no way a "Marxist," just as the Malraux of 1948 was in no way a "Fascist," if words mean anything.) I maintain that *Les Noyers de l'Altenburg,* insofar as this book expresses Malraux's fidelity to his recurring themes, can perhaps reveal the secret of his thinking, and perhaps even of his action.

If some people were amazed, beginning with *Les Noyers de l'Altenburg* and *La Psychologie de l'Art,* to see Malraux "go over" to esthetic criticism, it is because they had not read his earlier works carefully. The success of *La Condition Humaine,* considered until the war to be Malraux's great novel, has clouded our outlook and impeded a true comprehension of his total output. There is nothing more disputable than the

[3] *Les Noyers de l'Altenburg,* published in Switzerland during the war, was reprinted in a temporary and limited edition by Gallimard in 1948.

[4] A stenographic copy of this lecture, given 4 November, 1946, on "L'Homme et la culture artistique," revealing even the speaker's vivacity, appeared three days later in the weekly, *Carrefour.* It is from this text that I am quoting.

recent studies devoted to Malraux that divide his writing into successive periods and make him appear, in his final transformation, as a tired adventurer or a retired novelist at last, in his remaining day of leisure, entering "the world of art." As it happens, Malraux entered "the world of art" at the age of 18 and has never left it since.[5] The adolescent lover of Oriental art who, around 1920, attended courses at the École du Louvre without credit, and lectured at the Musée Guimet, became in 1923 the young explorer of Banteai-Srey, and then, during the intervals of public life and revolutionary activity, developed into what I venture to call the most professional of estheticians. To Malraux's name have been fastened all sorts of labels, some accurate, some invented. The most accurate would be that of the profession he has always followed, editor of art books.

Is this constancy manifest in the work itself? The question has not been asked often enough. But once asked it immediately evokes the answer. From the 25-year-old philosopher who published his first book in 1926, *La Tentation de l'Occident,* to the critic of *Les Voix du Silence,* including the novelist whose books spread out over some fifteen years, Malraux has never ceased being the man who, in the paintings and statues of the world, seeks the face of the gods. Of what gods? Those whose infinite procession revives and recommences as soon as the museum ceases to be a museum and becomes a participation; as soon as the painting once again becomes a dream and the statue a ritual object. "Almost barbaric figures in which a great harmonious suffering was petrified. . . . I visited the galleries of your museums; your genius filled me with anguish. Even your gods, their grandeur stained like their images with blood and tears, are animated with a savage power." So speaks the Chinese, Ling, as early as 1926, in *La Tentation de l'Occident* (p. 30). Two years later, the revolutionary Garine, in *Les Conquérants,* during a moment of delirium, sees looming up before him a hallucinating procession of gods: "At Kazan, on Christmas eve '19, that extraordinary procession. . . . What? . . . They are bringing all the gods in front of the cathedral, huge figures like carnival floats, even a fish goddess with a siren's torso. . . . Two hundred, three hundred gods. . . . Luther too. The fur-covered musicians are making a god-awful racket with the instruments they found. A tall pyre is aflame. On the shoulders of the guys carrying them the gods are going around the square, black against the pyre, against the snow . . ." *(Les Conquérants,* p. 159).

This dates from 1928. But everyone was doubtlessly more concerned with Garine's revolutionary romanticism, his obsession with the absurd, his desperate eroticism, than with his visions of mythological processions. Nevertheless, the texts are there, from the beginning of Malraux's career, all of them translating the preoccupations that will be developed, fifteen or twenty years later, in *Les Noyers de l'Altenburg* or *La Psychologie de*

---

[5] "How long have you worked on your art books?" an acquaintance asked Malraux last year. "All my life," he answered. (Flanner, *The New Yorker,* November 13, 1954).

l'Art. "It is history's mission to bestow a meaning on the human adventure—like the gods. To relate man to infinity . . ." says Möllberg (NA 98). And the conclusion of *Les Voix du Silence,* in 1951, "Let the gods on judgment day set up before the forms that were alive the people of statues" (p. 624).

Here then is what the young André Malraux learned in the museums after the war. Between 1917 and 1921 three revelations struck this mind nurtured on Nietzsche (but more by *The Birth of Tragedy* than by the declamatory *Zarathustra*): the October Revolution, the destruction of Europe, and the art of the Orient. And all three—Lenin, the 1918 armistice, and the Musée Guimet—proclaim the same thing: history changes, the gods die. From one culture to another, from one period to another, the difference between men seems immense, ineluctable. Problem: Is the difference between men greater than the similarity? And when the gods die, does the society—nation, civilization, or church—that created these mortal gods crumble with them only to reappear in another form, another place, another time? "The Greeks believed man distinct from the world, as the Christians believe man linked with God, as we believe man linked with the world," Ling observes in *La Tentation de l'Occident,* in a line, although written twenty years earlier, that could come from *La Psychologie de l'Art.* The Greek, the Christian, the Oriental are men, but are they *the same man?* "The museum," says Ling, "teaches, alas, what 'foreigners' expect of beauty. It stimulates one to compare, and above all to feel, in a new work the difference it presents. . . . Emotions, unexpected color harmonies, the esthetic dreams that my ancestors found in our paintings will, in death, unite the reveries that toys evoke in children. . . ." And further on: "The world is invading Europe, the world with all its past and present, its offerings made up of dead and living forms. . . ." On the following page they are named: "The charioteer of Delphi, the brooding Kore, the romanesque Christs, the heads of Sais and Khmer, the Wei and T'ang boddhistavas, primitives of every land . . . the stream of living forms. . . ." Who does not now see the import carried by these lines of 1926? There is nothing, even to the words—obscure for some, scandalous for others—of the Sorbonne lecture in 1946 ("to find out whether man is dead or not"), that is not already prefigured in *La Tentation de l'Occident.* One need only have looked; but who was aware of it then? Ling's letter to his French correspondent: "For you, absolute reality was God, then man; but *man died* after God, and you seek with anguish someone to whom you can entrust his strange heritage." (TO 48, 77, 88, 105)

And so the central theme of the entire work was formulated from the beginning. Nor did it alter, even though the author altered, from a militant revolutionary to an active anti-Communist. It goes without saying, however, that the question is less meaningful than the answer. Behind the Ling of 1926 and the Möllberg of 1943, both of whom affirm man's death, who is speaking, who is resigned to their erudite despair? The disenchanted conclusion of an historian who has estimated the distance between cultures, or of the ethnologist who has sojourned among the "primitive" tribes of Africa and the Pacific—is that all there is to Malraux's anguish? The pessimism of a scholar, of a curator? The problem would never be posed if there were not some inherent ambiguity. I have referred to the astonishing article by Pierre Debray that attributed Möllberg's conclusions to Malraux and accused him of rupturing the unity of man. In the literary press of 1948, from *Esprit* to *Lettres Françaises,* one can find many analogous remarks. Let us, therefore, re-read Möllberg's observations:

Humanity's successive psychic states are irreducibly different since they do not affect, develop or involve the same part of man. On basic issues, Plato and St. Paul can neither agree nor convince each other; they can only convert each other. A Christian king and a prehistoric moon-king do not have two *ideas* of destiny; in order for the Christian king to feel, to comprehend destiny, the other's psychic world must have disappeared. I doubt that there is any dialogue between the caterpillar and the butterfly.

Because he thought he had discovered, after many years of sociological illusions, this fundamental disparity between men, the ethnologist Möllberg denied the humanistic faith that he had "affirmed for years." The pages of his manuscript, *Civilization as Conquest and Destiny,* thrown to the winds of Africa, lay dispersed between Zanzibar and the Sahara. The book disappeared on the same soil that destroyed his idea of man. (NA, p. 103, 79)

At first, I, and several others as well, seemed to perceive in Möllberg a fictional projection of Oswald Spengler. The major theme of *Der Untergang des Abendlandes* (published in 1917) is, after all, less concerned with the decline of the Occident as such, than with the possible and fatal decline of *all* civilization. No subsequent culture can ever find the same values, the same symbols, the same feelings, the same men. But one day Malraux wrote me: "Physically, Möllberg is Léopold Chauveau; ideologically, Frobenius (in so far as the characters of a novel are ever anyone)." Léopold Chauveau has not left a particularly great name in literature. However, his memory remains alive for many. A surgeon who no longer practised, an author of regional novels and children's stories, Chauveau belonged to the Pontigny group (that so highly resembles Altenburg). But why should Malraux have transformed Chauveau into Möllberg? One can venture a guess. In one of the Altenburg episodes, we see the little figurines that the ethnologist carries with him everywhere. He has sculpted them himself. Fantastic animals, squirrels with fins, birds of prey with simian bodies, cat-faced penguins, as sad as the phantoms of Goya. Möllberg calls them his monsters and gives them names. One should now read the memories of Chauveau, in *Galerie Privée,* by the old lady who, for half a century, was at the center of French letters and who hid under the pseudonym of "M. Saint-Clair." [6] Chauveau too sculpted "half-human monsters." Were they, queries the memorialist, "the indirect, exasperated expression of an inner collapse, of an element of malice?" Who can know, now that Chauveau is dead. However, in fashioning these strange figures that become in *Les Noyers* the sarcastic symbol of human metamorphoses and the irremediable difference between cultures, Chauveau provided a concrete figuration of the problem that has haunted Malraux since 1926.

As to Leo Frobenius, he probably marked Malraux's thinking during the postwar years—between 1918 and 1923—at which time his renown in Europe was at its peak. The German ethnologist, born in 1873, published his first volumes toward the end of the 19th century (*Die Weltanschauung der Naturvölker* dates from 1898). He did not begin his African explorations, based in the German Cameroons, until 1904, but his analyses of Negro cultures had already become internationally famous before 1914. At the end of the war he founded at Frankfurt the Institute of Cultural Morphology. His *History of African Civilization* was translated into French at the time when jazz and Negro sculpture were the vogue in Paris. The collection, *Sculptures nègres,* by Guillaume, appeared in 1917; the book by Clouzot and Level on *L'Art nègres et l'art océanin* in 1920; the French translation of Einstein's *African Sculpture* in 1922. Thus, André Malraux, at the age of 20, led by the vogue, encountered a fascinating work in which human universality dissolves in the kaleidoscope of mores.

I should like merely to outline the parallel Frobenius-Möllberg; it is revealing. "We have just considered," says Möllberg after his long report to the intellectuals at Altenburg, "the societies that are ignorant, in the case of the first, of our concept of destiny; the second, of our concept of birth; the third, of our concept of barter; and the last, of our concept of death. . . . Between the men we have just discussed and the Greek, medieval man and, let us even say, ourselves, what is there in common?" (NA, pp. 96-97). And Frobenius on the concept of death?

> The notion of dying, the knowledge of death, the idea of the complete annihilation of the living, the thought that any human being . . . could possibly be extinct tomorrow, all such notions are utterly and entirely foreign to the animistic period, that, for instance, of the Bushmen. . . .

The concept of eternity?

> The Dyak knows nothing of eternity.

[6] Gallimard, 1947. "M. Saint-Clair's" *Il y a quarante ans* was also published by Gallimard.

The concept of belonging to the same species as other men?

For the man who has advanced beyond the lowest grade of culture and planted his foot somewhat higher, the "other species" begins at the neighboring village, so that his neighbors are to him "fair game."

And the conclusion drawn from all this?

These pygmies have not yet realized the differences between men and animals. We must take them, we must understand them, as they live in their own way, in their solitude. Primitive nature and themselves. . . . They will have naught of each other. They do not understand the notion of individuality . . . *Under such conditions, what is there to study in mankind? What have we to learn from other men?* [7]

Like all powerful ideas, the ideas of Frobenius have held Malraux in their grip since 1926. But one would have to be blind (or deliberately close one's eyes) to equate Malraux with Möllberg. Just because one considers the problems formulated by Nietzsche, Marx, or Bergson is one necessarily Nietzschean, Marxist, or Bergsonian? There would then be no difference between thinking and enrolling. Let us rather see what a Malraux, compared to a Péguy or a Valéry, gleans from the problem of civilization. In 1905, Péguy remarked that "whole civilizations are dead. Absolutely, entirely, totally dead. . . . And in this modern civilization, the little culture that exists in the modern world is itself essentially modern. It is that much more mortal, that much more exposed to death because it is less profound, less ingrained in the heart of man." [8] Paul Valéry's naïve declaration in 1919, that so greatly contributed to making him famous, "We civilizations now know that we are mortal," loses in this light much of its originality. Valéry emerges as an intellectual *reactionary*, insofar as he identifies his own viewpoint with the success of rationalism, that is, with a particular and fragmentary conception of man. The thinker who in 1919 believed he had made the discovery that civilizations are impermanent, emerged from a tranquil half-century during which history had remained more or less inert. If Valéry detested history, it is because he dreamed of maintaining our civilization within the limits of an untragic period, in which problems could be posed in terms of individual intelligence and not of rupture and collective destiny. Petit bourgeois of a happier age, Monsieur Teste wishes to suffer only within his own mind, in which he has installed, by a delightful play of mirrors, the Palace of Mirages of the untainted consciousness. Malraux comes on the scene and puts an end to these solitary pastimes.

[7] Leo Frobenius, *The Childhood of Man*, Philadelphia, London, pp. 154, 264, 476, 133-134. My italics.
[8] *Par un demi-clair matin*, 1905, *Nouvelle Revue Française*, July, 1939.

To Frobenius' problem, *does the concept of man have a meaning?* one can reply yes or no. Or one can not reply at all. The Marxists, racists, and Fascists of any allegiance only see in man the product of external necessities—economic, genetic, cultural. Valéry denies himself all possibility of replying. And there are those, atheists or believers, Spanish anarchists or Christians, Cheng-dai of *Les Conquérants,* Kyo of *La Condition Humaine,* Berger of *Les Noyers de l'Altenburg,* who believe that man is what he does, not what is done to him. Malraux was much too impressed by Marx and Hegel not to consider, from the beginning, this Hegelian viewpoint according to which the hero judges himself not by the significance of his acts, but by his manner of intuiting and espousing the movement of history; the servant and administrator of history. It is against this perspective, which became the perspective of Marxism, that Kyo protests, in as early a work as *La Condition Humaine,* "Each time fate precedes will, I am on my guard." When Malraux starts agreeing with Frobenius, Malraux is no longer a Communist.

"Already," André Malraux wrote me, *"little of what I dramatized in* La Condition Humaine *holds true."* But the central problem of the novel has outlived a once significant historico-political conjuncture. *"I think,"* he also wrote, *"that you are right in insisting on what you call my permanence. Not that I am particularly concerned with it: the evolution of Nietzsche carries somewhat more weight in the history of ideas than the constancy of such and such. But I do think that Altenburg, rewritten, would only pose more clearly the problem that underlies everything I write: how to make man aware that he can build his greatness, without religion, on the nothingness that crushes him. 'In that prison we draw images from ourselves that are powerful enough to negate our nothingness,' says Walter."* Images? That, it seems to me, is the meaning of *La Psychologie de l'Art.*

The amazing pictorial documentation assembled in the three volumes of the Skira edition (unfortunately too greatly reduced in *Les Voix du Silence*) takes on its full significance in this light. Quattrocento paintings, sculptures from New Ireland, jewels and bronzes from the steppes, Celtic coins, Macedonian staters, ritual masks, Gothic stained glass windows, dogon masks, illuminations, tuppence-colored, Byzantine mosaics, Pompeiian paving blocks, drawings made by lunatics or children, Christs, boddhisatvas, Sumerian bas-reliefs, Tavant frescoes, objects of magic, stone figures, lekythoi, dolls, Cézanne, Magnasco, Goya, Giotto, all proclaim both the fatality that explains the works and the liberty that produced them. Across so vast a panorama of strangely different lines, from the women of Botticelli to the straw dolls and spider's webs of the Moi savages, human differences interweave with the profound unity of man. What link is there between Phidias and the grimacing art of Japanese lacquers, between Leonardo and the idols of Basutoland? None, if not that they all express the same combat against the contrary forces that have always been present in man, a common reaction, however multiform, in the face of destiny, solitude and death. In this museum into which Frobenius introduced twenty different human species with their fetishes, their feathers, their incommunicable dreams, Malraux met a man alone and naked, threatened and immortal, a Man.

Malraux and the Demons of Action

by Nicola Chiaromonte

History. History haunting Europe even as Buddha's interrogation overwhelmed Asia.—Malraux, *Le Musée Imaginaire*

I

André Malraux has been on the scene for over twenty years. He is still a "public figure" in the most emphatic sense of that term, being dominated by the resolve *both* to obey and to express the imperatives of world history, or, as he would put it, the *destiny* of contemporary man. The author of *Man's Fate*, former Assistant Secretary-General of the Kuomintang, colonel in the Spanish Republican Air Force, commander of the Alsace-Lorraine Brigade first in the underground and then at the front, now intellectual lieutenant of General de Gaulle, has in fact turned the will to be "public" into an ethical principle. From the point of view of a Kierkegaard as of anyone who values "inwardness" above all, this is a most wrongheaded attitude. But then, one of Malraux's main contentions is precisely that modern man has lost all objective (i.e., intellectually justifiable) possibilities of turning inward to a "spiritual reality" of some kind. Nothing is to be found in that direction except formless ambiguity. Modern man must, literally, *do* or die. His situation is an extreme one. Nothing short of a jolt of passionate energy will save him.

It is the constant assertion of this sense of urgency, expressed in a style of exalted intellectual lucidity, that has won Malraux the admiration of so many young (and also not so young) Europeans. Having been forced into one extreme situation after another on the stage of world history, those youths look up to Malraux as to an elder brother who, in a time which has been throughout "a time for despising," succeeded in leading a proud life, one in which doing and thinking were not split but rather extolled as two aspects of the same energy. Whatever one's opinion of his deeds or works, one cannot help admiring in the French writer the quickness of that faculty of the soul which the Greeks called *thumos*, "the spirited element." It is precisely because it retains a quality of youthful

"Malraux and the Demons of Action," by Nicola Chiaromonte. Part I, *Partisan Review* (July 1948); part II, *Partisan Review* (August 1948). Copyright 1948 by the *Partisan Review*. Reprinted by permission of *Partisan Review* and Nicola Chiaromonte. A revised version has appeared in the Italian in *Tempo presente* (August 1960).

recklessness in its very errors that Malraux's adventure has the quality of being "exemplary." Or, if one prefers, typical in a very eminent sense.

Malraux's first important work was *La Tentation de l'Occident* (1926). Before that, in 1921 (at the age of twenty-six), he had published *Lunes en Papier*, a kind of dadaist fairy tale. But, together with a later work, *Royaume Farfelu*, a fantasy on the theme of an exotic Nowhere, *Lunes en Papier* has been repudiated by the author and never reprinted. In themselves, these pieces were not particularly significant. If they become significant at all, it is in the light of Malraux's later work, insofar as they help us to catch a glimpse of what he has since consistently striven to keep away from: the realm of aimless sensations and daydreaming, "the fishes of darkness . . . the beings that torment us, the Beasts. . . . They are born out of our boredom and breed boredom" (*Royaume Farfelu*). Irrelevant imagery, daydreaming, recur only once in Malraux's work: Kassner, in *Days of Wrath*, being in prison, is *forced* to yield to the upsurge of stray reminiscences. But, however forcefully controlled, and even repressed, the sense of the aimless and the grotesque continues to be a strong undercurrent in his writing. Out of it comes a character who is artistically most successful, the one who represents all that Malraux's heroes do not want to be: Baron Clappique of *Man's Fate*.

La Tentation de l'Occident is written in the form of an exchange of letters between a Chinese traveling in Europe and a Frenchman living in the Far East. The Chinese criticizes the West in terms of a strongly westernized outlook, the Frenchman corrects this in him on the basis of his own awareness of the contrast between the two civilizations. Both know Nietzsche's considerations on cultural nihilism. In fact, they both represent a single character: Malraux thinking of Europe from China. The argument is as tense and as elliptical as anything Malraux has written. The conclusions, if any, are those of an anguished relativism. From Rome, the Chinese writes: "I understand the message of these ruins: he who sacrifices himself participates in the greatness of the cause to which he has made the sacrifice of his life. But I don't see any greatness in the cause except what it owes to the sacrifice. In itself, it is without meaning. . . . Is barbarism the less barbaric because it is powerful?" To which the Frenchman replies with a striking definition: "The will to power . . . the consequence of a reverie which would borrow from intelligence the means to force upon the world the acceptance of its folly. . . . [We] are a race committed to the test of the *act*, hence pledged to the bloodiest fate."

Here Malraux is already stating what will continue to be his main theme. The very statement of this theme also contains a radical questioning of it. The Frenchman's remarks imply, in fact, the psychological notion that a man's soul is, to start with, nothing but an excess of dreams and formless desires. The permanence of the external world makes out-

lines of possible acts from the swarming images. From dream to act, however, there is no rational transition. Dreams breed dreams indefinitely.
Only the jolt of choice, action, can put an end to the "pestilence" of
desire. After which, what was inane foolishness becomes bloody madness.
But man *must* choose between being an individual and being, literally,
nobody. Only in action can he find some clear necessity, if not rationality.
Such is, briefly stated, the problem of action and its ultimate meaning
which all of Malraux's work illustrates.

A number of remarks in the short essay "On Certain Young Europeans"
(1927) take us a step closer toward André Malraux's point of departure
as a novelist and a man of action. Our civilization, having rejected security in, and submission to, the Catholic Church, and having "lost the
hope of finding the meaning of the world in science . . . has been deprived of any spiritual aim." This means the breakdown both of the world
in which we live and also of the self, the only reality from which we can
start any search at all. The situation is absurd. "Lacking a doctrine, [the
young European] has nothing left but a resolute will to give battle. *And*
there is nothing in that will except weakness and fear. Our epoch . . .
does not dare reveal the core of its thought, which is nihilistic, destructive,
fundamentally negative."

An amazingly lucid confession, and one which seems to leave little room
for anything but bad faith. One should not forget, however, what is
implied in this trend of thought; namely, that the moment we are confronted with a situation in which we *may* hope for a meaningful issue,
intellectual evidence becomes irrelevant. History, the event, the occasion,
transcend all truth. The humiliation of the intellect, in fact, makes Malraux gamble on the deed even as the weakness of the human condition
made Pascal gamble on God. "To tie oneself to a great action of some
kind, not to let go of it, to be haunted and intoxicated by it" (*The*
Conquerors, 1928) is the only issue. A man of any magnanimity cannot
do less. And it is Malraux's contention that in our time a "great action"
can mean only one thing: *a battle,* and a reason for it.

When he described Fabrizio searching for the battle of Waterloo and
not being able to find it, Stendhal was expressing, in his own nimble way
one of the great insights of nineteenth century sensibility. It was a flash
of pure wonder at the utterly paradoxical relation between an individual
destiny and whatever general significance might be attached to a "histori
cal event." In fact, it was the splendid illustration of a myth which no
historical venture, and no amount of sophistry, has thereafter been able
to obliterate from our consciousness. The "epic" moments of *War and*
Peace: Prince André lying on the battlefield of Austerlitz; Alapatych a
Smolensk; Pierre among the prisoners, comprise a most vigorous appre
hension of the same meaning, and of the same myth. The myth is abou
man and history: the more naïvely, and genuinely, man experiences

historical event, the more the event disappears, and something else takes its place: the starry sky, the other man, or the utterly ironical detail. That is, the unhistorical: Karataiev and his footgear appear infinitely more significant than Napoleon or Mother Russia. Yet man is inside the event as in a trap. History does not reveal its meaning, but gives way to destiny. We have the paradox of an irretrievable disproportion. For Stendhal, as for Tolstoy, the revelation brings with it an instant of catharsis. Something might or might not follow from it, but the moment of illumination and wonder has a value of its own, and can never be forgotten, or explained away: a stark question has been addressed by the living individual to the historical whirlwind, however mighty or majestic.

Now André Malraux is perfectly well aware of the ambiguity of history. Yet, he depends on the historical to give clarity and form to human action. He is a Stendhalian character determined to have his battle, a Jacob who claims to know the name of the angel even before the angel has appeared to him. To start with, he self-consciously asserts the supremacy of the impersonal event over the individual, and the fact that there is only one language that is decisive: the language of history. But this does not make him any less aware of the original paradox. The question raised by Stendhal and Tolstoy is as constantly present to Malraux as his passion for what obliterates it: the rationality of action itself, knowing no other measure than the will to conquer. But, in the end, what remains is the question. The angel appears to Jacob, and he has no name. Malraux's complete works could well bear the title of his latest, unfinished novel: "The Struggle with the Angel."

It is in the light of such radical self-consciousness, and not simply as an egotistic utterance, that one should interpret Garine's exclamation in *The Conquerors*: "I consider my youth the card on which I gamble. If I could cheat, I would cheat." It is Julien Sorel, aware of his own destiny.

Malraux himself began his gamble in Indochina. He had gone there as an archeologist in 1923, on a fellowship granted him by the École des Langues Orientales, where he had been a student. The demon of action pushed him in two quite different directions. One impulse drew him to make common cause with a group of Annamite students belonging to the nationalist Young Annam League. Malraux wrote articles for their papers and helped them in their underground work. For the local French authorities, this was abominable treachery, especially since the young scholar was using Government facilities to carry on his archeological work. And it was in the course of this work, in 1924, that Malraux was tempted by the realization that there were unchartered regions, in the jungles of northern Annam, where one was almost sure to find ruins of ancient Buddhist temples. Together with a French rough-rider, he conceived the plan of going there and of appropriating whatever examples of Khmer sculpture they could find and take away with them. When he came back, the French authorities lost no time in having him prosecuted for theft of Government property. That would teach the amateur revolutionist a good lesson. Malraux's line of defense was that, since they were not indicated on official government charts, the temples and their bas-reliefs were nobody's property. But this legal point would have been of very little avail without the devotion of a small group of friends and of his first wife, who succeeded in having the prosecution withdrawn in the face of a violent campaign by the reactionary Parisian press against the "Communist thief."

"There is a decisive way of being shut off from the human community: it is humiliation, shame," says one of the scholars gathered to discuss the "essence of man" in *Les Noyers de l'Altenburg* (1945), the first part, and the only one published so far, of *La Lutte avec l'Ange.* In Indochina, Malraux came to know humiliation both in his own person and in the fate of the oppressed Indochinese. At the same time, he had the opposite experience of being drawn to others and of finding that he could count on their fidelity; the comradeship which tied him to the Indochinese rebels and to those who stood by him in the moment of humiliation was decisive. The context was an act of revolt against the established order and its rules.

Malraux never wrote a novel about the struggle of the Indochinese. But (until, in 1946, political expediency apparently cautioned him to remain silent) he consistently defended the cause of the Annamite rebels. The "Appeal for Those in Indochina," published in 1933, was as ringing an indictment of French colonialism as has ever been written.

As for his adventure in search of artistic treasures, it became the theme of *The Royal Way* (1930). Centered on an enterprise whose meaning can hardly go beyond that of a resolute egotistic drive, the novel lacks scope. It has, however, strong and revealing moments. Significantly enough, Perken, the German adventurer who is the hero of the story, and with whom the young Claude has associated himself, is not interested in treasures. He is going into the jungle in order to find a friend of his, who has been lost for months. Perken has conceived the strange plan of founding a native state capable of fighting French domination. What he wants is "to leave a scar on the map." "Hostility toward established values, . . . a taste for the actions of men together with the consciousness of their vanity. Above all, nonconformity . . ." are his motives. But, deeper than this, what Perken refuses to submit to is "limited, irrefutable destiny, falling upon you as a set of rules on a prisoner. . . . The certainty that you will have been *that,* and nothing else . . . my human fate: that I should become older, that time, this atrocious thing, should grow in me like a cancer." What he wants above all is "to exist against all this." And that is why he finally meets the absurd: death from a poisoned wound, among savages.

Many of Malraux's critics (both of the Right and the Left) have spoken of his "egotism," or of his "estheticism." It is becoming more and more obvious that, if one must have recourse to formulas, one should rather say that Malraux was the first to introduce into French contemporary culture the themes that have come to be popularized under the label of "existentialism." He did this, however, at a moment when Heidegger was hardly known outside of Germany, and with a concreteness and a directness that are those of an artist haunted by metaphysical problems, but who depends very little on professional philosophy as such. Certainly, Malraux's intellectual formation owes much to the friendly influence of Bernard Groethuysen, a philosopher of great erudition and wit who enjoyed something like a Socratic position in the Paris of the Twenties and Thirties. Groethuysen had been a pupil of Dilthey and was very well informed about philosophical novelties. He certainly told Malraux about Heidegger. But Malraux's problems were, in any case, peculiarly his own.

There is plenty of egotism in modern culture, as well as in the "existentialist" trend of thought. Malraux's egotism, however, is of a peculiar kind since it strains continually to break through the barriers of the self and to establish an authentic relation with the world of men, as well as with the universe.

As for estheticism, Malraux is an esthete in the sense that art (especially plastic art) is for him the only realm in which man can meet fate on equal terms. But art as a superior form of delectation does not mean much to him. Once again, what he is interested in is the victorious form. In *The Royal Way*, Claude remarks: "Making, as we do, of the artist himself the essential value, we fail to see one of the poles of the work of art: the condition of the civilization which looks at it. As if, when it comes to art, time did not exist. What interests me in works of art is their deeper life, the life made up of the death of men." This is, in fact, the starting point of the recent and very characteristic book, *Le Musée Imaginaire*: the battle of art through the ages, recounted by Malraux.

To carry out consistently the impulse of revolt which had taken hold of him in Indochina, Malraux went to China in 1925, where he remained for nearly two years. There, for the first time, he encountered history in the making, a "great action": the Chinese Revolution, or rather the series of insurrections connected with the rise of Chiang Kai-shek to the head of the Kuomintang, which ended up on one hand in the Shanghai massacre of April, 1927, and on the other in the formation of the Communist Army which for twenty years has been successfully challenging Chiang's power. Without becoming a member of the Party, Malraux worked with the Communist wing of the Kuomintang, first in Canton, then in Shanghai, where he performed the functions of Propaganda Commissar of the Revolutionary Committee. Out of this experience came *The Conquerors* and *Man's Fate* (1933).

Those who labeled Malraux an "esthete" or an "egotist" have also

questioned the meaning of the public allegiance he gave for nearly four-
teen years (from 1925 to 1939) to the Communist cause. The right-wing
critics (from Brasillach to Thierry Maulnier) repeatedly asserted that he
could just as well have been a Fascist, since he finally was only interested
in violent action and warlike virtues. To which Malraux replied that he
objected to Fascism precisely because it made of warlike virtues the
supreme virtues, while to a Communist they were only the tragic means
to an end which was the opposite of war or domination. From the left,
Malraux was often accused of being kept by "egotistic" reservations from
giving a genuine allegiance to the cause. To this, he answered that if
revolutionary fraternity meant "indulging in First Communion emotions," he would have none of it. But if it meant to make of human
dignity and of human culture the highest values, then it was his chief
concern. As for discipline in action, nobody could accuse him of not being
aware of its necessity. But this was definitely not a subject of speculation
or for artistic enthusiasm.

The truth is that Malraux's connection with the revolutionary cause
was of a complex kind. No book of his throws a more direct light on this
complexity, and on the ambiguities it involves, than his first novel, *The
Conquerors*. Here is the hero, Garine, observed from the outside: "If by
a bolshevik you mean a revolutionist, Garine is doubtless a bolshevik.
But if you mean . . . a particular type of revolutionist, who, among other
characteristics, possesses that of believing in Marxism, then he is not a
bolshevik." "Doctrinal trash" exasperates him. For Garine, "the revolution cannot be born except from its actual beginnings . . . is, above all,
a state of affairs."

The true Bolshevik is Borodine: "a great business manager . . . a man
who, before each and every thing, has only one thought: 'Can I utilize
it, and how?' " Garine obeys Borodine's orders, but this is what he thinks
of him: "He wants to make revolutionists the way Ford makes automo-
biles. This will end in disaster, and before long." There is no doubt with
whom Malraux's sympathies lie.

Garine is a man of action unleashed. To him, "there is only one reason
that is not a parody: it is the most effective use of force," and there is
only "one thing that counts: not to be defeated." He says of himself that
he has put "a complete lack of scruples at the service of something which
is not my immediate interest." An adventurer? Of a sort. But since he
does not seek personal profit, since he has chosen a cause and not a career,
Garine finds himself bound by laws that he cannot control. He is committed to his action and to the demons evoked by it. He cannot simply
kill and send people to be killed. He must account for his acts, to himself
as to others. He must follow to the bitter end the course he has chosen.
If he had wanted just adventure, then he is indeed trapped: "Those who
want to soar above the earth soon come to realize that the earth sticks to
their fingers."

The actual fate of the "great action," the Chinese Revolution, to which Garine together with Katov and Kyo of *Man's Fate* are committed, can be described in a few words. The Canton insurrection, which Garine organizes, is connected with the great boycott of Hong Kong, which threatens the very life of the British Empire. Any successful development of the situation depends on Chiang Kai-shek on one side, and on the Comintern on the other, simply because these are the main forces behind the events. The revolt, one must add, is mainly a revolt of the Chinese against foreign imperialism. The Japanese are looking at it with great interest, but they are as worried as the Western powers by Russia and its Comintern. As for the Communists *on the spot,* they think they can turn the whole situation into a proletarian revolution. When his victories bring Chiang to the point where he must either have a showdown with the Western powers or appease them by dropping the Communists, whom he wants to ged rid of anyway, he chooses appeasement. Stalin, on the other hand, has ordered the Communists to get along with Chiang at all costs, because Chiang is winning, and because the Soviet Union must prevent the Japanese from being the only ones to profit from Chiang's rise to power.

This being the case, clearly the revolution is doomed. But could what seems so obvious after the fact have been realized by people involved in the day-by-day events? The answer (even in Malraux's account) is "yes." If Garine is so furious at Borodine, it is not because he takes a sentimental (or ideological) view of the "people's cause," but for the simple reason that he considers Borodine's mechanical strategy to be in contradiction with the logic of reality itself. As far as the line from Moscow is concerned, Garine finds himself in a rather "Trotskyist" frame of mind. In *Man's Fate,* the same is true of Kyo, who is so critical of Vologin, Borodine's double: "The Blues are giving the bourgeois what they promised the bourgeois. We don't give the workers what we promised the workers. . . . We will all be massacred, without even maintaining the dignity of the Party."

To the man who is committed to an action because he sees in it the way toward the realization of his idea, the *detail*—any fact that contradicts the logic of his faith—is not just a disturbing incident. It is an utterly distressing and *fundamental* reality. It puts everything in question, and makes the man stop and think, a posture that he will not be able to bear for long. At this point, the question is raised: "What then?" Here is the rub. Should one give up, and withdraw from an action that has become worse than wrong, that has become senseless?

To understand the kind of answer his characters give to this question is to get to the core of Malraux's attitude. The first thing to be said is that neither Malraux nor his characters accept for a moment the idea that one can withdraw from an action in which one has chosen to be involved. By withdrawing, one would become a comedian, renouncing the very substance of identity, which requires acceptance of the fact that life is essentially tragic, not a game whose rules the individual can change at will. The next thing to observe, however, is that the question raised refers not so much to what one should *do* as to what one should *think*: a question of consciousness and of meaning. Admitted that Garine and Kyo have no choice but to carry out the mission they have undertaken, we still want to know what has happened to their doubt, how it is being followed up in their minds, and, eventually, in what way it influences their actions. Especially since we are in a novel. (But even in real life that would be an essential question, or wouldn't it?) Otherwise, what kind of doubt would such a doubt be? Purely discursive? Just for the sake of argument?

The fact is that this doubt is never answered in Malraux. It is cut short by action. Not by the *logic* of action, but by the obscure, overpowering force (really, a demon) to which men like Garine and Kyo have yielded the moment they chose their place in history. With Garine, it is his passion for efficiency and power. With Kyo, it is something more vague: the *emotion* of the Revolution in act. Garine has drastic doubts about Borodine's orders. But these doubts do not prevent him from having the terrorist Hong executed, and the moderate Cheng-dai poisoned. Garine wants to eliminate all obstacles to a Communist triumph which, on the other hand, he knows is being jeopardized by the very policies he is carrying out. Clearly, he is not obedient to any practical reason, but is simply offering up victims to a nameless fetish which he calls "Victory." Garine's consciousness might be infected with "Trotskyist" thoughts, but his acts already announce the crazed Stalinist commissars who, in Spain, will make of the slaughter of their ideological adversaries a dogma to which practical reason itself must yield. As far as truth is concerned, Hong is right when, to Borodine who tells him that "the Revolution means to pay the army," he replies: "Then it does not deserve the slightest interest." And probably Cheng-dai is no less right when he calmly tells Garine: "I like to read tragic tales, but I don't like to contemplate their spectacle in my own family. I cannot see without regret my people transformed into guinea pigs. . . ." But then, the argument here does not relate to what is true and what is false.

When Kyo, after his discussion with Vologin, goes to take his place in the insurrection which his reason tells him is doomed, he thinks: "Moscow and the enemy capitals of the West could organize their opposing passions over there in the night and attempt to mold them into a world. The Revolution, so long in parturition, had reached the moment of its delivery: now it would have to give birth or die. . . ." And then he is "seized by the feeling of dependence, the anguish of being nothing more than a man, than himself." Kyo is here falling on his knees, performing an act of submission to a suddenly revealed God: the new Allah, the God of History. In fact, Kyo is reminded "of the Chinese Mohammedans . . .

prostrate on the plains, covered with sun-scorched lavender, howling those songs that for thousands of years have torn the man who suffers and who knows he is going to die." But, Voltaire would say, "the pain of that angel does not heal us." There is a strange gap between Kyo's interrupted political argument and his sudden communion with the age-old sorrow of man. The one is no answer to the other.

Malraux's novels are characterized by a unique achievement: in them, action, the most opaque and ambiguous of all human facts, is observed and analyzed with the utmost vehemence until it becomes immaterial and transparent, almost one with the workings of intelligence itself. However poignant Malraux's descriptions of violence and death may be, he is not the only modern writer who has been attracted by such themes. What is unique is the resolve to show the mechanics of the action itself *as a historical whole, and* the ideas that move his characters as parts of the action. He says in his essay on Choderlos de Laclos, that Laclos' characters, foreshadowing those of Balzac, Stendhal, and Dostoevsky, "accomplish acts that are *premeditated* in function of a general view of life." Whether it is true or not of those novelists, this certainly applies to Malraux himself. Garine, Hong, Cheng-dai represent not so much Malraux's hesitations as his unmodifiable views of the event in which his characters are actors as well as victims. The conflict between the Communist, the anarchist, and the sage, masks another and deeper conflict: the one between the man who accepts the iron rules of historical action, the individual who rejects them precisely in the name of the impulse which pushes him to act, and finally the person who, like Cheng-dai, "is only capable of a particular kind of action: that which demands the victory of man over himself."

As in Stendhal and in Tolstoy, in Malraux the relation between the individual and the event is a paradoxical one. Malraux's paradox could be stated by saying that the individual moves in an ordinary space, while the event proceeds according to a pluridimensional geometry. There is no knowledge of such geometry save the one that springs from the resolve: do or die. This is why Malraux rejects "doctrinal trash": Marxism, insofar as it claims to be a prescience and not simply a resolve. At the same time, he cannot help surreptitiously giving a kind of advantage to the man who, like Garcia in *Man's Hope,* is ready to say: "In times like the present, I'm less interested in the reasons men may have for giving up their lives than in the means they have for killing off their enemies." Garcia is superior to the anarchist because he is prepared to neglect "reasons" in order to organize "means." In the same novel, Manuel appears endowed with a superior kind of rationality because he is ready to take upon himself the death of the two stragglers who are going to be executed so that discipline may be restored in the ranks of the People's Army.

Where Stendhal and Tolstoy **stop and** wonder because they cannot forget the *detail* out of which springs the revelation of an irretrievable irony or absurdity, Malraux makes allowances for wonder and proceeds. What fascinates him is what lies beyond any individual detail or thought: the general shape of historical destiny in our time and the will to master it. Communist tenacity and ruthlessness interest him in that they represent a peculiar way of bringing together a "reason" which is universal in character and a will which is essentially absolute, knowing no obstacles and no scruples. Yet, the same sage, Gisors, who had said: "Marxism is not a doctrine but a will," added: "You must not be Marxists in order to be right, but in order to conquer without betraying yourselves." There is, so it seems, a point where one must "stop and think": betrayal. But then, how can a will ever be proven wrong as long as it lasts? Where should the resolve to conquer stop, except in victory, or in defeat? And which is the traitor: the man who jeopardizes victory because he refuses to yield his "reasons" for wanting it, or the one who is ready to suppress these "reasons" as hindrances, and thus jeopardize the *meaning* not only of victory but also of defeat?

In Malraux, when defeat comes, darkness is complete. Hope or tragic lament would appear equally futile. There is room only for a last flicker of humanity: the gesture by which Katov gives up to two fellow victims the cyanide that would have spared him the torture of the furnace.

André Malraux is, in fact, the poet of violent defeat. But he shows a significant unwillingness to accept his roles. At the end of *Man's Fate,* he has one of his characters, Hemmelrich, make his escape to Moscow and find some solace in the Five-Year Plan. Surely, this is weak, since it presumes the acceptance of a "First Communion" attitude toward such an abstruse enterprise as the Plan. It is curious to see a poet of tragic actions trying to avoid the implications of tragedy. *Man's Hope* was published at the end of 1937, when the Spanish Republic was being subjected to a slow agony, and Stalin had already judiciously stopped all help. Yet Malraux made a point of ending the book with the victory of Guadalajara. Manuel and Garcia could find justification only in victory. They would have become just two more images of human impotence if the author had waited until 1939 and, for example, chosen to end his novel with the scene that took place in a Madrid square a few moments before the entry of Franco's troops: some of the last defenders forming a circle, standing at arm's length, and shooting each other.

II

What were the intellectual motives of Malraux's allegiance to Communism *as an idea* from 1925 to 1939?

The strongest one was probably the notion of "virile fraternity." Insofar as it took the form of "revolutionary combat," Communism for Malraux gave back to the individual, made sterile by bourgeois egocentrism, "his fertility," the absolutely fundamental sense of *belonging* to a definite time, a definite place, and a specific milieu, without which authentic norms of conduct, and even a true understanding of the self, cannot be born. This was a strong idea, and a deeply felt need. Its psychological roots could perhaps be found in what Kyo says at one point in *Man's Fate*: "Men are not my brothers: they are those who look at me, and judge me. My brothers are those who look at me, and love me." "Virile fraternity" means a type of human relationship cleansed of both sentimentality and suspicion, in which the individual will feel both "left alone" and trusted, hence essentially encouraged: "fertile."

This is, for Malraux, the ideal social situation. Its opposite is bourgeois individualism, in which the individual (like the capitalist Ferral in *Man's Fate*) is the prisoner of a loathsome kind of narcissism, can never see in the other person anything but the reflection of his own self, is condemned either to use the other individual as an instrument or to yield to masochistic sentimentality in his presence.

Because he condemned this kind of individualism, Malraux also condemned the equivocation by which, since the second half of the nineteenth century, the cause of art had become identified with that of individualism. "Artistic individualism," he points out in the preface to *Days of Wrath*, "is justified only insofar as it is applied to the domain of feeling and dream. . . . What destroys the work of art is not passion, but the will to prove." The consequence was that it was perfectly legitimate to think not of a "Communist art," which was absurd, but of an art inspired by the acceptance of a "Communist situation."

Malraux's *intellectual* position with regard to Communism and the Soviet Union in the late Thirties could be summarized by saying that he was perfectly willing to accept them as starting points, but not at all ready to adopt the official ideology that was supposed to be corollary of such a stand. Hence, in 1934, at the Soviet Writers' Congress in Moscow, he launched an attack against "Socialist realism," and also against the notion that the artist should bow to a "line": "Art," he said, "is not a submission: it is a conquest . . . if Marxism is the consciousness of the social, culture is the consciousness of the psychological. . . . The refusal of the psychological, in art, leads to the most absurd individualism. Every man, whether he wants it or not, tries to *think* his own life. The refusal of the psychological can mean only one thing, namely that he who will have reached the deepest consciousness, instead of transmitting his experience to his fellow men shall keep it to himself."

The argument was a telling one as far as it went. But, of course, the attempt to draw a line between state dictation in society and in art was doomed. In order to connect the Soviet Union with *his* ideal of a new *culture* based on "virile fraternity," Malraux had to overlook a fact which is central in modern times, namely the implications of total state power. Yet the argument was significant insofar as it revealed the one value on which Malraux was not ready to compromise: the *quality* of human experience, and its highest form, art. Art was going to appear to him more and more as the supreme form of human energy: a "conquest" superior to all others.

Malraux was a strange Communist anyway. He did not only contend that party officials had nothing whatever to say in the matter of culture and ideas. He also maintained that Stalin, Thorez, and Aragon could *do* what they liked, but they shouldn't try to tell him, Malraux, what the *meaning* of Communism was. The claim was insolent, and the Communist hierarchy (which had no authority over Malraux, since he was not a party member) answered it by keeping this peculiar spokesman for Communism under constant suspicion, and spreading a number of slanderous rumors against him. The writer haughtily ignored the slander, and went his way, maintaining a self-imposed discipline which consisted of a single rule: he would call himself a Communist, and not raise any political fuss, as long as it was at all justifiable to consider the C.P. the instrument of a universal cause, and the Soviet Union as the power center of this cause.

What Malraux expected from Communism was not any leap from necessity into freedom, but a redeeming transformation of Western culture. In 1935, speaking at the anti-Fascist Writers' Congress in London, Malraux described the Communist task as follows: "To recreate the phantom heritage which lies about us, to open the eyes of all the sightless statues, to turn hopes into wills and revolts into revolutions, and to shape thereby, out of the age-old sorrows of man, a new and glowing consciousness of mankind."

Surely, those were a poet's reasons. If one had asked Malraux how he could prove that there was a necessary connection between his grandiose vision and the peculiar style of the C.P., between Stalin's transcendental philistinism and the "sightless statues," the answer would no doubt have been: "I don't see any other *force* in the world, today, which could reasonably be connected with the realization of such a hope. Do you?" A *realistic* vision, then. Or should one say: a visionary realism? It was, in fact, in the name of an apocalyptic dream of Hope and Power coming together like the Lion and the Lamb in Isaiah that Malraux rejected as irrelevant the prosaic warnings of common sense and factual evidence: the objection raised by the particular against the general.

It was not Hope, however, but the *will to act* in the face of impending doom, that pushed Malraux. In 1935, to one of those pathetic Popular Front crowds that used to meet at the *Salle de la Mutualité,* in Paris, he announced not Bread, Peace and Liberty, but the Coming War. "We may die in it, but we shall not die without having been in it," he cried. If war was inevitable, then surely ideologies, party lines, and the naïve hopes of the crowds were mere details. The real question was that of Western culture as a whole, of Western man and his future: whether, in our time, man could find a way of mastering history, or would succumb to it.

Malraux's break with Communism came in 1939, with the Hitler-Stalin pact. There, unmistakably, was *betrayal*: the official notice served to the world that from then on the Soviet Union (and its agencies, the Communist parties) meant the Soviet State, and no longer a universal cause. Malraux then decided that there was only one thing for him to do: to be in the war against Hitler. That was the only way to be consistent with the logic of history betrayed by Communism. He enlisted as a private in the Tank Corps.

Before the Pact, however, there had been the Spanish War. There, really, the "sickness unto death" of the European Left, and of Europe itself, had begun. There also, in spite of appearances, and of what he himself would have been willing to admit, Malraux found himself for the first time at odds with the logic of Stalinism.

Malraux was in Madrid when Franco's revolt broke out. He saw something unforgettable: the first, almost miraculous, upsurge of popular spontaneity and courage. The Canton and Shanghai insurrections might have appeared as engineered and led from above. But in Barcelona and Madrid, the people had taken everything into their hands, and won, *almost*. Malraux went back to Paris, and told the popular audiences there of two things: the extraordinary courage of the Spaniards, and the powerlessness of courage against the instruments of modern warfare. He launched the slogan "Planes and guns for the Spanish people," and, with a group of influential friends, started out to organize the smuggling of planes, guns, and volunteer pilots into Spain. The French C.P. remained aloof, and recommended the sending of ambulances and bandages. Later on, when Malraux had begun to form his escadrille, the Spanish Communists circulated the rumor that the planes had really been sent by Thorez & Duclos. Malraux could hardly have liked that.

Yet, without Soviet tanks and planes, Franco would have won in 1936. Before this fact, all the rest became secondary for Colonel Malraux. He accepted the Communist line in Spain as being identical with the supreme necessity of war. He refused to see that military logic meant turning the Spanish war into a senseless slaughter. He refused to consider the fact that things like the massacre of the Barcelona anarchists, in May 1937, were not only debasing the dignity of the Spanish cause, but also attacking its physical energies. It was logical that, in March 1937, when, in connectioñ with the Moscow Trials, Leon Trotsky asked Malraux to state publicly whether or not he had seen him, Trotsky, in Royan in 1934, Malraux refused to answer. It was logical, since the writer considered himself bound by discipline not to say anything on such "controversial" matters as the trials. But surely, there, logic was preventing Malraux from acting rightly. Since he had always had great admiration for Trotsky, he could hardly have failed to feel the sting of the incident.

In Spain, once again, while siding with man, Malraux pleaded the case of fate. Spain, however, and the true nature of things, avenged themselves. *Man's Hope* is a halting, uncertain, fragmentary book. The case of cold-blooded efficiency is argued again and again, inconclusively, with nothing like the vigor it had when it was defended by Garine. There are too many characters, too many people; so many that it becomes clear that the event is anonymous, or rather, a purely collective one. Hence, the opposition between the Communist, the anarchist, and the intellectual, which was so vigorously stated in the preceding novels, becomes uncertain, and finally breaks down. The characters seem to be themselves aware that there are too many sides to the question, too many disturbing details, for any logic to claim a conclusive victory. Finally, what Malraux has to say is that the first moment of hope, confidence, and heroism (what he calls the "apocalypse") in a popular insurrection is a marvelous and unique manifestation which the rationality of war cannot take seriously. What follows is the wasting away of hope. But this implies that the Communist, the man concerned exclusively with the "means," is, at best, a taskmaster. He arrives when fate has already spoken, and sets up a bureau to enforce its decrees. As far as the real substance and meaning of the story are concerned, he can only play the part of Doom.

Insurrection may be romantic, but war is, after all, a frightful drudgery. Drudgery once accepted, an earnest man cannot avoid the next discovery, namely that if there is any significance in it, it comes from the patience, the sorrows, the humble dignity of the people who are the instruments and the victims of the bloody toil. The individual, with all his incongruities, and his ungovernable virtues, reasserts his presence; within the behavior of the individual, the community's presence is shown, the bonds between one man and the other, which no written law has created, and which no taskmaster's injunction can really control, but only crush. We come upon the mystery of man, in the gap between History and the myriads of stories that go to make it up.

"The mystery of man" is the theme of Malraux's latest novel, *Les Noyers de l'Altenburg*. There is no ideology in this book, which treats two episodes from the two successive wars that have laid Europe waste. The narrator, a Frenchman, is taken prisoner, in 1940. Around him, his fellow prisoners, Arabs, Senegalese, Frenchmen, hungry and cold, write letters to their families, make up grotesque myths about the war. Like Kassner in *Days of Wrath* (but not *alone* in a cell, like Kassner), the narrator is *forced* to contemplate and wonder. "A writer, what has haunted me for ten years, if not man? Now I am here, confronted with the original stuff. . . ." He thinks of his father, a scholar who, after the failure of a strange adventure in Turkey, had come back to Europe just in time to become a German officer in the First War (he was an Alsatian).

Before going to war, he had had the time to test, in the company of several eminent scholars, how brilliantly inadequate were the attempts of Western intellectuals to find a definition of man beyond the utter relativity of historical knowledge. In the war, this M. Berger had had two fundamental experiences. The first was nausea while witnessing the efforts of a German intelligence officer to get a small boy to reveal the identity of a woman spy, supposedly the child's mother. Then, M. Berger participated in the first experiment with mustard gas, made by the Germans on the Russian front. The scene (easily the most poignant image of pity and horror described by Malraux) is preceded by a significant insistence on the quality of the "raw material" of history: the German soldiers who are going to "exploit" the effects of the gas on the enemy. Like the prisoners of 1940, they tell dirty stories, play cards, mythologize about the war: between them and what is going to happen there is an utterly sardonic disproportion. Finally, the gas is launched, the German infantry sent out. The landscape remains empty and silent for a while. Then all of a sudden, on an earth on which nature itself has been monstrously killed, a few figures appear, followed by more and more, until the whole scene is crowded with German soldiers, coming back each with a scorched Russian on his shoulders. The horror has been too great. Everything collapses under the weight of a speechless pity. M. Berger also picks up a stricken Russian, then realizes that he is himself poisoned: "there was nothing left in him except a forlorn hatred against everything that had prevented him from being happy."

However, it is not pity that gives poetic meaning to the scene. Beyond pity, what we have is a glimpse of doomsday: humanity transgressing into the inhuman. (The book was finished before Hiroshima.) Clearly, that collapse is only an incident: those men will be as incapable of stopping the machinery of which they are both the tools and the victims as they are unable to withstand the first shock of that new horror. They simply don't know what they are doing, or what's happening to them. Hence, if there is any salvation, it must come to them from the outside, in the form of some extraordinary act, a messianic intervention of some sort. Pity is of no avail.

The last part of the novel focuses again on the prison camp, in 1940, and it closes on a contemplative note: "The mystery . . . which connects through an overgrown path what is shapeless in my comrades to the nobility which lies ignored in man: the victorious part, in the only animal which knows that it must die." In the village, barns, ploughs, wells recall the Bible and the Middle Ages, become symbols of the immemorial "works and days" of man. The smile of an old woman announces "the discovery of a simple and holy secret."

Simple perhaps, and also general. Between Malraux and the particular incident, or the particular individual, there remains the same everlasting distance as between Achilles and the tortoise in Zeno's paradox. Nobody in particular is behind that smile, or in that village. Face to face with the "original stuff," the narrator sees in it symbols of the permanence of the "simple" beyond the turmoil of history. The "simple" could be the native soil, France; it could be the notion that, no matter how fateful, a historical event is only the surface, not the core, of human existence; or it could be both. The "discovery" remains ambiguous, a private affair. In any case, we can hardly believe that the smile of an old woman is an answer to Malraux's transcendental (and ultimately unanswerable) question. Who, in fact, but an exceptional individual, an artist, a hero (or a saint?) could bridge the gap between History and man, retrace the "over-grown path" that connects the shapelessness (and the helplessness) of the ordinary individual with "the nobility that lies ignored in him"? A revelation seems to be needed, or rather, a redeeming act.

Should we relate this to the notion of the "liberal hero" to which Malraux has made a reference in his conversation with James Burnham? The "liberal hero" is, it seems, the man who unites "strength of will," energy, decisiveness in action (hence contempt for the opportunism of the liberal politician) to a clear consciousness of the "nobility" of man and a profound respect for cultural values. A kind of humanized (and humanistic) Garine. Significantly enough, Malraux sees the prototype of the "liberal Hero" in T. E. Lawrence, the soldier of fortune and Oxford intellectual who (like Perken of *The Royal Way*) almost succeeded in leaving "a scar on the map."

Lawrence's, however, was a definite dream of political accomplishment in the Middle East: "hustling into form the new Asia." Malraux's own enterprise is the most general a modern intellectual can conceive of. Its themes are not only the dialectics of will and destiny; the mystery of man; the ambiguity of History; Western values, but the rescue of all this through action: the "restoration of structure and vigor" to Western culture, and the sense that this must be accomplished in an extreme situation, hence through a series of violent acts.

Malraux now attributes such an aim to de Gaulle with respect to France, which he would not do if he had not first thought of it himself, in a much broader context. Aside from mutual sympathy and respect, Malraux and de Gaulle find what is probably their deepest reason for agreement in the fact that they both conceive of contemporary politics in terms of the inevitability of the Third World War or, in any case, of the global struggle between East and West, and of the role France is called to play in it. The rest, for both of them, is only a function of this central fact. Malraux never liked political liberalism and democracy anyway. On this, no doubt, he found it easy to agree with the General. On the other hand, since he has gone through the experience of totali-tarian politics, and of its demand for the unconditional surrender of culture; and since he is perfectly aware that, after Hitler, people expect something besides appeals to authoritarian messianism, Malraux now

isists on "cultural" democracy and "cultural" liberalism. "To seek pro-
:ction for freedom today through a liberal political structure is pure
olly," he told Burnham. The only choice left is to trust the "liberal" will
f the "man of destiny." Finally Malraux's strongest argument in favor of
·aullism is the same he eventually gave in defense of his Communist
and, namely that there is no other *force* capable of doing what has to
e done. Once Communism is rejected, Gaullism is the only possible bet.
nd, when one is Malraux, one has to bet.

Like all political realists, Malraux (in his own peculiar way) applies to
ιe present social situation the principle of the excluded middle. But, as
aléry once said, "there is always a middle term, and it cannot be ex-
uded." In social matters, this seems to be particularly true, since society
what least resembles a logical problem, or a *Kriegspiel*. There are
ιillions of people in Europe, today, who feel bewildered, disillusioned,
ιd worse, and who still resist the either/or logic which the situation
ems to impose. They are too distressed to believe in wholesale solu-
ons. In fact, for many of them wholesale solutions are synonymous with
ιtastrophe. They may occasionally cast their ballots for this or that party,
ιt at bottom they are filled with doubt. Their doubt, too, is a sort of
ιmble. Namely a gamble on the chance that some sensible choice might
ε offered to them: a choice that makes sense in terms of their own daily
:istence rather than in the abstract language of geopolitics. If, in the
.eantime, they are confronted with Fate, they will, of course, be unable
› do anything but bow to it. These people may not be a political force,
ιt they certainly constitute a political fact. Couldn't even a man of
:tion be tempted to take up their cause? In any case, such people can-
ɔt be treated with contempt just because they are too scattered and un-
·rtain to constitute a mass. After all, Western culture owes much of its
vigor" precisely to the fact that, in the face of dogmatism, Western man
ιs known how to insist on the positive value of doubt and disbelief.
oubt, of course, is not a political act. But the burden of the proof falls
ι him who asserts. When Malraux proclaims that only by making the
ate strong can freedom be saved, his is an assertion which, in 1948, is
lequately answered by disbelief.

The truth of the matter is that Malraux may be proved right only in
ιe sense: the weakness of the Third Force, combined with the disinte-
·ation of the Left so successfully brought about by the Stalinists, might
ell result in de Gaulle's coming to power. As for the rest, there is no
ore connection between the "restoration of structure and vigor" to
Vestern culture and the State machine which de Gaulle might be able
› build up, than there was in the past between "virile fraternity" and
ιe Communist Party. The two orders of facts are related now (as they
ere in the past) only by Malraux's own decision that they be so. Eventu-
ly, Gaullism cannot be for him anything but the latest development of
ιe implacable need to act by which he is possessed.

In his *Aesthetic of the Cinema* (1946), speaking of the search for move
ment in Baroque art, Malraux writes: "What the frantic gestures of th
Baroque world are calling for, is not a modification of the image, but
succession of images . . . the cinema." This search for dynamic move
ment, and the cinema, are in their turn connected with "the fanatica
need for the *Object* itself, essential to the West, and related to its politica
conquest of the world." Here, Baroque art, and the cinema, come t
occupy a place in the same view of history which led the young Malrau
to say that the West is "committed to the test of the *act,* hence pledge
to the bloodiest fate"; and also to wonder "what could become of
reverie which would borrow from intelligence the means to force upo
the world the acceptance of its folly."

What indeed, except Malraux's own enterprise, and the visionary rea
ism on which it is founded? The "cinematic" urge he attributes to th
Baroque is also his deepest drive. It is what gives his ideas the peculia
quality of being not simply ideas, but outlines of gestures calling for
succession of external movements; and also what makes his vision deman
so imperiously to be acted out, made into an object belonging to the re
world.

Finally, André Malraux has pushed to its extreme consequences tha
modern pragmatic impulse which tends to see in the world of action th
only reality, and, what is more, to reject any proposition which cannot b
directly translated into a force, an act, or a series of acts; hence, as
matter of principle, to give preference to the possibility of a gesture ove
the elusiveness of a meaning—an impulse which obviously stems fro
a radical despair of truth.

Quite logically, Malraux sees the climax of such a passion in wor
historical action. But then action appears to him as the ground of chanc
and fate: discontinuous in essence and, from the point of view of th
individual who is inevitably seeking a unity of some sort, absurd. Caug
between the irrational test of the act, and the will to escape the ambigu
ties of pure thought, where can a man find a norm excluding sheer "folly
except in a zone intermediary between truth and dream, in a sense c
quality suggested not by any abstract idea but by a pattern of images:
plastic form of some sort?

This is the sense in which one can speak of estheticism, in Malrau:
He is too keenly aware of the implications of his own attitude to see i
action anything but the occasion of a struggle whose motives must b
those that are most avowable in human history: cultural values an
qualities. Qualities and values are what is at stake in action. Their mea
ing, however, lies beyond its sphere, and can be found only in the form
which visibly express it: the forms of art, man's supreme "conquest
Because art appears to him the highest form of action, Malraux cann
avoid seeing the ultimate intent of his enterprise mirrored in the wor

of artistic forms as in a strangely baroque frieze illustrating the *battle* between Man and Destiny.

Malraux's latest work is *The Imaginary Museum.* The book expresses Malraux at his best. It is a unique attempt to reinterpret the whole history of art from the point of view of modern art and its effort to come to grips with the world outside of all conventions and canons. It is impossible to summarize the wealth of dazzling *aperçus* and bold generalizations which make of this volume a kind of extraordinary intellectual rhapsody. One can only isolate from it the dominant theme, which is the ambiguity of modern man as reflected in his artistic adventure. On one side, Malraux sees in the modern artist "the will to submit everything to his style, beginning with the rawest object, and the barest. His symbol is *The Chair,* by Van Gogh." On the other side, this will to control the given, and to impose on the world of appearances the rigor of style, reveals itself to be a demonic will to destroy all forms rather than yield to the deceitful seduction of external appearances: "The artists know how false has become any accord of man with himself (and with the world). . . . The accord of man with himself has become *the* lie, the infamy that must be crushed. From Cézanne to the surrealists, the modern painter is a fanatic. . . . (The artists) look for all sorts of worlds except the one that is imposed on them."

Because of a profound need for truth and autnentic expression, art has ceased to be a representation of the external world submitted to the canons of the "ideal beauty." The disappearance of the world, however, means the emergence of the obscure and of the demoniacal, rather than of any truth. "The domain of the demoniacal is the domain of everything which, in man, aims at his destruction. The demon of the Church, the demon of Freud, and the demon of Bikini, have the same face. . . . Satan paints only in two dimensions. . . . If compared to the nineteenth century, our century appears as a Renaissance of Fate. The Europe of ghostlike cities is not more devastated than the idea of man it had created."

No sooner has Malraux said this, however, than he tries to show the opposite, namely the existence, in modern art, of a classical urge: "A humbly imperious simplification, the same which made the authority of Cézanne, and which has brought about the resurrection of Bach, connects in a common style the works of Piero della Francesca, El Greco, Latour, Vermeer, Goya, with the frieze of Olympia and the Romanesque statues. Emerging together with the barbaric Renaissance, hailed and recognized with it, this style is possibly the greatest style created by the West."

At this point, one cannot help noticing how much more forceful than this attempt to discover the signs of a new classicism is Malraux's description of the demoniacal, and his response to it. It is hard indeed to see any community of style between Piero della Francesca and Goya, Cézanne and the Greeks. Or, if such a community exists, then where is the border line between the demonic and the classical?

Not even in the domain of forms can Malraux forget the question that haunts him. He needs a norm for his action, an indication about the future, a principle of "structure and vigor." Driven as he is by the demon of the act, it is to the classical that he aspires. The world of forms appears to him agitated by the same Furies as the world of action. Yet he is determined to find in the artistic consciousness of our time the signs of a classical urge. If they could be clearly discerned, such signs would be far more convincing to Malraux than intellectual speculations, or the gamble of action. Questioned by him, however, art echoes his question. David's harp could ease the frenzied Saul. In the whole pageantry of art, André Malraux finds the assurance that his demon will stay with him, and keep him wide awake.

Malraux the Fascinator

by Claude-Edmonde Magny

> The true role of a critic is to free the novel from the artist
> who created it. . . .
> —D. H. Lawrence, *Essays on Classical American Literature*

In the light of recent essays that have been devoted to André Malraux,[1] one is tempted to wonder if literary criticism, as practiced today, is not, despite its quotations and interviews, an art of falsehood, or at least of willful blindness. Behind the many masks of eroticism and heroism—whether he seems momentarily to express Communist or Gaullist ideology, whether he chooses the novel or the essay as his means of expression—Malraux (perhaps like most great writers) has reiterated only one point under the most diverse forms: the absolute impossibility for any individual to communicate with any other, even with those who belong to the same group. But probably the characteristic fascination of his art has blinded readers and critics alike, even preventing them from clearly understanding the essence of his message and from judging it.

The book in which this message, the inexorability of human solitude, appears most clearly—and which is also the most successful of his novels—is without a doubt *La Condition Humaine*. Gabriel Marcel at one time reproached him for not having fulfilled the promise of his title, too vast for its actual content, and for not having provided us with an exhaustive, 'essential" description of the human condition, probably meaning by that that Malraux's analysis of the human condition is considerably different from Gabriel Marcel's. In any case, one can say that for Malraux the human condition is defined by its incommunicability.

No one understands anyone, in Malraux's universe, not even himself. Gisors, whose passion is understanding others, fails; he understands Tchen better than he understands his own son, Kyo, whom he loves. Conversely, and as though his own lucidity reverberating around him prevents others from seeing him clearly, everybody misunderstands him:

"Malraux the Fascinator," by Claude-Edmonde Magny. (Translated from the French by Beth Archer.) The article first appeared in *Esprit*, No. 149 (October 1948). Reprinted by permission of *Esprit*.

[1] Marcel Savane, *André Malraux* (Richard-Massé); Claude Mauriac, *Malraux ou le Mal du Héros;* Gaëtan Picon, *André Malraux* (Gallimard).

"For twenty years he had been using his intelligence to make others love him by justifying them, and they were grateful to him for a goodness they did not suspect was born of opium." He even feels alien to himself. "It has happened to me to find myself in front of a mirror and not recognize myself," he says to Kyo, who does not recognize his own voice when he hears himself on a recording. Even if he knew himself, this knowledge would have no denominator common to the knowledge he can have of others; these two heterogeneous orders of knowing, derived by different means, would serve only to enclose him deeper in his solitude. One understands neither those whom one loves nor those whom one does not love. The day he learns that May has been unfaithful to him, Kyo discovers that what he mistook for a deep comprehension was only complicity; his wife is as much a stranger as though she were deranged or blind, or as though he had never loved her. "One only knows of people what one has changed in them," says Gisors somewhere; but when his son comes to him, Kyo finds himself unwillingly changed: "his will was transformed into intelligence." Alienated from their loved ones by love itself, or by the influences they have unwillingly felt, men become alienated from themselves. Clappique, destined for opium, drinks instead: "One is even mistaken about one's vices," says Gisors. Only when the door closes behind Kyo, whom she had signaled to leave without her, does May discover that "if she gave him the sign to leave alone, it was because she thought she was making the last—the only—gesture that might decide him to take her along." Unaware of their true motives, their true feelings, consequently separated from themselves within the span of a moment, men are even more separated from themselves within the span of time, by action as well as by the will to know: it is axiomatic that they complete an action for all reasons but the ones which made them undertake it in the first place. The pivot of the plot of *La Condition Humaine* is a scene in which an individual finds himself cut off from his true volition: Clappique, who is not a gambler, who loves Kyo and has decided to save him, lets the wheel spin past the moment when he could warn Kyo not to go to any meeting, bewitched as he is by his own fascination, normally unknown to him, with the motion of the ball. "This ball whose motion was about to die down was a destiny, and first of all his destiny. It was not struggling against a creature, but against some kind of god, and this god was also himself." All his life, Clappique has sought in alcohol and in mythomania a means of destroying himself, of negating himself; suddenly he discovers that what he has really wanted, like all men, is to be god, and that he was not only mistaken about his drug but about his vocation. Obliquely, he sends Kyo to his death.

One could multiply the examples, borrow them from other books as well, evoke various solitudes—Garine's, or Perken's in *La Voie Royale*, particularly in the scene in which he has a woman for the last time, or in his conversation with the opium-addicted English doctor who cannot refrain from telling him "You can't sit still" (which contrasts the two intoxications—drugs and action), or Kassner's solitude in his cell (which, through an exception that turns out to be only momentary, is materially and spiritually ended by the sacrifice of a stranger)—and come back to Ferral, who, whether it is Valérie or another woman, never seeks through others, never possesses anyone but himself. Malraux's fictionally individualized characters are nomads, like islands separated by uncrossable abysses; even when their will is not (as is Ferral's) driven to affirm itself against everything else and to emphasize its distinction, they never succeed in meeting except for brief moments and usually derisively: Kyo takes leave of his father probably to go to his death; both father and son know this but pretend to ignore it—"Both of them knew they were lying, and that this lie was perhaps their most affectionate communion." Hemmelrich has to find his wife and child blown to bits by a grenade in his shop in order to discover that hatred is also a means of communication with others: "Now he too could kill. It was suddenly revealed to him that life is not the only mode of contact between beings, that it is not even the best; that he knew them, loved them, possessed them better in vengeance than in life." And Kyo suddenly reconsiders and comes back looking for May so that she might die with him: "Before opening the door he stopped, overwhelmed by the fraternity of death, suddenly aware to what degree, in the light of this communion, the flesh is ridiculous in spite of its passion. He now understood that to lead to his death the person one loves is perhaps a total expression of love, an expression not to be surpassed." But to die truly *together* is not within the power of man.[2] Kyo dies alone, far from May—wishing only that she forget him—in the playground of a school, among his wounded comrades, some awaiting torture, others execution, living beings as isolated one from the other as he, when he becomes a corpse, will be from them.

In *La Condition Humaine,* the incommunicability between men reappears at every level, in every form, as an obsessive certitude, the only one there is, along with death, of which it is doubtless the epiphany. Men are fundamentally separated one from the other by being distinct individuals. But this enormous misunderstanding reappears between human groupings and the forms of life they incarnate: the Communists, Ferral's consortium, and the Kuomintang are irreconcilable, not only on the economic or political level, but in their social and ideological structure; these are metaphysically incompatible existences. Similarly, Garine and Cheng-dai in *Les Conquérants,* and in *L'Espoir* the anarchists (the Négus), the Catholics (Ximenez, Hernandez), the Communists (Manuel),

[2] This is a theme often brought up in *L'Espoir,* particularly with reference to Hernandez' death in the very scene that prefigures the conversation with Moreno. "There is no hero without an audience. As soon as one is truly alone one understands this." In the same conversation, the story of the mouse is an example of man's strangulation of himself.

the leftist volunteers (Magnin), the "warriors" (like Karlitch), all represent formations that can only conclude temporary alliances in terms of the common struggle; their incompatibility will necessarily reveal itself in the course of time, as in the case of Hong and Garine, or Chiang Kaishek and Kyo's friends.

I shall cite only two examples significant in their very triviality, of metaphysical misunderstanding in the day-to-day relations of individual men. Two individuals involved in the same situation, thus seemingly united, are suddenly at different levels, which accentuates their estrangement. During the final meeting between Garine and Hong in *Les Conquérants,* Garine, who likes Hong and understands him, shrugs his shoulders when seeing Hong brought before him, as one would at the outburst of a child. Hong interprets this gesture of tenderness as contempt, and falls on Garine in an attempt to kill him. Then, there is the scene between Tchen and Kyo, in *La Condition Humaine,* in which Tchen, having just spoken to Kyo about the octopuses that haunt his dreams in an attempt to make Kyo share in his anguish and most secret exaltation, makes an unfortunate remark which reimmerses Kyo in the personal suffering of which Tchen knows nothing. At best, in Malraux, contact between human beings is unilateral; that is, illusory.

The impossibility of communication through intelligence, love, or death is expressed by Malraux's novelistic technique in both the manipulation of episodes and his style.

As early as *La Tentation de l'Occident*—a book significant in subject and even in technique, since it is a dialogue between a European and an Oriental in letters which never really reply to one another—the rhythm evokes the cadence, line structure, and even the punctuation of Rimbaud's *Illuminations.* At least, the extreme discursiveness of the Frenchman's letters contrasts with the somewhat studied affectation, almost *à la* Valéry, of those of the Chinese. I am in no way suggesting an influence. What there is of Rimbaud in the young Malraux is innate: in both writers one finds the style of a visionary whose vision is only fragmentarily clear. The commas, periods, and paragraphs merely reproduce as accurately as possible the primary intuition, without trying to re-establish between two flashes an arbitrary and false continuity. Young A. D.'s visions are granted in this way; that they are inexplicable and filled with surprising details is both the nature and the guarantee of their authenticity.

Tall banners dominate everything, covered with very ancient black characters. Long ago.
The mob—so many blind men—move back quietly. Near the horizon, on wild grass, a line of bones devoured by ants, marks the passage of time. Near the fires, black witches have seen the future.
Foxes run by. . . .

One recognizes in this jerky cadence, in these sentences that deliberately ignore the rules of antecedents and clauses, subordinate or connecting, the aphoristic style that will develop into the great essays, the preface to *Sanctuary*, the essay on *Les Liaisons dangereuses*, and *La Psychologie de l'Art*. I am selecting at random in *Le Musée Imaginaire*:

Tragedy, in this case, deceives us. The fatality of the house of Atreus is above all the end of the great oriental fatalities. In tragedy the gods are as concerned with man as man with the gods. Its mysterious figures do not emerge from the eternity of Babylonian sands; they cast it off at the same time as does man, and in the same way. In the destiny of man, man begins and destiny ends.

Jean Cassou, I believe, has said of Éluard's poetry that it was composed entirely of stresses. One might say of Malraux's essays that they, too, are made up of a series of stresses. Juxtaposed disconnected affirmations are held together by no logic, no syntax, but by the rhetoric of periods and paragraphs, just as his novels set up characters beside and in front of one another (often too, at least in conclusion, one against the other) each of whom is a unique existence, imprisoned at times unwittingly in the separateness that makes him fundamentally incapable of living harmoniously with others. Perhaps the various "ideas" around which Malraux composes his essays are no more compatible with each other than Ferral's world with Hemmelrich's, the aims pursued by Kyo and the Kuomintang, Garine, and Cheng-dai, or the divergent mentalities of Hernandez, Karlitch, Leclerc and Scali, Manuel and the Négus. Can this series of lightning flashes that leaves us blinded as well as overwhelmed when we read *Le Musée Imaginaire* or the speech for UNESCO be reconstructed by critical examination? Once the transitions between them are re-established, can they provide a coherent system?

The disjointedness that exists in the sentence and in the style reappears in the composition of whole works. Even the most hurried reader of the novels cannot fail to notice that the classic continuity of plot is replaced by a juxtaposition of sometimes simultaneous, more often successive scenes that unfold in various places and involve various characters. One passes without transition from one to the other, as in the projection of slides, by means of a series of flashes, and this choppy quality of the narration (which does not clarify the sequence of events) is further heightened by the breaking up, within each episode, of the scene described into a series of *shots,* similar to those in the movies, and doubtless inspired by them. This cutting up heightens the relief of the story at the cost of its continuity, the mind being less able than the eye to recompose what it has perceived in flashes. Clearly what is involved is not a mere artifice, and the novel is elevated above mere story-telling by this clash of episodes that the author deliberately, so to speak, brings into collision in order to compose from the various sparks and noises the meaning of his book, to be extracted by the reader. This discursiveness, however, seems fundamental to Malraux, who is probably incapable of saying what he means in any way other than in the exclusively aphoristic style of his essays, or in such beautiful, disconnected, and truly disordered novels as *Les Conquérants, La Condition Humaine, L'Espoir* and *Les Noyers de l'Altenburg*. These are wholly devoid of that abundant connective tissue, that dense and compact pulp by which the French and the English nineteenth century tradition taught us to recognize the "true" novel. One understands why *Les Conquérants,* for example, disconcerted its early readers, and for a long while was considered avant-garde: with this work begins a truly revolutionary concept of literature which no longer entails simple consumption, but achieves a kind of cooperation between the author's production and the public. The latter are invited to contribute to the creation of the work through an effort at prolongation and reconstruction, since the book exists beyond its material aspect and has become not only a novel but a *super*-novel; it is anything but an object of precise specification. Defined once and for all, it is an invitation to our participation.

Malraux's works, made up then entirely of *stresses,* limited to the presentation of vehement characters or to the description of moments of crisis, oblige the reader's imagination to supply the *rests*—the repose, the dull and relaxed parts of the story in which time passes normally languorously, with nothing important happening; in short, the connective tissue of reality. When, by chance, the *rests* are indicated in the story because of the structure of the novel, they are padded, so to speak, with the recollection of scenes as violent and uncontrolled as those that actually take place, or by snatches of dialogue in which the antagonistic, irreconcilable viewpoints cross as in swordplay. Nothing, however, emerges from these dialogues, and one can scarcely call them conversations, since each interlocutor ultimately sticks to his own argument—even Gisors, or Garcia in *L'Espoir,* who are, as it were, the representatives of intelligence. When Ferral says to Gisors "Don't you find it characteristically stupid of the human race that a man with only one life should lose it for an idea?", he affirms an irrefutable truth. But equally irrefutable is Gisors' reply: "It is very rare for a man to tolerate, what shall I call it, his condition as a man." This reply engenders a position like Kyo's, for whom all human effort is an attempt to justify this condition by endowing it with dignity. There is also nothing to counter what Gisors says elsewhere: "The hallucinating sickness, of which the desire for power is only an intellectual justification, is the desire for godliness: each man dreams of being god." But, on the other hand, as a character in *L'Espoir* says, it is with this desire to be god that bastardy begins. All Malraux's works are thus torn, without hope of resolution, between at least two positions: a basic antihumanism (which is represented, depending on the circumstance, by intellectual pride, the will to power, eroticism, and so on), and an ultimately irrational aspiration toward charity, a rationally unjustifiable choice in favor of man.

The energy he exerts in placing metaphysically irreconcilable positions face to face without betraying them, or demeaning them, and in allowing them to preserve all their virulence and stamina, creates the power of Malraux's novels and gives them their quality of shock, of gripping violence; it also accounts for the weakness of the position, taken as a whole, in his essays. It was Gaëtan Picon, I believe, who first commented on the total absence in Malraux of truly *evil* characters. Few writers since Corneille have revealed themselves so totally inept at representing low, vile, or even simply nasty characters. Cruelty is omnipresent in Malraux's world, but no individual appears as basically, fundamentally cruel. With him we live in an age of contempt and see people treated with contempt, but those who are contemptible do not appear on the scene. If they do, it is furtively and they are not individualized. They are the springboards of action, the purveyors of contempt or cruelty, but as though by accident or circumstance, and without their having a definite face which would at once become the very face of contempt or cruelty—realities that must remain abstract. These mechanisms of the plot are only glimpsed in the meandering scenes that employ them. The capitalist, Ferral, is viewed with as much sympathy (or as much objectivity, if one prefers) as his adversaries, Kyo and Tchen; he is the instrument of their defeat and their agony. However, we do not see him in that light, which would be negative, but rather as a personality as strong as they, and ultimately as valid. Malraux himself has commented that Nazis do not appear as such in *Le Temps du Mépris*; they are only seen as hangmen, consequently as instruments, their existence being implicit, not explicit. He provided the justification for this in the preface with this significant remark: "If I had had to give the same importance to the Nazis that I gave to Kassner, I would evidently have done so in the terms of their real passion, which is nationalism." We are to understand by "real passion" that which is affirmative and not destructive in them. Similarly, in *L'Espoir* we see of the Falangists only the result of their actions; we never see them as *persons,* except by chance and almost abstractly, as for example in the remark Scali makes to himself about the Italian he is interrogating on the subject of the Fascist morgue. One might say that Malraux refuses to grant to evil the concrete, tangible form of a human being. Within the realm of Malraux's fictional creation, as in his ideas, there is no room for anything purely negative. Incapable of observing anything but light, he cannot represent or conceive of nonbeing, as though his pen refused to express it in any manner whatever.

And certainly it is from this purity—in the chemical sense of the word—that his writing extracts its grandeur. Dostoevsky, Baudelaire, even Bernanos or Balzac, did not emerge without compromise or taint from their plunges into the depths of the human soul. But angelism—and what aviator is not something of an archangel?—is a dangerous attitude, especially when it is inborn, exposed as it is to the double peril of pride and ingenuousness: ingenuousness, because one imagines one can save the world without major difficulty, a world in which only that which *is* exists (it is only through action that Garcia discovers the ultimate Manicheism of existence); pride, because those beings made up entirely of light and thinking themselves free of the taint of sin, believe they can do without transcendence, and by their self-affirmation, finally affirm themselves against God. Even for non-Christians, Malraux's philosophy is characteristically lacking in humility, with the same kind of pride and ingenuousness, manifested by the increasing impossibility of his writing tragedies in a world he believes amputated of the forces of evil. The spectacle of contemporary history has evidently prevented Malraux from committing the same mistake on the theoretical level. But it must be admitted that the relationship his writing establishes with reality becomes more and more abstract beginning with the journalistic method of *L'Espoir,* in which the events are simply transcribed without any attempt at synthesis.

Probably, synthesis is impossible. Nowhere is this more apparent than when Malraux offers us fragments of that vast, and unfruitful, attempt at recreating the history and evolution of humanity in its entirety, an attempt that produced *Les Noyers de l'Altenburg* and *Le Musée Imaginaire.* This latter work, an essay, and the last of his published works, seems indeed to constitute, in the guise of a history of art, the launching of a temporal system of the world, a veritable ontology of history. He is trying to rediscover through the diverse and incomparable forms of art the civilizations that engendered them, and behind these civilizations, the mental, social, or religious structures that defined them, in order to reintegrate them all within the framework of one dialectic, namely, the relationship between man and the world, which ultimately becomes the relationship between the individual, the *Me,* and everything opposed to it. Greece, for example, placed between the Orient that precedes it and Christianity that succeeds it, epitomizes all civilizations that liberate man by restoring to him the whole of the cosmos, including Nature and Destiny. "In contrast to the petrified enslavement of the figures of Asia, the movement (the first known to man) of Greek statues is the very symbol of freedom. The Greek nude develops without congenital defects and without heredity, just as the Greek world, which conquered its enslavement, is a world that might have been created by a god who had not ceased being a man."

But in spite of these influences, these vestiges, these resurgences (such as those that relate Greek forms to the statues of Amiens or Reims, or to those of Giotto, those "forms of a world without destiny"), the different universes thus defined remain incommunicable. Already in *La Voie Royale* Claude Vannec says to the director of the French Institute, "Basically, every civilization is impenetrable to every other. But objects remain, and we remain blind to them until our myths are attuned to theirs." When Malraux attunes his myths to those of the Greek sculptor who first represented the acanthus—that stylized (which, according to him, means humanized) artichoke—or when contemporary artists hail African or Polynesian arts as anti-Baroque—seeing in them what they seek themselves, "arts of expression without gesture"—is his interpretation not purely arbitrary (even subjective)? Does this make them penetrate any further the density and profundity of a civilization?

The interlocutors assembled at Altenburg, with Möllberg and Frobenius at the forefront, would doubtless say no, with the exception of Count Rabaud. No single, indivisible, universal notion, like those created through the ages by various civilizations, can apply to the different (though biologically homogeneous) beings called human. There is the ant man of protohistory, the potlatch man, the man of matriarchal societies, the man of religions which believe in a duality, the man of mythology, Gothic man, and innumerable others. And these formulas, borrowed by Malraux from his earlier writings (the essence of the thesis "men, rather than man" is to be found textually in the essay written ten years ago on Laclos), doom his undertaking in advance. If there is no idea or essence of man, but merely different types of mentalities, incommunicable because they are irremediably linked to civilizations without a common denominator, if the history of the human race is limited to the description of the various stages of a metamorphosis, stages as dissimilar as the caterpillar and the butterfly, what value can there be in the interpretation given by an art historian—a man of the twentieth century —of forms which, by hypothesis, are incomprehensible to him? What truth lies in such a sentence as ". . . the Polynesian tympanum of Autun, and even the portal of Chartres, attack first of all Western optimism."?

Malraux would probably reply that in no way did he wish, in *Le Musée Imaginaire*, to reintegrate within the center of a single mental universe the dissimilar types of man that developed throughout history or prehistory. It remains nonetheless evident that such is the implicit intention of an undertaking like his; for intellection, comprehension, or the possibility of speaking or writing, impenetrability need not be absolute. Frobenius understands, within certain limits, the civilization that gave rise to the Babylonian king related to the stars, or the process that led, in a society unaware of the relationship between birth and copulation, to filiation on a maternal basis. Malraux certainly thinks he understands the meaning of the Asiatic figures and their "petrified enslavement" or that of the Japanese paintings that seek only to capture the secret meaning of the world and reveal it to the spectator. But, perhaps out of the fear of unintentionally breaking down the barriers that isolate civilizations and the human spirit, he prevents himself from developing completely and concluding the attempt at comprehension and integration that he initiated, and from giving it its full stature. It is as though, once and for all, he decided on the theory of noncommunication, and had chosen to show only those aspects of the world that harmonize with what fascinates him. Of course, it is as impossible to deny the reciprocal isolation of individuals, the difficulty of understanding someone else, the conflicts that inevitably arise between men who can affirm themselves only by further exaggerating their fundamental individuality, as it is to deny the findings of ethnology or art history. But it must be pointed that Malraux—as when he utilizes the investigations of Frobenius—elevates into metaphysics what was only a method, transforms a working hypothesis into a judgment on Being. The artist's privilege is to liberate himself from his personal obsessions by incorporating them into the fabric of life, by blending them so thoroughly with other objects that we too are forced to become aware of them, so that he is no longer alone, shut up with his anguish in a horrible *tête-à-tête*. But it is also the reader's privilege, once he has fallen under this fascination (which he later cannot forget, any more than he can forget the figure of Garine in any of the hallucinating scenes in *Les Conquérants*), to attempt in turn to liberate himself from these obsessions, having seen all that lies on the outside, all that borders the hallucination, in order to criticize it, dominate it through thought, and restore to the world its equilibrium.

So much for Malraux's vision of the world insofar as it is expressed in the novels. When it tends to become a philosophy, reproaches more serious than mere partiality can be made. Any page of Malraux teems with ideas; anyone would agree to this. But these ideas do not get on well with each other. I indicated earlier that if one postulates ethnology (or art history) on the absolute heterogeneity of civilizations, one immediately destroys the very science one has tried to establish. The method used in *Le Musée Imaginaire* is questionable. It exudes an odor of death, of catacombs filled with this accumulation of fragments, of debris juxtaposed in an "art album," taken from all civilizations, all ages of the globe, stripped of their flesh by reproduction, taken out of their context, deprived of all purpose, separated from the circumstances that gave rise to them, in short, stuffed by the taxidermy of photography in order to become that thing unknown until the nineteenth century, "the work of art"—the crucifix that is no longer a crucifix because it is no longer prayed to, the close-up taken out of the context of moving pictures that unduly arrests our attention, the portal of a cathedral amputated of all architectural or symbolic meaning in order to be likened to great fetiches according to the whim of the archeologist. It makes one think of a Buchenwald of plastic arts: in this spot gold teeth standing in a huge pile, over there the corner for tattoos . . . an immense cemetery into which sank five continents and fifty centuries of tender, living, and *human* creation, a cemetery paralleled by the Altenburg colloquium with its imaginary museum of mythologies and ideologies. In this instance ethnology serves as the crematorium, as does museography in the other. The interlocutors assembled in Altenburg do not really converse with each other any more than Ferral with Gisors, Pradas with the Négus. And I fear that however ingenious, however brilliant they seem, Malraux's diverse "ideas" are equally incapable of dialogue. It is not by chance that he borrowed the eighteenth century method of writing—most strange for a thinker—which consists in skipping two ideas out of three, as though to force the reader to re-establish the transitions. The unfortunate thing is that in his case, as opposed for instance to Montesquieu, the restoration of the mutilated pieces of the papyrus becomes impossible. A detailed analysis of the famous (and indeed admirable) essay on *Les Liaisons dangereuses* would easily reveal this. Two pages after having declared, "Like all writers, Laclos did not become master of his techniques until he had escaped from the style of the period. And he doubtless felt in some confused way that he could only escape if he escaped falsity. His characters, and the author as well, write badly as soon as they lie, . . ." Malraux goes on to define eroticism as resting entirely on the compulsion (itself immediately incorporating persuasion as one of its forms) effected in *Les Liaisons* by the lie. Must one then conclude that the book is badly written the more closely one examines its essential parts?

Even more serious than these contradictions is the characteristics from which they arise: the constantly peremptory manner, without justification or explanation, in which all affirmations are presented, and which often makes them questionable from the moment they cease being obscure.[3] The unequivocal affirmation regarding a religion based on a belief in the possibility of spiritual change—"however profound the Christian experience of the world, it always culminates in solitudes"—is at the very least surprising. The weakness of discursive thinking, that perpetually jumps from one idea to another, is that it sometimes goes beyond the control of the author; by virtue of its refusal to present its credentials to anyone, it finally succeeds in duping its creator as well.

Malraux's ideas have no underside; like his characters, they are purely positive. Having emerged full blown from the head of their author, they were not dearly acquired by folly and error, their weight in foolishness surmounted but not paid for. Like money acquired through gambling or speculation, they have no consistency, no real density. They remind one of sorcerer's gold—gleaming at first glance, supernaturally brilliant, the next day turned back into dead leaves. They are disappointing on

---

[3] For example (still in the essay on Laclos): "One need only think of the best mythology in our literature, *Les Misérables*, or *Jean-Christophe*, or Eugène Sue, and what there is of Eugène Sue in Balzac. In the case of almost all mythological creations, one senses their derivation from the realm of poetry."

close examination. As Alain says somewhere, "I am suspicious of prose that says true things. It is not difficult to tell truths, a whole desert of truths opens up. There is probably no truth, in the fullest sense, but that of a broken idol." It is this "desert of truths" that we see gaping before us in *Le Musée Imaginaire.* Perhaps Malraux has missed the experience of being foolish sometime in his life, or of formulating some silly idea later painfully set straight. Lacking this, his most brilliant flashes leave us unconvinced; too easily attained, they come in with the flute and go out with the drum. It is commonly said of him that "he has ideas." It would be more correct to say that he is had by his ideas. For one moment they nest in his brain, his style sets them down on paper, then they fly away, to be replaced by other ideas as uncommunicable to each other, as incapable of engaging in a dialogue, as are, according to Möllberg, a Christian king and a protohistoric king linked with the stars, or else Plato and Saint Paul, who are no more able to constitute themselves into a system than is Clappique capable of acquiring a true human experience, lacking the capacity for the mutual integration of each other's diverse acquisitions.

One might be tempted to say the same of Malraux himself. It is amazing that almost all the themes to emerge from his later works (particularly those in the essays) are already contained in *La Tentation de l'Occident,* including the formulas, as well as a few lines that criticize in advance the viewpoint expressed in *Le Musée Imaginaire*: "The particular pleasure one has in discovering unknown arts ceases with the discovery and is not transformed into love . . . other forms appear that will move us and that we shall dislike, like sick kings to whom each new day brings forth the most beautiful gifts of the kingdom, and each evening brings back a constant and desperate avidity." Nor has Malraux ever developed a character who changes and really grows: the Garine rediscovered in China by the narrator of *Les Conquérants* is still the same as the Swiss student accused of complicity in an abortion case; the rapid biographies of Tchen and Hong flung at us in passing give the impression of summing up an essence, rather than describing an evolution. There is only one character the author wished us to see progressing toward a gradual maturity—Manuel in *L'Espoir*—and his mutations are shown to us in snatches, in two or three successive flashes. And at that, they are as oriented toward disintegration as toward integration, since a part of his maturing lies in the gradual discovery, as Garcia says, that "between any man who acts and the conditions of his act there is a boxing match."

Individuals never succeed in integrating with each other, nor in forming communities other than temporary ones; ideas are never constituted into a system. Happily, in Malraux's world, there are a few opiates (I do not mean drugs). The first, and ever-present, is the Night and the World.

One thing only is common to all the characters created by Malraux—the Universe that envelops them all, in the broadest and quasi-pantheist sense of the term (a universe perceived at least with pantheist sensibility), a vast reservoir of cosmic forces in which even the loneliest participate. From this emanate the sudden bursts of lyricism that, coming at the end of the tensest scenes, relax the atmosphere and make the situation tolerable. Man's hell suddenly drops anchor in the Night, the Chinese night in *Les Conquérants* and in *La Condition Humaine,* the Spanish night in *L'Espoir,* nights that are so many epiphanies of the great interstellar night that enters in great billows as though to fill the gaps between beings left by even the most passionate of caresses, and to supplement the inescapable mockery of human contact. It is into this night that May and Kyo walk, the same night whose silence, in the scene of the light switch between Valérie and Ferral, bestows on the instant that has just passed a dimension of eternity, the only dimension possible. "The vast sleepy silence of the Chinese night, with its smell of camphor and of leaves, extended all the way to the Pacific, enveloped the night, outside time: not a ship call, not a rifle shot. . . ."

This is probably the best of what China taught Malraux—the meaning of a universal life of which we are merely the condensations, arrogantly taken with ourselves as though organically rebellious against the great billow from which we stem, and which mercifully returns now and again to assuage us. But in this, as in *La Tentation de l'Occident,* Chinese wisdom and Western pride alternate or are superimposed on one another without achieving the *harmony* that would establish a superior order. Man's communion with the world merely provides him with the repose, the moments of relaxation that are no more functional to his tense life of action than that "liberated universe" that opium restores to Gisors after his fifth pipe.

Music also plays a role somewhat analogous to that of Night, but is less frequently evoked. More significant, and more so even than the myth of "virile fraternity" is the theme of Charity. All readers of *La Condition Humaine* will recall Katov and his vial of cyanide at the end of the book. Not by chance is Katov one of Malraux's rare characters who, along with the "representatives of intelligence" (Gisors or Garcia), arrives by sole virtue of his charity at an attitude that integrates even more than it transcends all other attitudes, and that momentarily dispels the curse of noncommunication. I am thinking of the episode of the armored train, which is less spectacular than many another because it concerns a collective body rather than a particular individual, but because of that, all the more meaningful. Each officer is powerless in his turret, a telephone in one hand, a revolver in the other (two instruments equally useless for murder or for communication); each soldier behind the metal plate listens to the noise of revolutionary artillery as though to the very sound of death. And the train itself is paralyzed, isolated, rooted to the rails that it rocks with its agonized heaving, and held by those rails as though by a strait jacket. Only Katov is capable of experiencing the scene and seeing it as it should be seen (the scene, in fact, is seen entirely through his eyes), because he has an imaginative sympathy strong enough to overcome for one moment—but how derisively—the damnation of solitude.

In the final analysis, charity remains as empty, as ineffectual, as incapable of refashioning a communion as intelligence, night, or music, voices from another world (in which Malraux does not believe); it submits to the fundamental solitude of man without being able to end it permanently. It is noteworthy that *Les Noyers de l'Altenburg* is divided into two distinct parts connected only by the personal bridge of Vincent Berger's common presence: one is the Odyssey of Vincent Berger, vainly seeking in Islam that mythical, imaginary reality of the Touran [Holy War], an adventure whose simultaneous emptiness and meaning are revealed in the Altenburg colloquium, the apocalypse of total noncommunication between men. The other (the German soldiers carrying behind their own lines the gassed Russians), which by the way was omitted from *Les Scènes Choisies,* is the revelation both of human fraternity and of its impotence.

Gaëtan Picon sees in this last novel a progress over its predecessors, in that eroticism no longer appears and cedes its place, apparently definitively, to the exaltation of charity. Less optimistic than he, I do not find Malraux's position notably changed from that of *La Tentation de l'Occident* or *Les Conquérants;* it is still made up of the same two or three irreconcilable truths, maintained with the same energy all the way, that he successively espouses, jumping from one to the other, without any hope of resolution. It is simply that the accent has been shifted, and the absurdity of existence (the leitmotif of *Les Conquérants*) is evoked somewhat less often than the grandeur of sacrifice. However, the human fraternity is still confronted with the opposing affirmation that has not varied since *La Tentation de l'Occident* and that Möllberg, with the full strength of his intellectual power, formulates: *not man, but men.* The human race has no existence other than biological (and even that . . .). In the name of what community, what similarity are men henceforth to participate in fraternity?

Charity, in Malraux's world, thus remains a completely gratuitous affirmation. Its almost *experimental* aspect, appearing as something whose existence and value one attests to without explaining, is responsible for both the grandeur and the weakness of Malraux's position: grandeur, in that its very absurdity, its inexplicable character guarantee the authenticity of the experience in which charity is encountered; weakness, in that one does not see the meaning behind the sacrifice of Katov, Kyo, and Hernandez if, on the one hand, there is no life but this one, and, on the other hand, men are as different from each other as from the chimpanzee or the ant. In *La Condition Humaine,* there is no *order* (in the sense of the Christian order of charity) into which a temporally inefficacious act of charity can fit. Also, the examples of the reversibility of values that one encounters in Malraux remain isolated; their momentary brilliance flashes across the evanescent world in which we live, without lasting long enough to produce a coherent pattern. They edify nothing.

I am concerned here not with reproaching Malraux for not being a Christian, but simply with pointing out the intellectual fragility of his position. As he foresaw it at the end of *La Tentation de l'Occident,* the immediate consequence of the "death of God" which occurred in the nineteenth century is the impossibility of the authentic and coherent continuation of "humanity." If, as Tauler said, "man is a nothingness capable of God," then by suppressing God man is also suppressed, at least as a clearly defined notion capable of unequivocal application to man's many varieties.[4] Man died at the same time as God. A curious consequence of the "death of God" within Malraux's creation is the truly symbolic position given to the theme of fraternity. The relationship between Kyo and Gisors, between the narrator of *Altenburg* and Vincent Berger, is a kind of transposition on the human level of the ancient relationship between man and God, the fountainhead of all good, the intangible incarnation of values. Both men speak of their creators with the same reverential intonation. Corresponding to the remark proudly written by the adolescent Kyo—"This lecture is one of my father's . . ."—is the admiration with which the young Berger notes the attention granted Vincent by the intellectuals gathered at Altenburg—"Everybody waited for my father to resume. . . ." And there are those paternities, more of the spirit than of the flesh, if not wholly of the spirit (these men do not have children, it is said in *Le Temps du Mépris*), that relate Jaime to Alvear, Hong to the anarchist Rebecchi, Tchen to the Lutheran pastor who formed him.[5] But this relationship does not,

---

[4] "For you, absolute reality was first God then man," says the Chinese to the Frenchman, "but *man is dead,* following God, and in anguish you are seeking someone to whom to entrust his strange legacy."

[5] And the tie that binds Malraux's characters to their creator should not be overlooked. That Garine, for instance, speaks most often with Malraux's own voice is quite evident. It is even more interesting to observe the manner in which he lends his ideas to his heroes, in the strictest meaning of "lend," since he later takes them back. He took back Claude Vannec's possessions (the quotation appears above), he takes back from Vincent Berger, in order to put it in *Le Musée Imaginaire,* the line on the stylized artichoke-acanthus, not to mention Uncle Walter whom he quotes without reference, and in such a fashion that one might see in it an adaptation of Prospero's monologue—a quotation suitable for an anthology: "The greatest chance is not that we were thrown by chance into the profusion of matter and of stars, but that out of this prison we drew from within ourselves images powerful enough to negate our nothingness." Just as he successively coincides with each of his ideas, so Malraux successively incarnates himself in each of his characters, his only means for consecutively living through incompatible existences.

any more than any other, permit men to bridge the chasm that separates them (God the Father was transcendent in relation to man; here the separation is reciprocal). Kyo dies and Alvear cannot face the vacant eyes of his blinded son. Even the most spiritualized paternity cannot achieve the abolition of a universe of absolute separation.

A view of the world that seeks to impose that universe as the only real one is not only biased but dangerous, and politically. Without doubt the human race is constantly menaced with division into groups; an inherent fragility is the price paid for this extreme differentiation, this plasticity, this capacity for change. Most societies have known in one form or another a system of castes, which is the simplest sociological expression of this compartmentalization. Ethnological progress has added to this grouping within groups the idea of the fragmentation of the human race, a breaking up no longer into castes, but into mentalities or different civilizations.

But this kind of centrifugal fatality has, at various moments in history, been countered (happily) with a centripetal force that perpetually renews the ever-threatened unity of humanity. Christianity and Marxism (among others) both have the merit of being reintegrating movements. Christianity is not only essentially a religion that grants each man the feeling of possessing an individual and distinct life in the eyes of God, but a promise made to *all* men without distinction, including slaves and women (whom Malraux treats as a foreign and incomprehensible race in most of his novels). Marxism reaffirmed the membership of the proletariat within the human race, and sought the means by which that membership might become effectual and not merely theoretical. And intelligence ought ceaselessly to reduce these inevitable divisions with the help of a constantly growing comprehension of others, and to refuse, no matter how difficult it is, to accept as definitive the successive partitioning, whether ethnological, racial, sexual, or social, that Malraux seems too easily to endorse.

In the face of this dreadful universe presented by Malraux's works, in which there is no understanding between men and women, fathers and sons, men of action and intellectuals, anarchists and Communists, Chinese and Europeans (and doubtless blacks and whites as well), Christians and non-Christians, and so forth, a number of contemporary attempts at reconciliation equally vast in scope come to mind. Vittorini in his novel *Uomini e no,* refuses to admit, even taking into account the SS brutes, that there are beings with the faces of men who should definitely be banned from the human race; Alain attempts, in *Les Idées et les Ages,* a vast synthesis of man's spiritual heritage, including stupidity and superstition, outworn mythologies, the god of a religion with no more believers; Keyserling tried to comprehend India and China. (It does not matter whether these attempts were successful or not; it is in fact certain that they can never be completely successful, since the effort of integration and unification can never be achieved once and for all, but must constantly be renewed and eventually undertaken by each man for himself.) Even those poetical, more "literary" attempts, Eliot's *Wasteland* or Joyce's *Ulysses*, are efforts to reincorporate in the modern mind those great myths of the past (the Holy Grail, Isis and Osiris, the Odyssey, the Flood, Genesis, and even the symbols of playing cards), in order to restore life and immediacy to them, instead of proclaiming in every key, and accepting as immutable evidence, as do the scholars of Altenburg, the incommunicability of the man of potlatch and the man of capitalism.

Probably Malraux secretly enjoys these tragic convictions; he feels attuned to the sundered universe he presents to us—as Chateaubriand was attuned to death and to the insanity of his lady loves, or Barrès (to whom Mauriac rightly compared Malraux) to the putrid odor of Venice or Aigues-Mortes. However, emerging from the domain of literature, we must emphasize the danger of such a vision of the world. To set up with equal force against one another two irreconcilable truths incarnated in man or in groups of men, is to accept a situation that only war, carried to the total extermination of one of the groups, can resolve. Ferral and Kyo cannot converse; one must eliminate the other. So with Pradas and the Négus, or Cheng-dai and Hong. Finally, a society that accepts as irremediable the bipartition of the human race, whatever the form— Aryan and non-Aryan, capitalist and proletariat or proletariat and capitalist, black and white, men and women, Yahoos and supermen—places conditions on itself that inevitably lead to a concentration-camp universe, in which half of humanity (whether the majority or the minority matters not at all) will slowly kill off the other, unless it has sufficiently powerful means to exterminate it in one fell swoop. An atomistic concept of the world logically gives rise to the intervention of the atomic bomb. Of course, I do not mean to imply that Malraux consciously and deliberately thinks at this time of the barbed wire behind which the enemies of Gaullism will be placed. But it is not accidental (and he has been praised for it) that he was one of the first to prophesy the coming of a "temps du mépris" (age of contempt) and of a world of concentration camps, of an era in which the fraction of humanity that has seized power (in whatever form it may be) will attempt either to suppress those without power or to deny them their humanity so as better to exalt and deify themselves.

Malraux: Passion and Intellect

by Victor Brombert

> Qu'est-ce que tu veux que me fasse ta pensée, si tu ne peux
> pas penser mon drame?
>
> Garcia in *L'Espoir*

I. *"Death to Intelligence!"*

What good is your thinking . . . ? Bitter words with which Garcia,
a spokesman for the besieged city, reproves Miguel de Unamuno, the
philosopher who preferred absolute truths to political commitment. What
are absolute truths in the face of Madrid's heroism? What common measure is there between academic meditations and an apocalypse? Just as
inadequate as words in the presence of a shelltorn body, so the intellect
itself appears defeated before it can even begin to account for man's instinctive choice of tragedy, for his *amor fati*.

We cannot avoid the question: does Garcia's exclamation, which
ironically echoes the far more brutal outcries of the Salamanca Falangists ("death to Unamuno," "death to the intellectuals," "death to intelligence," "long live death"), mark the bankruptcy of reason? Certainly
this is a key question not only for Malraux and his readers, but for an
entire generation haunted by the conflict between thought and action.
Malraux himself, according to Emmanuel Mounier (*L'Espoir des
désespérés*), was no more motivated by ideas or by an idea when he sided
with Gaullism after the war than when he espoused the cause of Communism in the Thirties. "He has little esteem for ideas," writes Mounier.
But can we agree that Malraux really feels or ever felt that ideas only
serve to evade or betray decisions, and that at best they set up fake
dialogues between individuals or cultural groups who, in fact, have nothing to tell each other?

A convincing case (but how honest?) could no doubt be made to
prove that Malraux does indeed hold a skeptical view of intelligence as
such. His novels are all clearly in rebellion against the long tradition of

clinical analysis on which the French novel prides itself from Mme. de Lafayette to Gide and Proust. Few writers—and certainly few novelists—are more remote from the atmosphere of the salon conversation. His early novels (*Les Conquérants, La Voie Royale*) are perhaps even a little excessive in their lyrical praise of the adventurer. No wonder Gaëtan Picon calls him and his generation romantic. But even in his later and more mature works, he consciously shuns the analytical novel, both introspective and retrospective. His is a literature of the present, a literature of "extreme situations," as Sartre calls it; a literature of war and death, in which evil, as represented by the sadistic will to degrade, remains pure and consequently unredeemable. In the revealing preface to *Le Temps du Mépris*, Malraux fervently takes issue with the cerebral (and pathologically impartial) kind of novelist who, obsessed by the notion of individualism and individual antagonisms, forever explores the "inner world" of his characters, but neglects what alone in man is great: his ability to take sides and to find solidarity in common action.

For the lack of such a sense of solidarity Unamuno, in *L'Espoir*, is called "immoral"; he has turned his back on a just war because no armies can be just. He has refused action. If the word *intellectual*—which occurs so often in the work of the author—has pejorative connotations, it is precisely because of this separatist tendency, this unwillingness to *be with*. Few characters in his novels come so close to being thoroughly hateful as the scientist in *Les Noyers de l'Altenburg* who arrives at the Russian front with his bottles of phosgene gas to supervise their utilization and observe the results. He has so completely divested himself of any *human* quality that even the most hardened German officer considers him an "enemy" who, with all his impersonal talk of phosgene, mucous membrane and respiratory tracts, seems to have appeared at the front to destroy the very notion of courage. But Professor Hoffmann is a caricature—and an exception. Most often, the scholars in Malraux's novels are merely incapable of action or ineffective. Unamuno retires to a kind of cell, lies in bed, bitter and sullen, surrounded by books. In *Les Conquérants*, Cheng-dai—the Chinese Gandhi—prefers the role of advisor to that of leader. Tired old Gisors, in *La Condition Humaine*, although he has formed revolutionary disciples, is obsessed by the thought of death ("his memories were full of tombs"), refuses to participate in the action and withdraws into the world of art and opium while his son dies in a hopeless struggle.[1] In *L'Espoir*, Alvear, professor of history of art and father of the blinded aviator (the sons are decidedly more committed than the fathers), reads, drinks and recites a sonnet by Quevedo while passively waiting for death in his Madrid apartment. The intellectuals who meet for a symposium in *Les Noyers de l'Altenburg* perorate endlessly on the

---

[1] W. M. Frohock puts it very well: "[Gisors] is powerless against his own paralysis. The physician cannot save himself" (*André Malraux and the Tragic Imagination*, p. 78).

concept of man to the accompaniment of the "idiotic cackle" of hens coming from the outside. As to the ethnologist, Möllberg, he denies the very concept of man, and symbolically destroys the manuscript of his work, *Civilization as Conquest and as Destiny,* the sun-scorched pages of which probably hang scattered on branches between Zanzibar and the Sahara.

Without indulging in hostile caricature (he does not share Edouard Berth's views—*Les Méfaits des intellectuels,* 1914—that intellectuals represent a morality of cowardice), Malraux nevertheless seems to intimate that professional thinkers tend to be incorrigible dreamers. "Intellectuals are like women, my dear! soldiers make them dream," says one of the characters in *Les Noyers de l'Altenburg.* Dreamers who also suffer because they are the first to believe (although they would not admit it, even to themselves) that thought is inferior to action. When, exceptionally, one of them turns out to be an adventurer of the T. E. Lawrence type, all the others inspect him with curiosity and admiration. More revealing still: when such an adventurer-intellectual delivers a series of lectures, it is on "The Philosophy of Action." Needless to add that this emancipated individual (is there a faint memory of the Michel of Gide's *L'Immoraliste?*) has become far more interested in action than in philosophy. As for the others—those who have remained faithful to their books, and to the glib and oily art of learned colloquies—they are condemned to dreams and talk: *"les intellectuels sont bavards. . . ."*

Throughout Malraux's work—from *La Tentation de l'Occident* to his recent studies on art—there seems to be a tendency to devaluate the intellect which finds its most succinct formulation, in *Les Noyers de l'Altenburg,* at the moment of greatest revelation: "thought" is but a "monstrous fraud." Kyo knows that his father deludes himself, that action seldom stems from thought and that one cannot use one's *knowledge* of the "inner life" of others to make them act: "what is deepest in a man can rarely be used to make him act." Moreno, in *L'Espoir,* has learned that neither thoughts nor deep truths exist when shells begin to fall. The most damning commentary on the Altenburg symposium is that it remains exclusively a dialogue with culture, not with life (or death). "An idea never grew from a fact, but always from another idea."

Unable to give birth to action, or to account for it, the intellect, especially in its analytical function, seems moreover to possess disturbing powers of corrosion. Recently, in an irritating though challenging article on our "exhausted" civilization, E. M. Cioran has again blamed our lucidity, and shown the danger of unmasking the fictions which alone can make us bold.[2] The idea is not a new one: Sartre, in the preface to the first issue of *Les Temps Modernes* (1945), called for the death of the

---

[2] "Sur une civilisation essoufflée," *Nouvelle Nouvelle Revue Française,* May, 1956, pp. 799-816.

analytical mind: "We are convinced that the spirit of analysis has out-lived itself and that its only remaining function is to disturb the revolutionary consciousness and to isolate men. . . ." But Malraux had already pointed to the same dangers. Kyo in the presence of his father (symbol of absolute intelligence) always feels that his will to action softens or even disintegrates. "As soon as Kyo came into his presence, his will to action was transformed into intelligence, and he found this rather disturbing." It is again Vincent Berger who puts it most tersely when he tells von Bülow's envoy that dreams corrupt action.

All the values most prized by Malraux and his heroes—courage, audacity, love (?) and fraternity—seem, at first sight, to be at odds with intellectual prowess. Kyo discovers that to judge others is less beautiful than to love them, and that virile fraternity is a more exalting refuge than the mind. Tchen, the terrorist, knows that death is greater than the meditation on death. Similarly, the behavior of the peasant-soldiers in *Les Noyers de l'Altenburg* convinces Berger that it is the common man, not the intellectual, who perpetuates life.

This tendency to humble the mind—like most of Malraux's themes—is already present in his earliest writings. *La Tentation de l'Occident* (1926) questions the very "intelligence" of Europe which, according to Ling, the Chinese observer, suffers from the myth of order (a confusion of order and civilization), from a chaotic sensibility (where order would be required), but most of all from a disease diagnosed as the *maladie de la pensée:* the mind turning in a vacuum, like a beautiful machine spotted with blood. A. D., Ling's French correspondent, compares European culture to a self-contemplating madness, while Ling is even more contemptuous as he calls the intellect an evil ornament (a *"néfaste parure"*).

Finally—and this is perhaps the most devastating criticism leveled at the mind—Malraux seems to make it very clear that the truly fundamental experiences of man are not known but perceived. The body is frequently a more adequate means of communication than language. Desperate (but eloquent) clutchings of hands! Visceral participation in a human communion of suffering and pity! "What these men were doing, my father now understood: not with his mind, but with his body. . . ." This is how Malraux describes the moment of revelation during the gas attack on the Russian front when the German assault wave is metamorphosed into an "assault of pity," and every German soldier returns to his lines carrying a Russian victim. And *revelation* is no doubt the proper word here. Germaine Brée and Margaret Guiton put it very well: according to Malraux, the fundamental aspects of human experience are "mysteries that cannot be elucidated but only revealed." [3] Malraux himself refers to the insight into "a mystery which did not give away its secret

[3] *An Age of Fiction,* p. 189.

but only its presence." And when the meaning of this mystery is revealed to Berger, he can only find one telling word to evoke his former cerebral search for philosophical significations: *crétin!*

II. *Scholars in Action*

Crétin . . . and yet. And yet, as someone has observed (was it Gide?), idiots are conspicuously absent in Malraux's work. The educated, the articulate, and even the erudite occupy a privileged position in his novels. In spite of their ineffectiveness, Malraux does not truly disavow the intellectuals of the Gisors-Alvear type. They all are, in one way or another, the repositories of some important truth. Alvear, for instance, knows that at best man can involve in an action only a very limited part of himself. And as for Gisors, it would seem that Malraux, far from disavowing him, has placed him at the very center of the novel: radiating tenderness and understanding, he is simultaneously outside the action and at the heart of the meaning of the novel. Kyo, Tchen, Ferral—all come to consult him. He is the mirror where all action reflects itself, a conscience where all thought finds an echo and a prolongation. He is a beginning (after all, he formed a generation of revolutionaries), but he is also the one who outlives tragedy, for he remains alive after Kyo and his comrades have died: his suffering, his consciousness—above all his meditations—constitute the novel's epilogue.

And what about the myth of the intellectuals' ineffectiveness? Paradoxically, all of Malraux's heroes (the most adventurous, the most competent, the most violent, the most "heroic") are precisely intellectuals. The list is quite impressive. Garine, in *Les Conquérants,* has studied literature, directed the translation department of a Zurich publishing house and meditates on Saint-Just. Claude Vannec, in *La Voie Royale,* has studied Far Eastern languages and published articles on Oriental art. To be sure, Kassner, the militant Communist, in *Le Temps du Mépris,* who undergoes torture in a German prison, is the son of a coal miner; but he too has had an intellectual formation: a scholarship student at the university, he later organized a workers' theater, became a writer and the colorful reporter on the Siberian civil war. The main characters in *La Condition Humaine* are even more clearly "intellectuals": Kyo is the son of a university professor; Tchen is the former disciple of Gisors at the University of Pekin; and even Katov—the hero of several revolutions and survivor of a White Army firing squad—has studied medicine in Odessa. But it is no doubt in *L'Espoir* that we meet with the greatest concentration of intellectuals in action: the aviator Scali, who was professor of the history of art in Italy and has published the most important study on Piero della Francesca; Garcia, one of Spain's foremost ethnologists, and now one of the heads of the Loyalists' military intelligence; Magnin who, like Malraux himself, organized and leads one of the air squadrons, and whose gestures (the way, for instance, he takes off his glasses) betray *"la marque complexe de l'intellectuel."* Three generations of Bergers have devoted their energies to books and ideas. And not only the major characters, but also the figures in the background would, under less dramatic circumstances, feel not at all out of place in a writers' or artists' conference: Gérard, in *Les Conquérants,* has been professor at the Hanoi lycée. Pei, in *La Condition Humaine,* writes for Chinese magazines and prepares an apologia of terrorism. Shade, the journalist, and Lopez, the sculptor, discuss the problems of contemporary art in *L'Espoir.* As for Guernico, the deeply moving leader of the Madrid ambulance corps, he is one of Spain's well-known Catholic writers, now walking through the nightmarish streets of a besieged city in search of the living presence of Christ. Even characters not unduly afflicted with idealism have not escaped the contamination of books: the power-crazy erotomaniac Ferral, president of a super-capitalistic consortium, is the son of a learned jurist, obtained an *agrégation* in history, and directed, at the age of twenty-nine, the first collective history of France!

Malraux is not the only writer who has taken the scholar out of his study and placed him in the midst of a struggle; he is not the only one who has transformed his peaceful and slightly ironic contemplation of life into a scorching meditation, a dialogue, a battle of ideas—and promoted him to the rank of tragic victim or hero. The contemporary French novel is peopled with artists, journalists and teachers who think, discuss, analyze and accuse—and above all who indulge in what Henri Peyre calls a new-romantic *mal du siècle:* the sense of metaphysical anguish.[4] According to Emmanuel Mounier, all of Malraux's characters are *"métapraticiens":*[5] neither pragmatists obsessed by the notion of efficiency nor hysterics in search of thrills, but "explorers of the unknown" by means of action. Mounier has diagnosed them well. For Malraux's characters are not merely concerned with solving the problems of their time or suffering from their own sense of inadequacy. Theirs is not the mire of shame and guilt through which flounder the victimized professor-martyr Cripure or Sartre's scruple-ridden Mathieu Delarue. They are about the only intellectuals in the recent French novel to get involved in action out of a clear choice, with a clear faith and an unmuddled sense of destiny. (Roger Vailland's Resistance heroes in *Drôle de jeu* are either priggish political fanatics like young Frédéric, or ironic and somewhat Stendhalian picaresque figures like Marat.) The heroes in the world of Malraux may be the heirs to the same ironic culture which finds its culmination in the arrogance and disincarnation of a Monsieur Teste, but they are also willing to sacrifice momentarily such a culture if that is the price they have to pay so as not to betray. Only the elder generation of intellectuals, those who belong to the Alvear type (Roger Stéphane has shown that for

---

[4] *The Contemporary French Novel,* p. 183.
[5] *L'Espoir des désépérés,* p. 28.

them the idea of Revolution is inseparable from a systematic skepticism),[6] are unwilling to make such a sacrifice and consequently are doomed to succumb without hope and without faith, superannuated representatives of an epoch whose moral criteria no longer apply. Dr. Neubourg, as he leaves a sullen Unamuno in his room, has the impression "of taking leave of the nineteenth century."

Dramatically (given the themes and concerns of his novels), the presence of intellectuals is a force indispensable to Malraux: they heighten the artistic and moral consciousness within the novel. The ordinary peasant-soldiers may be the key to the problem of the unity of man—but it is after all Berger, not a peasant-soldier, who discovers and formulates this eternal unity. Moreover, in order to give the *common* man an aura of eternity, Berger (or rather Malraux) has recourse to artistic allusions and metaphors: a soldier's mention of Bamberg suggests the "German Chartres"; peasant faces recall Gothic statuary (the scene takes place in Chartres); joyful gestures bring to mind medieval farces or scenes painted by Breughel. This technique is not unlike that used by Proust for ironic and poetic effects when he compares a maid to a Giotto "charity," a courtesan to a figure by Botticelli and an old servant to the statue of a saint in her niche. But the most important function of the intellectuals in the novels of Malraux is that they discuss the very problem of intelligence and incarnate the central conflict between passion and intellect. It is Garcia, after all—an ethnologist, an "intellectual"—, who finds Unamuno immoral.

III. *Being and Doing*

The awareness of this conflict between passion and intellect, between vitality and lucidity, permeates nearly every page of Malraux. And not only of this particular conflict, but of any dialogue: contradictory myths which demand the allegiance of man, alternating voices of hope and of doubt, clashes between thinking and doing which become particularly dramatic in times of revolution. At every moment, man has to *choose*, caught—as Claude Mauriac has shown[7]—between two treasons. No matter how unworthy it may be of man—and Garcia is the first to suffer from it—the world man faces is Manichean. But to be able to choose is also beautiful: through choice alone man becomes a hero. The Greek knew it: "Of my own will I shot the arrow that fell short, of my own will," declares Prometheus to the Chorus. Similarly, Vincent Berger proudly declares that the home of any man who can *choose* is where the darkest clouds accumulate. For a Stendhal, this would be Cornelian *"espagnolisme"*; for a Sartre, it is only "heroic parasitism" (the hero demanding of fighters who have not chosen their fight to legitimize a death

---

[6] *Portrait de l'aventurier,* p. 120.
[7] *Malraux ou le mal du héros,* p. 208.

which he, the hero, has chosen)—but in any case the choice, and the desire for the choice, stem from a sense of the heroic.

If Malraux is a romantic, it is primarily through this awareness of fundamental antithesis—an awareness which manifests itself on the artistic level through antithetical images: the Loyalist prostitute carrying a rifle is contrasted with the perfumed Fascist women who round out the pleasures of a banquet by going to watch the execution of prisoners; homeless children are asleep beneath giant floats of Mickey Mouse and Donald Duck while Franco's flotilla bombards the nearby port; Manuel evokes his first lesson in the military art with toy soldiers while all around him the living or dead flesh of real soldiers is carried on litters. One of the most unforgettable scenes in *Les Noyers de l'Altenburg* is Walter Berger's description of Nietzsche's mad, but sublime chant, in the obscurity of the St. Gotthard tunnel, to the accompaniment of the rhythmical clatter of the train's wheels and the mechanical pecking of a chicken belonging to a peasant traveling in the same compartment. Malraux is a master of dramatic contrasts and of grandiose images: the growing shadow of Katov as he walks to his death; men with wounded arms in plaster casts gliding by like spectral statues of violinists pushed through the corridors of the hospital; ghostlike figures building barricades during a misty night—all these create an effect of enlargement and of tenseness.

Ever since *La Tentation de l'Occident* (there is an astonishing unity to his work), Malraux has been obsessed by the "hopeless conflict" between man and that which man creates, between the thinker and his thought. This tragic cleavage takes many forms. Ling discovers that in Europe the man of passions (*"l'homme passionné"*) finds himself in disharmony with the very culture he has forged, that the erotic pursuit is nothing but a desperate attempt to be at the same time oneself and *the other*, that thought and emotion are forever divorced. A. D. quite agrees: "with a calm sense of anguish, we become aware of the opposition between our actions and our inner life." In *Les Noyers de l'Altenburg* (written some fifteen years later), Malraux is still concerned with the many shapes of this same conflict: knowing and living; action and talk ("In Tripolitania, my father had acted; here, he was talking"); the very problem of the definition of man. Is man what he *hides*, or is he what he *does?*

It is in *L'Espoir*, however, that this sense of conflict between being and doing, between the intellect and the passionate commitment to action finds its clearest and most artistic formulation. Critics have not always been fair to this very beautiful book, the greatest unquestionably to come out of the Spanish Civil War. Claude Mauriac complains that the characters are too numerous and not sufficiently individualized. Others have deplored the excessively rapid shifting of scenes and the consequent impossibility for the reader to remember them. Yet there are many unforgettable scenes in *L'Espoir:* Colonel Jimenez limping across the

Barcelona square to give the signal for the final attack on the Hotel Colon; the machine-gunned fireman on a ladder fighting off the enemy planes with his water hose; the distribution of cigarettes and razor blades to the besieged Falangist officers in front of the Toledo Alcazar; the execution of Hernandez; the spontaneously heroic defense of Madrid— without mentioning the famous airplane scene (with the peasant) over the Teruel front and the extraordinary descent of the wounded aviators from the mountain. Nearly constantly lyrical, no novel of Malraux so clearly elicits our enthusiam, nor gives us such a powerful feeling of participation. What reader has not, for a moment at least, imagined that he was there, with Siry and Kogan, on that foggy November morning, when the International Brigade in Madrid's West Park halted Franco's Moors? Some of this enthusiasm and nostalgia is due, no doubt, to the prestige which, from the very first, the Spanish War acquired in the eyes of many European intellectuals—a prestige which is well summed up by the hero of Roger Vailland's *Drôle de jeu:* "Everybody knew immediately what side to take; it was the purest of recent wars, the one in which dying came most easily." It is perhaps because so many of the characters in *L'Espoir* have chosen freely to die that the readers, whose common destination is also death, can—as Malraux has said in relation to another work of art—"contemplate with envy characters who for a moment are the masters of their destiny." [8]

The antithesis passion-intellect is worked out on several levels in *L'Espoir.* On the most "sentimental" one, passion takes on its etymological significance (*passio:* to suffer), and ideas are shown as thoroughly inadequate in the face of physical anguish. Magnin knows it: "What is the weight of an idea when two legs have to be amputated?" Scali knows it too, after having seen works of art besmeared with human blood. "Paintings . . . lose their force."—"Art is weak in the face of suffering; unfortunately, no painting can stand up against a pool of blood."

It is, however, on the level of politics (much more so than on the level of sentiment or psychology) that the dialogue between thought and action is most cogently developed. This dialogue centers around three key problems: (1) *Being versus doing* (or political purity versus political efficacy). A whole section of the novel is entitled *"Etre et Faire."* Garcia knows that a revolution has to be "organized" even though the very discipline endangers the ideas of the revolution. Manuel, the apprentice-leader, learns first of all to be more concerned with what people *do* than with what they *are.* But not all agree (Hernandez, for instance) that the justice of the instrument depends exclusively upon the justice of the cause. (2) *Can an intellectual take sides?* To what extent does an intellectual ("the man of the nuance, of quality, of truth as such, of complexity") betray the values of culture by taking sides in what is necessarily a grossly

[8] "Laclos" in *Tableaux de la littérature française, XVIIe, XVIIIe siècles,* pp. 417-428.

oversimplified Manichean concept of a world sharply split between total good and total evil? Alvear and Unamuno refuse the sacrifice and the betrayal. But is not this refusal an even worse spiritual treason? (3) *A nostalgia for a synthesis,* perhaps most clearly felt and expressed by Garcia. Asked by Scali what is man's noblest effort, Garcia answers: "To convert as wide a range of experience as possible into conscious thought."

These discussions and these formulas, when lifted out of their dynamic context of shell explosions and battle reports, may sound unbearably abstract. But if the novel is successful, it is precisely because Malraux has given these discussions life by placing them in the midst of action and moreover used the very structure of the novel to lend concrete meaning to the dialectics of thought and passion. And this is no doubt the reason for the multiplicity of characters which has so much disturbed some critics. For it becomes obvious, as the novel progresses, that Malraux alternates scenes of war with philosophical and political conversations, and that to do so, without falling into monotony, he had to vary the couples. There are altogether fifteen major conversations in *L'Espoir,* each one separated from the other by scenes of action, each one centering on a different topic and shuffling the participants: Ximenes–Puig, 25-28 (courage, anarchism, religion); Shade–Lopez, 34-39 (the new art); Ramos–Manuel, 64-67 (the function of the Spanish army); Manuel–Barca, 69-72 (the impossibility of neutrality); Garcia–Magnin, 81-87 (revolution and the problem of discipline); Magnin–Enrique, 112-115 (the Communist Party); Manuel–Alba, 122-125 (the problem of leadership and trust); Ximenes–Manuel, 125-128 (the problem of leadership); Garcia–Hernandez, 153-156 (the need to organize the Apocalypse); Hernandez–Moreno, 162-166 (experience of prison and awareness of the absurd); Garcia–Guernico, 221-227 (churches, faith, Christ and Spain); Scali–Alvear, 228-235 (man, war, art and the intellect); Garcia–Dr. Neuburg, 272-275 (Unamuno); Garcia–Scali, 281-286 (intellect versus action); Garcia–Magnin, 359-361 (Communism and the Communist Party).[9]

Even a cursory inventory of these conversations reveals that they are more or less evenly distributed, that they are all of about the same length (on the average, four pages) and that there is considerable variety in the combination of participants (Garcia, with six conversations, seems to be the most talkative). Moreover, it is interesting to note that half of these conversations take place *in movement.* "Ximenes liked to talk as he walked." All the characters seem to share this taste for the somewhat nervous promenade-conversation-meditation when both body and mind are pressing forward. Ramos and Manuel are "walking on the embankment" on the Sierra front; Magnin and the Commissar Enrique are pacing up and down the Loyalist airfield; Manuel and Alba "walk among the rocks" in the direction of the Fascist lines; Ximenes and Manuel "walk

[9] Pages refer to the Gallimard edition, 1937.

toward San-Isidro"; Garcia and Hernandez deambulate through the death-infested streets of Toledo; Garcia and Guernico cross foggy unreal Madrid where groups of shadows seem to participate in a tragic nocturnal ballet; Garcia and Scali walk through the "black streets" in the direction of the Prado—so that, within the "conversational" pages, the contrast between action and thought continues to be felt, just as it is felt through the very structure of the novel. The book closes on a meditation-promenade among the shambles of a liberated town.[10] Neither the characters nor the reader are ever permitted to forget the world in which men hope, act and die. As they walk and talk, the intellectual heroes symbolically stumble against loose stones or are interrupted by the sound of a passing ambulance. Even when the abstract dialogues take place in an apparently secluded apartment, the outside world continues to impose its presence: cars shifting gears, the smell of a burning perfume factory, or—more ironically—the voice of a blind man singing the words of hope of the *Internationale*.

Dramatically indispensable, given the central themes of his work, the intellectual also appears as fully endowed with tragic attributes. Malraux's novels (perhaps this is true of all great novels) represent simultaneously an action and a commentary on that action, a sequence of tragic events and a meditation on tragedy. But the intellectual is not merely the commentator, he is also the victim. There is sometimes pathos in this sense of victimhood, in the meek acceptance of one's condemnation: "Guernico would not fight; he would be killed." Yet there is also a hard lucidity (the very kind of lucidity which impels the tragic hero to stare into the unadorned face of his destiny): the lucid inventory of despair. And there is also the more resilient feeling of justification which comes from the awareness that thought means suffering ("each one suffers because he thinks"), and from the Pascalian pride in this ability of man to *comprehend* and consequently to rise above the forces that crush him: the victory of being "the only animal who knows that he must die." But above all, there is a quest for wisdom, that wisdom which—as the chorus in Greek tragedy knows—comes only through suffering. All of Malraux's heroes—he first of all—seem to discover and announce some fundamental truth. Like Dostoevski and Goya (on whom he wrote an admirable study), they speak the "obscure and pressing language" of modern prophets.[11]

IV. *Toward a Synthesis*

"The basic problem lies in the conflict between two systems of thought: the one which questions man and the universe—the other which sup-

---

[10] Malraux's technique is not unique. James Joyce also likes to promenade his characters. Harry Levin writes: "It should be noted that the principal action of the *Portrait of the Artist*, whether in conversation or revery, is walking" (*James Joyce*, p. 43).

[11] *Saturne*, p. 113.

presses all questions by a series of actions." Malraux wrote these words, in 1933, in a letter to Gaëtan Picon.[12] But is the conflict really so hopeless, and has not Malraux himself attempted to resolve it? Does not all of European literature in the past twenty-five years, while keenly aware of precisely such a divorce, yearn for a new synthesis? Armand Hoog—at a time when most critics were baffled by Malraux's Gaullism (some even accused him of having surrendered to Fascist pessimism)—very perspicaciously affirmed that the author of *Les Noyers de l'Altenburg* was striving to bring out of chaos a new and *justified* man.[13] Sartre (in "Qu'est-ce que le littérature?") defines the new "metaphysical" literature not as a sterile discussion of abstract ideas, but as a dynamic effort to apprehend *from within* the human condition in its totality. And is it not highly revealing that *Les Noyers de l'Altenburg,* the first part of *La Lutte avec l'Ange* whose biblical title suggests a metaphysical struggle, ends on a note of total harmony between man and the universe?

Without going in search of metaphysical unity, it is clear that Malraux has become increasingly concerned with the unity of the individual. He admires Laclos for having created the *"personnage significatif,"* but he too has given life to what might be called *representative* characters—so representative indeed that they sometimes lose their individuality. (What do we really know of Kyo, Katov or Garcia?) Above all, he has striven to represent *complete* man. That is why he so repeatedly returns to the savage in man, and insists on erotic sadism and torture: not to analyze hidden complexes, but because he is determined to leave nothing outside the human. Because he does not want it to be said: here man ceases to be man. In the preface to *Le Temps du Mépris,* he accuses nineteenth century literature of having sacrificed the will to create *"l'homme complet"* to a fanatical taste for subtle psychological differences.

The unity of the individual depends moreover on the very unity of culture. To prove—or to affirm—the interrelation, or even the interdependence, of all civilizations has been one of Malraux's most constant efforts in recent years. In a speech delivered in the Salle Pleyel, in March, 1948, he put it very firmly: "There are irreducible political conflicts: but it is absolutely false to say that cultural conflicts are irreducible by definition." [14] In this light, the entire *Noyers de l'Altenburg* is a refutation of Dr. Möllberg's pessimistic view that civilizations are separated by hermetically sealed cultural barriers, that a dialogue is as impossible between them as between the caterpillar and the butterfly and that consequently the concept of Man is devoid of any kind of permanent reality.

It is not surprising that Malraux has turned (or rather returned) to studies on art: they carry his arguments for a possible unity and synthesis more convincingly than his novels, although, in a sense, they may properly

[12] *André Malraux,* p. 81.

[13] "André Malraux et la validité du monde," *La Nef,* March, 1947, pp. 121-126.

[14] "Adresse aux intellectuels," *Le Cheval de Troie,* July, 1948, p. 977.

be considered as a logical sequel to his fictional work. Kama, the painter in *La Condition Humaine,* already knows that art is a weapon against loneliness, a means of communion with life . . . but also with death. It is he, really, who seems to answer Reverend Smithson's question: what faith, other than Christianity, can account for the world's suffering or conquer death? More than any other of his novels, however, *Les Noyers de l'Altenburg* proclaims this faith in art. First of all the setting: the Chartres cathedral, an Alsatian abbey. But even more the conviction of the characters that salvation comes from art: "The first sculpture which represented a human face, simply a human face; liberated from the monsters . . . from death . . . from the gods. That day, man formed man of the dust of the ground." For Walter Berger, the first work of art was the first victory over the absurdity of the universe, the first and most lasting defiance of death. Through art, man escapes his condition ("our art seems to be a correction of the world"), and is delivered from space and time. Obviously, Alvear, on that gloomy night in his Madrid apartment, was in possession of some important truth.

Faith, salvation—these words suggest the need for a religion. Will Malraux convert to Christianity? It is certain that he is aware of the synthesizing virtues of the Christian religion. In *La Tentation de l'Occident,* he has Ling remark that Christians reach out toward God by "ordering" violent emotions, and that Christianity teaches a communion with the world through an "exalted consciousness of its fundamental chaos." Vincent Berger believes that the *coup d'état* of Christianity is to have installed fate *within* man and that it is consequently necessary to *know* man in order to fight the demon. His entire work is an effort at reconciliation and unification. Clearly, if ever Malraux is converted, it will be out of a cerebral quest for a synthesis between passion and the intellect. In the meantime, however, his intellectual heroes remain the indispensable witnesses of man's only possible grandeur in a meaningless universe: they know that we ourselves must create the concepts and the images which can "negate our nothingness."

Time, Art, and the Museum

by Maurice Blanchot

There are some people who regret that Malraux's books on *La Psychologie de l'Art* did not undergo more rigorous planning. They are found to be obscure, not in their language, which is clear—and even more than clear, brilliant—but in their development. Malraux himself, at the end of the essays, seems to have wished for better composition. Perhaps Malraux is right, but his readers are surely wrong. It is true that the ideas he develops have their whims; they are peremptory, sudden, they remain unresolved. They appear and disappear, and since they often affirm themselves in formulas that are attractive to them, they seem to think themselves thereby defined, and this achievement suffices them. But the movement that abandons them, calls them back; the joy, the glory of a new formula once again draws them out of themselves.

This movement—this apparent disorder—is most definitely one of the important aspects of these books. The ideas do not thereby lose their coherence; it is rather that they escape from their contradiction, even though these contradictions continue to animate them and keep them alive. I should add, it is not merely ideas that are perhaps not in any clear order. Someone has written—perhaps Valéry—"One must always apologize for discussing painting." Indeed, an apology is due, and he who discusses a book that discusses painting should doubtless apologize twice over. Malraux's apology does not lie in the passion he devotes to the art he discusses, nor even in the extraordinary admiration that he lavishes on it (for perhaps art does not always wish to be admired; admiration may also displease it). It lies rather in this unique merit: ideas, however they may tend, according to their own requirements, toward an important and general view of art, in their attempted dialogue with art works, with the images they accompany, succeed at the same time—without losing their explanatory character—in illuminating themselves with a light that is solely intellectual, in sliding toward something that is broader than their meaning, in achieving for themselves (and for us who are destined to understand them) an experience that imitates art rather

"Time, Art, and the Museum," by Maurice Blanchot. (Translated from the French by Beth Archer.) This appeared as a somewhat longer essay, "La Musée, l'Art, et le Temps," in *Critique*, Vols. VI and VIII, Nos. 43 and 44 (December 1950 and January 1951). Reprinted by permission of *Critique*.

than describes it. Thus ideas become themes, motifs, and their somewhat incoherent development, often criticized, expresses instead their truer order, which is to constitute and test themselves in their contact with history through a movement whose vivacity and seeming vagrancy make us perceive the progression in history of art works and their simultaneous presence in the museum in which culture today assembles them.

Doubtless Malraux does not think he has made a discovery when he shows that, thanks to the progress of our knowledge and subsequently to our techniques of reproduction—but also for deeper reasons—artists for the first time draw on universal art. Many critics before him have considered this "conquest of ubiquity" and, to mention him again, Valéry (speaking it is true more of a foreseeable future than of the present) said, "Art works will acquire a kind of ubiquity. Their existence in the present or their return to any former period will be determined by our command. They will no longer exist only in themselves, but all of them will exist wherever there is someone." He concludes, "One must expect that such tremendous innovations will transform the whole technique of the arts, will consequently have an effect on creation itself, will go as far, perhaps, as to modify the very notion of art." This is all marvelous, but Valéry resisted the marvel which in any case he wanted barely to perceive through the dim consciousness of a half dream. Just as he did not willingly accept history, so he disliked the museums that Malraux called ethereal, in which Valéry saw waxy solitudes that stem, so he said, from the temple and the salon, the school and the cemetery. In these domains of incoherence he seemed only to notice the unfortuitous invention of a somewhat barbaric, somewhat irrational civilization; but even his disavowal was mild and he did not insist.

Not only does Malraux insist, but with persuasive power he makes of the Museum a new category, a kind of force that, in our era, is simultaneously the end of history—as it is expressed and achieved by art—its chief conquest, its manifestation, and even more. The Museum is the very conscience of art, the truth of artistic creation, the perfect moment in which artistic creation, at the same time as it attains reality in an art work, refers to, summons and transforms all other art works. And in relating earlier art works to the more recent ones, which does not always reject them but always illuminates them differently, artistic creation induces them into a new metamorphosis from which it itself does not escape. By way of a brief reminder, *Le Musée Imaginaire* symbolizes first of all this fact: that we know all the art forms of all civilizations that devoted themselves to art. We know them in a practical and convenient fashion not with the ideal knowledge possessed only by few, but in a real, living and universal manner (through reproductions). And finally, this knowledge has some unique characteristics. It is historical, it is the knowledge of history, and of a series of histories, that we accept and assemble without judging them for any value but their own past. At the same time i is not historical, it does not concern itself with the objective truth of history, the truth of the moment in which any period was accomplished. And this is the knowledge we accept and even prefer. We know that all of ancient art was different from what it seems to us to have been. The bleached statues deceive us, but if we restore their painted surfaces, it is then that they appear false to us (and they *are* false, for this restoration denies the power and truth of time which has effaced the colors). A painting ages; one ages badly, another becomes a masterpiece because of the effects of time that have decomposed the colors, and we know the benefits of mutations—the Victory whose wings were gained only by the flight of Time; the heads from Bardo of mediocre artisanry that the sea resculpted and made fascinating. Furthermore, the very means of our knowledge transform almost at will that which they help us to know. Through reproduction, art works lose their proportions—the miniature becomes a full-size painting, the painting separated from itself, fragmented, becomes another painting. Fictive arts? But art, it would seem, is this very fiction.

Other even more important results occur. One must further add that these results are not dormant and inanimate effects, but the very truth of the Museum, the fundamental meaning that permitted it to evolve simultaneously with art's greater awareness of itself and of the freedom of its discovery. The Museum, we understand, assists in the affirmation that animates all culture. This is not immediately clear so long as the Museum, incomplete, glorifies only one art, sees in it not one art but perfection and certitude. Thus Greek art or Renaissance art are examples with which the artist can compete, but even if he equals them, he does not reconcile them; he is dedicated to himself; he takes his place outside of time along with them. That is why the only Museum is a universal Museum, so that "all is said," "everything is seen" signifies that whatever is admirable is everywhere, is precisely an "everything" that triumphs only when the incontestable has disappeared and the eternal has ended. On the other hand, as soon as the Museum begins to play its role, it means that art has agreed to become a museum art—for some a great innovation, for others a great impoverishment. Is art poor because it is simply itself? This is open to discussion, but the evolution is evident. The plastic arts are first devoted to religious sentiments and to the invisible realities around which the community perpetuates itself. Art is religion, says Hegel. At that time, one finds it in churches, in tombs, under the earth or in the sky, but out of reach and in a sense invisible. Who *looks* at Gothic statues? We do; the others invoked them. The disappearance of prayer resulted in the appearance of monuments and art works, made of painting an art available to our eyes.

The Renaissance began this evolution. But it was absorbed by the visible world it discovered. Certainly it was not merely satisfied with reproducing appearances, nor even with transforming them according to a harmonious understanding that it called Beauty. The whole of the

Renaissance did not take place in Bologna, for who better than the Florentines minimized the decorative, the pleasure of anecdote, and even the delight in color, so as better to capture the meaning of form—conceptions they do not owe to antiquity, but that are as native to them as the hunger for meaning? It remains that the Renaissance, if it renders art real, immediate, seems through its success and through the ambiguous nature of this success, to link this immediacy with the ability to represent reality. It is from this that all the misconceptions arise, and have yet to be abolished, but in the final analysis they are fortunate misconceptions since so many great works emerged from them. These great art works continued to belong to the church; they had a place in the palaces where, in some cases, they played a political role. They were intimately bound up with the life that sought to use them. A portrait, in the house of the model, remains a family painting. But when all these works enter the Museum, in fact or in idea, it is precisely life that they renounce; it is from life that they divorce themselves. "Artificial places," it is said of Museums, in which nature is banished, and the world is shrunken, solitary, dead. True, death is there, at least life is no longer there—neither the spectacle of life, nor the sentiments or modes of being through which we live. And then what happens? What was formerly a god in a temple becomes a statue in a museum; what was a portrait becomes a painting. And even dream, that absence in which the world and its images are transfigured, becomes dissipated in this new brightness which is the day light of painting.

This is the way that the transformation, the verity of an art work, is momentarily accomplished. Modern art, in the Museum, is aware of its truth, which intends it to be neither a function of the church, nor of anecdote, nor of history, nor of a personage, but to ignore contemporary life—the props of appearances—and perhaps all life, in order to discover itself in the life of art. The painter serves painting, but painting apparently serves nothing. The curious thing is that from the moment the artist makes this discovery, his interest in art, far from waning, becomes an absolute passion, and the works that mean nothing seem to incarnate and reflect that passion. Why, one may well ask?

Malraux himself asks this question, and supplies various answers. But first, one must look more carefully at the meaning of this evolution, this revelation, caused by history, which manifests itself in two forms—the imaginary museum and modern art. It is true that in many ways the views Malraux applies to the plastic arts are inspired by the discoveries of our time, and are movements of a philosophy whose principles originate in Hegel. Certainly, there are many differences, but the analogies are interesting. When one points out that today, for the first time, art has so to speak doubly unveiled itself, the words "for the first time" have an evident significance. They indicate that a conclusion has been reached and this conclusion, if it does not conclude time, nonetheless permits the observer who speaks of this first time to speak of time as of a concluded factor. It is clear that for Malraux, and doubtless for each of us, our period is not—insofar as the plastic arts are concerned—an era like the others. It is the radiating world of "the first time." For the first time art is revealed both in its essence and in its totality—both closely related. Art abandons everything it was not and extends to everything it has been. It reduces itself, it gives up the world, the gods, and perhaps even dreams, but this poverty enriches art with its own truth and subsequently with the vastness of the works that its former self-unawareness had prevented us from reaching; this great expanse of works that had been misunderstood, neglected, and even despised. The imaginary Museum is thus not only the contemplation of modern art and the means of its discovery, it is the very work of this art—one might even say its masterpiece, if it were not also necessary to say, almost in a whisper, its compensation. Were art no more than its own passionate affirmation, the absolute glory of the single moment when art marvelously becomes itself, it might not be tolerable unless it were still more, unless gliding across time and the civilizations of the world, like the purity of dawn, it suddenly revealed, with all its works, that marvelous fact that our art is universal, which means that all works of all times are also ours, are the works of our art, which for the first time unveils them to themselves, reveals them for what they are.

Perhaps we are going farther than Malraux's formulas would permit. But if today, for the first time, art has arrived at an awareness of itself (a primarily negative awareness—art no longer imitates, imagines, or transfigures; it is no longer in the service of values foreign to it; it is no longer—this is the positive side—anything but painting and its own value, though this is still difficult to grasp); if, in addition, this awareness, far from placing art in a temporal environment, links it to the passage of time and is the meaning of this passage of time which at a given moment materializes and manifests itself absolutely, then it is true that this moment is highly privileged. It can look back on all other moments, shedding on itself and all other moments total clarity—the light in which they reveal their purity and truth. Doubtless things are not so simple. Art is perhaps not a comet whose shimmering head—modern art—carries in its wake and illuminates the duller, dimmer beauty of its immense orbit. If today's art works help us to become the "heirs of the entire world" and, more than heirs, the creators and conquerors of all possible art works, they themselves depend in turn on this conquest and on this creation.

This dependence is not one of dry causality, but a dialectic that Malraux calls metamorphosis. Art—and by this is meant the entirety of art works and that which makes each one an art work—is essentially unrest and movement. The Museum is in no way made up of immutable survivors and eternal corpses. Statues move, we know; just as Baudelaire was frightened to see unreal images undergoing a startling development. With each decisive art work the others tremble; some fall, in a death that promises future resurrection. This movement would seem to be infinite, for if as Schiller said, "what lives in song must die in life," then that which immortality maintains, holds, and supports is this very death which has become creative negation and labor. At the end of his three volumes Malraux writes, "The first universal artistic culture that will no doubt transform modern art, *until now* oriented by it . . ." Modern art is thus destined, promised or condemned to the power of metamorphosis from which it issued, or, to go even further, whose purest expression for one exclusive moment it seemed to be. Its future is the unknown. But in the meantime, because no moment is like any other, and because this particular moment both revealed and multiplied the power of metamorphosis, it seems possible to look to modern art for the meaning of the question to which all art is an answer, and to find out why this answer is both valid and decisive. This is the problem of Artistic Creation to which Malraux devoted the second of his books, the one preferred by some, in which civilizations become art works, and art works are composed and completed according to the secret of their own fulfillment which they reveal to us as if by transparency, and as if this transparency were precisely their secret. This impression, in fact, is merely the happiness of a moment, and what we have to say on the subject is rather the unhappiness that follows, the obscurity that closes in on this fleeting daylight, for when art becomes a problem it is also an endless torment.

Plastic art is fundamentally hostile to nature. This we know, but Malraux points it out with an energy and perseverance that at times is surprising, as though this truth continued to be questioned. It is because he wants to point out something else. When he writes, "All art that attempts to represent implies a system of reduction. The painter reduces all forms to the two dimensions of his canvas; the sculptor reduces all virtual or represented movement to immobility," this reduction he speaks of seems to send the artist right back to nature. Does the painting of a landscape reduce the landscape, transform it through technique, and consequently deliver it to the impartiality of art? Not at all. For then the purpose of painting would be to reduce this reduction, as has been unsuccessfully attempted by many schools. In reality, if "art begins with reduction" this means that the art work takes shape only when starting with itself, at the inside of this artistic universe in the perpetual state of becoming—history made art—that the Imaginary Museum symbolizes for us, and that has always been evident to the eye of an artist, however poor and limited this universe.

Art does not begin with nature, except to deny it. The origin of a picture is not always another picture, nor even a statue, but all of art as it exists in works admired and as it is intuited in works scorned. The artist is always the son of the works of others whom he passionately imitates until he passionately denies them. Why is Malraux so unyielding in those affirmations that oblige him, for example, to consider of little interest the drawings of children? Because, if a child draws a dog, he may not draw the dog he sees, but neither does he draw Tintoretto's dog (and perhaps so much the better). It would seem that Malraux must keep the artist completely separate, sheltered from and beyond the world, just as the Museum is a universe without origin, a single span of time, the only time that is free, the only kind that is true history, equal to the freedom and self-mastery of man. The more the new artist encloses himself in the Imaginary Museum to liberate himself, the more readily art is born out of this assembling of all the factors of artistic creation. How did Giotto discover his vocation? By looking at Cimabue's paintings and not at the sheep he was herding. How does any vocation develop? Through imitation, copy, until the moment when the burgeoning artist, through the passionate imitation of these learning materials, masters the plastic secret of art works, and slowly—sometimes late in life, sometimes never more than peripherally—experiences, creates, distills his own plastic secret, which Malraux calls the "initial schemes" of his art. These "schemes" are in the beginning means of rupture, intuitions that express —not abstractly or esthetically, but plastically—the desire to surpass, to transform the art and style that first brought the young creator into the Museum. And although set free thereby, he nonetheless remains a prisoner of his masters.

To find these schemes once more, to describe them, is to rediscover the progress, the revelations, the metamorphoses—in a word, the specific experience that is meaningful only in works of art. This meaning is the one least often betrayed—although still betrayed—when it is described in its most concrete and most technical aspects. The most convincing pages Malraux has written show in extremely evocative yet precise terms what sort of artistic itineraries were followed by such painters as El Greco starting out from the Venetian school, Tintoretto also starting out from the Venetian school, La Tour starting out from Caravaggio, and Goya starting out from his own work Goya, who until the age of 40 never realized he was that other artist, Goya. To come back to El Greco, it is not the moving pages on Toledo, solitude, and the somber twilight with which the artist encircled his own vision that bring us closer to his genius, but everything that reveals the focal point of his discovery, and that can be expressed in this way: to maintain the Baroque design of movement—the distortion of all outline—while at the same time eliminating what it grew out of, namely, the quest for depth.

Malraux seems irritated when he hears mention of the artist's "vision." This antipathy to vocabulary is remarkable. Just as he energetically excludes from art the idea of representation, so does he seem to exclude from artistic genesis the notion of image. Up to a certain point this is

logical (one might say that painting is a struggle to escape from vision)
and results in any case from certain formulas that he willingly repeats
"Plastic art is never born from a manner of seeing the world but o
making it." This banishment of vision holds for imaginary vision as well
for interior fiction, for anything that can make of painting the passive
subjective expression of a likeness, be it of an invisible form. In his thre
books, Malraux allots one sentence to surrealism, and that to dispens
with it. This scorn, which is strong but instinctive—it goes without say
ing that Malraux uses terms according to his own arbitrary pleasure, an
to take him at his word would be ridiculous—this scorn for the word
vision and *imaginary* tend, above all, to eliminate everything from plasti
art that might make its function and creative activity less evident. Th
painter is a creator of forms and not a visionary who slavishly copies hi
dreams; conception means nothing outside the picture, and is insufficien
inside it to explain what it expresses. For prior to the picture there wa
nothing but an already pictorial intention, since it is through contac
with other pictures that this intuition took outline, and through imita
tion that it developed. Painting is an experience by which a specific powe
affirms or seeks itself, is valid only for that art, and has meaning onl
in relation to it. It is a power that must nevertheless be defined, or a
least named, and that Malraux calls style. What is art? "The means b
which forms become style." But what is style? The answer is not wantin
and in some ways, it must be admitted, is surprising. "All style is th
shaping of those elements of the world that permit the orientation o
the world toward one of its essential parts."

One might think, and with good reason, that *La Psychologie de l'Ar*
is exclusively concerned with restoring to art the experience that belong
to it, the world that belongs to it, that Universe of the Museum (a win
dowless monad) which is created and sustained by the artist throughou
the infinity of time. It is a world absolutely self-sufficient, self-ordered
oriented solely toward itself, animated by the span of its metamorphoses
a solitude worthy of any passion and any sacrifice. And he who devote
himself to this world knows that he runs the greatest danger, for what h
seeks is the ultimate. Indeed, one can imagine that Malraux's investiga
tions might have taken such a turn, and that it might not disagree wit
his idea of "one of its essential parts"—that part that bound the worl
to painting and the plastic arts with real passion. But for this, Malrau
would perhaps have had to be a painter himself, would have had to b
interested in furthering painting rather than in justifying it, in doing i
rather than looking at it. It is also true that the more one investigates
problem, the harder it is not to express it in relation to all the question
that are of vital concern to one.

Malraux is interested in painting, but we know he is also interested i
man. To save one through the other—he was unable to resist this grea

temptation, a temptation all the more pressing since the problem itself leads one to that point. We must carefully consider this strange Museum in which we dwell and this even stranger history into which Malraux places us. What do we see there? Whatever we prefer—and what we prefer are those works that, like our own, ignore the physical world, do not yield to it, and create a totally different world whose strength and victorious singularity fascinate us. However, these works—such as those of Byzantine style, to take a well-known example—with their rejection of the physical world and the rupture expressed by them, were not brought to being by a quest for the plastic, were in no way produced by a quest for style, but by values foreign to art and even to the world, values to which we owe all our gods—those above and below the earth. These are surprising statements, but hardly unexpected.

If art is defined and constituted in its distance from the world, its *absence* from the world, it is natural that everything that questions the world—called by a now highly imprecise term, transcendency—everything that surpasses, denies, destroys, threatens the complex of stable, comfortable, reasonably established, and hopefully durable relations, whether pure or impure, proposed for man's salvation or destruction, insofar as this questioning shatters the validity of the ordinary world, *works* for art, opens the way for it, summons it. The gods thus become, in the greater part of the Museum, the astonishing illusion that has permitted the artist who was consecrated to their cult to consecrate art. Art at that moment is religion, which means a stranger to itself, but this strangeness that tears art away from profane, non-artistic values, is what brings art closer to its own truth, even if not manifest. In this context, one might say that the gods were only temporary substitutes, sublime but unbeautiful masks of artistic power, for as long a time as this power, through the dialectic and metamorphoses of history, remained incapable of conquering in the artist, finally face to face with himself, the consciousness of its own autonomy and solitude. The Pantocrator awaiting Picasso.

And now what? Now art is called Picasso, but it seems that Picasso is obliged to continue the Pantocrator, not only because to him falls the demiurgic task of creating forms and creating everything that is the life of the Museum, but also of relating painting to that "essential part," to that superior goal, that level of the eternal, represented by the golden image of the absolute for the men of the first centuries. For modern art and for Malraux, this is a bend in the road, a different moment. It is true that the conspiring gods have disappeared. They have gone back to a state of profound absence, to that other-worldliness that they once made appear, or more precisely proposed to art as the fierce realm—the emptiness—in which art could become its own master without however knowing itself. Absence, depth, destined to divert attention from the real world, to reject appearances, to substitute the conquering power of style for representation. However, from the moment that art gained awareness of its truth, was revealed to itself as the denial of the world and the affirmation of the solitude of the Museum, should not this very absence, this depth in which the gods abided in order to accustom the artist to do without life—which painting reconquered—should it not in turn vanish into painting, be painting, and nothing more? Should it not attest to the fact that painting is valid as painting, and nothing else? Indeed it seems it should. Yet, if one accepts Malraux's views, this absence does not agree to being dominated by art and still claims—under more or less high sounding names: human essence, ideal image of man, honor of being man, in short "the essential part of the world"—to be the exemplary force, the divinity that art cannot leave unexpressed without ruining itself.

The arts of the past most certainly had a relationship with the gods. They seemed, in expressing the gods, to be materializing what was invisible, what is inexpressible, is not material, and through this supreme pretension art became oriented not toward the invisible and shapeless, but toward pure visible presence and form, consequently only confirming itself. These are impressive results. The invisible, however, remained. It has not really given up its rights. It must be added that since for Malraux painting is not image, is not the pictorial conquest of this *absence*, which, before any technical reduction, changes everything seeable into the stupor of "this cannot be seen," "this is not seeable," and since, in addition, Malraux does not even wish to reintroduce the invisible as fiction (even though in his third volume he makes allowance for poetry), the invisible that is not pictorialized can only wander around dangerously under the name of *ideal* or *cultural values*.

This inflexibility is not deliberate, and is even a pathetic debate that Malraux seems at time to be carrying on with his different viewpoints. To what end does the evolution of time and metamorphosis of the Museum lead? To a painter who is exclusively a painter. To Cézanne who, compared to Goya, created painting liberated from metaphysical passion, from the dream and the sacred; painting which has instead become self-passion and self-creating. Malraux attests to this. Modern art imposes the autonomy of painting with regard to all tradition and even to culture. Painting that has become culture is a stage, a moment—a bad one—that corresponds to intellectuals seeing in the plastic arts only what is most visible: harmonious fiction, transfiguration of things, expression of values, representation of a human and civilized world. But can painting, even when its representational function has disappeared, when it is no longer constrained to seek its own values, still serve as the safeguard of a culture? "An art of great Navigators," yes, says Malraux. "But is a culture of great Navigators conceivable?" Elsewhere the doubt becomes the response. Picasso follows Cézanne, and the anguished questioning sets out toward annexation and conquest. But a culture made up wholly of questioning cannot exist.

This is probably true. Must one not then conclude that art, an impassioned questioning, in the same way as it has nothing to offer to this fixed ideal receives nothing from it, this collection of known values, of public truths and established institutions that is called civilization? The painter, the artist—as he is made to appear to us—is doubtless a divine creature. And we are hardly surprised, since he has taken the place of the gods. Even more than that, he is the truth of which the divinity was only the mask—the necessary caricature. "The gestures with which we handle pictures we admire . . . are venerating. The Museum, which formerly was a collection, becomes a kind of temple. Of course, a still life by Braque is not a sacred object. However, though not a Byzantine miniature, it belongs in the same way to another world and is part of an obscure god that one wishes to call painting but that is called art. . . ." Malraux adds with a repugnance that we share with him: "Religious vocabulary is irritating, in this context, but there is no other. This art is not a god but an absolute." An absolute, yes, but one whose truth is to be enclosed in itself, whose meaning and excellence are to be within itself—and from without, can only be deemed insignificant. This at least is what Malraux's views on modern painting seem to lead us to think. The god is now called painting, but at an earlier time, painting had recourse to a metaphysical or religious realism in order to escape the temptations of an esthetic realism. That is why painting was enamored of the gods. However, now that the gods have become paintings, that art is concerned with "the creation of a painting that considers itself only painting," metaphysics must also disappear from the picture and be no more than *this* particular picture, at the risk of transforming it into metaphysics, of consequently restoring another form of realism, or worse yet, of appearing above and beyond the painting as the purely moral duty and obligation to save civilization and preserve man.

This obligation, however, becomes more and more pressing in the course of the third book. And it would seem that art too assumes more and more willingly this obligation, which can be called its idealizing function, its capacity for "sustaining, enriching or transforming, without weakening, the image of himself that man has inherited." It turns out that this obligation—intended to be pressing, perhaps even inevitable—changes our entire perspective of the Museum, the world, and the artist. The Museum seemed to be the universe of the artist, not the history of art, but art as the freedom of history, as the expression of a specific period of time (which we have still to examine), the manifestation of an era *sui generis* that was illumined by the profound idea of metamorphosis. In this Museum all art works were present, and by virtue of the fact that modern art without interference or travesty expresses the truth, the language needed by these art works to be understood, one might say that in effect they formed a totality. From a certain viewpoint, they were also, consequently, one and the same work, whose true meaning—the purely plastic values—was only perceived and admired through the artifices of anecdote, fiction, and sacred values. Today, however, we finally see these plastic qualities in their revealed and manifest truth with understanding, penetrating vision. Of course, we know that Byzantine art was not an art for art's sake, but sought rather to elevate things to a sacred universe. However, our function is to substitute what Byzantine art is to *art* for what it once was to itself. As Malraux says in *Le Musée Imaginaire*, "For us Byzantine art is first of all a system of forms; any art that is reborn undergoes metamorphosis; it changes meaning; it is reborn without God." If so many diverse works today comprise our taste, if we are simultaneously able to enjoy African art and Poussin, it is, it would seem, because we are able to discover the elements common to art in works without community, and because painting has to appear as a specific language, an immediate language more or less expressive and manifest, whatever the representation, suggestion, or historical travesty to which that language is linked.

In fact, however, this is not so, and we delude ourselves about the Museum. "The place that gives the loftiest idea of man" is not only the Temple of images, but of civilizations, religions, ancient glories. And the Museum that we should enjoy is not the one Cézanne revealed to us— the museum of an art that is only painting, the negative and authentic rejection of any content, of any attachment to the world—but, if it may be said, the Museum of all content, the museum of history and of time. "Our time," says Malraux, "seemed at first to base the unity of the arts so recognized exclusively on the similarity of forms. But a great artist who only knew, beside contemporary works, the purely plastic qualities of works of the past, would be a superior type of modern barbarian, whose barbarianism is defined as the rejection of the human quality. Our culture, if it were limited to that extremely narrow culture of our sensitivity to color and form and to the works in modern art that express this, would not even be imaginable. But it is far from placing such limitations on itself, for an artistic culture without precedent is being established. . . ." And this artistic culture, Malraux informs us, cannot be, must not be *purely* artistic. Furthermore, as soon as art becomes culture, becomes the means, the tool of culture, it no longer belongs to itself. It once more succumbs to travesty and servitude—the wheel of values and knowledge.

It is nonetheless evident that Malraux does not so easily intend to reexamine what appeared to him to be the truth and the meaning of modern art. He does not even seem aware of the incompatibility of the affirmation of art as the negation of the world and of all values (other than its own), and the objective, the function, imposed on it as the safeguard of the quality of man and of his values. This is one of the embarrassing points in *La Psychologie de l'Art*. In order to understand this one must try to understand the situation of the Museum in relation to the history of art within the framework of time. When we are in a museum—perhaps as spectators and no longer as artists—it is true that our admiration and interest are attracted by the past as represented in the art works, not the past as it may have been, but as it appears in the present and is ideally radiated in the works. Is it Greece we see, or Sumer or Byzantium? Certainly not. Our historic vision is an illusion, a myth, but the myth is an enormous "spiritual wealth." This illusion represents the eternal truth, that part of the truth that exists in the vestige that remains present, accessible, that moves us, fascinates us, is utterly our own, as though this vestige acquired life through us and through this life outlived us. "The dialogue that links our culture with the ephemeral absolutes transmitted by resuscitated arts, reestablishes with the past it outlines the relationship between Greek gods and the cosmos, between Christ and the meaning of the world, between the numberless souls of the dead and the living. Every Sumerian art work suggests the Sumerian empire, partly intangible, partly possessed. Great museums satisfy our taste for the exotic in history and *grant* us a vast domain of human powers. But the long trail left by the sensibility of the earth is not the trail of history. It is not dead societies that art revives. More often it is the ideal or compensatory image they had of themselves. . . ." It can therefore be said that art perpetuates the spirit, that it plays the same role in relation to history as history, in Hegel's view, plays for nature. It bestows a meaning on history, and guarantees beyond the perishable and across the death of time the life and eternity of this meaning. Art is no longer the anxiety over time, the destructive force of pure change. It is bound to the eternal, it is the eternal present that, through vicissitudes and the means of metamorphosis, maintains and ceaselessly recreates the form in which "the quality of the world through man" was once expressed. A power Malraux never tires of celebrating in shimmering words: "However art may represent man, it expresses a civilization as that civilization imagined itself; it implants the civilization in meaning, and that meaning is stronger than the multiplicity of life." "On Judgment Day let the gods set up the statues of men over against the forms that were living. It is not the world the gods created—the world of men—that will testify to their presence; it is the world of artists. All art is a lesson for its gods." And finally, this decisive sentence: "The incomprehensible stubbornness of men in recreating the world is not meaningless, because nothing becomes *presence* again after death except recreated forms."

Where does this privilege come from, if it is one? For it could be that it is also a curse and the most tragic failure of art, a failure that art is perhaps only now becoming aware of. Where does this exceptional power come from that seems to make of the artist the sole torch-bearer, the sole master of the eternal? Malraux states it more clearly than he proves it. But it is nonetheless possible to perceive the reason underlying his thinking. The essential reason is that the artist, par excellence, is a creator.

For he is never subject to nature, neither when he seems to imitate it nor when he rejects it in order to submit himself to the gods. In relation to the gods themselves, the artist is free. He may ignore this liberty, but his work attests to it and confirms it. It has happened, and happens even today, that the artist allies himself with the powers of the night, and like Goya, with monsters, with horror, with the night, or like those "primitives" that haunt us, with the fascination of the amorphous and of chaos—a disquieting relationship that seems to imply being possessed rather than being master. But herein lies the wonder: through the art work the being possessed becomes the power to possess. Servitude wakes up liberated. "Although the expression of archaic sentiments, even when indirect, grants to the masterpiece a particular resonance, recourse to shadows implies continued subservience to some kind of tyranny: in art no monster is an end in itself. Mingled in our admiration are our feelings about the deliverance of man and the mastery of the art work." Goya's solitude is great but not without limitations, for he was a painter, and if "painting is for him a means of arriving at the mystery, the mystery is a means of arriving at painting." It is also a means of becoming the dawn, freedom, and the light of day. Van Gogh is mad but his paintings are pure lucidity, a superior consciousness. The artist is never dependent on his times, or on his own history, any more than his paintings are dependent on the common vision. Now we understand why, from his birth to his death, he has appeared to us within the sole existence of the Museum. Because he is absolutely free only in the Museum, his freedom is to belong to the art that belongs exclusively to itself, although when truly creative, art is always that which transmutes existence into being, subordination into sovereignty, and death itself into the power of life.

Malraux on Malraux

by Gaëtan Picon

Here indeed are works in the first person singular. But the "I" they dramatize is a good deal more than just the one who lived through experiences and recalls them. Far deeper than that, the "I" is the one who evokes the events, provokes them, constitutes them. The writings express a life, and the personality revealed by that life to itself. But that life has endowed itself with a personality that evades it even more than it belongs to it.

Malraux doubtless enjoys saying that a man is only what he does, that man does not discover himself by contemplating himself, that one discovers life as one discovers war, and that it is out of the whole of these discoveries that a personality emerges. He seems, evidently, to espouse a kind of "empiricism," or psychoanalytical "existentialism"—if it is true that one man begins where the *other* leaves off, that all of us, vis-à-vis the future, are like Manuel of the last page of *Man's Hope*—"*And Manuel would become another man, unknown to himself.*" An individual is no more than the light projected by life on a shadow which before that moment was nothing. However, through his style of living as well as of writing, Malraux suggests that man possesses life rather than that life possesses man. If man is what he does, he is first of all that which he wished to do: man is not determined by the event but by his own will. Malraux transforms an experience into consciousness; first, he transformed consciousness into experience. Everything thus encourages us to go beyond the images of the event, the material of the action, the setting of History, in order to attain and illumine the consciousness that seeks to materialize, to test itself, to possess itself by means of these things.

The fact is, the very events Malraux talks about rarely came across his path; he almost always had to go in search of them. All of his action unfolds under the banner of revolutionary involvement. Even the war of 1940 was experienced by him less as a soldier than as a resistance fighter.

"Malraux on Malraux." (Translated from the French by Beth Archer.) From *Malraux Par Lui-Même*, by Gaëtan Picon. Copyright 1953 by *Éditions du Seuil*. Reprinted by permission of *Éditions du Seuil*. The bracketed and italicized remarks are Malraux's occasional responses to M. Picon. In the original text these remarks appear on pages facing M. Picon's discussion; and this accounts for the title of M. Picon's book, which is literally *Malraux by Himself*.

Nothing is more striking than his sensibility, his harmony with his times, and one is tempted to see in him a singular and prophetic lucidity. But should one not speak rather of complicity than of clairvoyance? Malraux's epoch did not lie before him like an object to be discovered and understood by a totally free and, consequently, supremely lucid intelligence. The relationship was more of a reply to a call. Everyone knows to what degree the actual happenings magnified the works, which in turn prophesied the events of the twentieth century. But these events might have been different from what they were. Any contemplation of History, when done without bias, recognizes how much is contingent in the pattern of historic fate. If Malraux intuited the tragic era in which we live, it is because he was made for it. It also happens that this era came about. The occurrence of "the days of wrath," of the "classical period of wars" testifies less to the lucidity of the man (be it Malraux or Nietzsche) than to the role of chance in the literary or philosophical work. Malraux can only herald tragedy because he is himself a man of tragedy. Not that he likes unhappiness, rather, that he needs it to test himself. He summons great events (combat, not defeat; the exceptional and grandiose, not necessarily the tragic), because he is a man of extreme situations. His works might not have become a true image of the world. Their basic value would nonetheless remain because first of all they are the true image of their creator.

The era began to resemble the novels. And even the author's destiny. . . . Malraux does not always evoke what he really experienced. Very often, he evokes what he has only seen or skirted. Whatever haunts him he approaches more closely, though at times without making contact. At the time he wrote *The Conquerors, The Royal Way,* and *Man's Hope,* he knew what combat meant: the battle against the jungle, and the battle against men. But he had not experienced capture and torture. He had neither been Perken marching toward the Moïs, nor Kassner in his prison, nor Hernandez before the firing squad. If he relentlessly returns to these scenes, it is because they express his deepest obsessions—a fascination that is both fear and the impatience to be put to the test, a manner of forcing Destiny to take off its mask. It happened that the future held in store for Malraux a few of these tests. Like Kassner, he was to discover prison and interrogation; like Perken and Hernandez, he was to experience the moment in which man is faced with torture, or thinks he is. Premonition? More likely, will. Malraux set off on precisely those paths that lead to such tests. In addition, we see in the relationship between Vincent Berger and Enver—in *The Walnut Trees of Altenburg*—a prefiguration of what was to become the relationship between Malraux and General de Gaulle. It is also interesting to see that Alsace appears in his writing for the first time, only a short while before Malraux was to become Colonel of the Alsace-Lorraine brigade. [*Before the war, my only relationship with Alsace (to which I am now deeply attached) was as a tourist. Altenburg grew out of the necessity to transpose Flanders, the forest replacing the sea; then, out of the more pressing necessity to permit Vincent Berger's witnessing of the gas attack which occurred on the Russo-German front and which I did not dare displace. It was three years later that I was chosen commander of the Alsatian brigade by the heads of the Maquis, who, in the Central provinces, had organized the Alsatians who fled there.*

You know that later all the decisive events of my life were bound up with Alsace, even to the names of the streets on which they occurred.

This relationship between the work and life of certain writers is extraordinary. Victor Hugo wrote Marion de Lorme before meeting Juliette Drouet, and probably one should investigate areas that are more profound than chance "meetings." Life is less responsible for providing the invented event than for providing the author with its equivalent; it less probably discovers the fact than its incidence. And this incidence, seen after the artist's death, usually escaped the artist himself, the perspective of destiny not being that of life. If Dostoevsky found his true genius in prison, his condemnation was neither the misfortune nor the accident that everyone, including Dostoevsky himself, first saw in it. The language of destiny cannot be reduced to a language of traditional biography, but I am not convinced that it defies all analysis.] Life makes dreams come true, just as it confronts one with one's obsessions.

Malraux's destiny resembles him, just as his century resembles him, which is to say that the event does not mold the personality as much as it answers the call of the personality. The sole subject of this impersonal creation—that goes from the political history of the twentieth century to the history of artistic creation, proceeding via an analysis of the common human condition—is the imperious summons of this personality, by means of which it acquires the destiny it must have in order to become what it wants to be.

And this creation that rejects all psychology, all self-analysis, is none other, at heart, than a vast psychology of its creator.

He, always he, and only he. Events in history, movements in art, only respond as the echo of his anguished voice. Malraux requires of the creative gesture of the artist—who, like God, draws man out of clay and bestows meaning on the absurdity of being a man—the same defense against his demons as he demands of human energy, cruelly faced with the bloody trials of the times. And just as he is inseparable from everything he evokes, he is inseparable from each of his heroes.

It has often been noticed that the characters are differentiated from each other in that they oppose and incarnate irreconcilable truths. But it has less often been noticed that in many cases they belong to the different stages of human formation, and that consequently there is between them the distance that separates someone who has already been tested from someone who has not. The distance between Garine and the narrator, between Perken and Claude, is in no way a conflict (it is on the surface that occasionally the dialogue opposes them), but a hierarchy: the distance between the adolescent and the mature man, and, if not between the disciple and teacher, then between the weaker and the stronger. This theme of predecessor and the intercessor is not to be overlooked since, already present in the earliest of Malraux's works, we find it again in *The Walnut Trees of Altenburg* in the story of the son retracing his father's steps ("How I see my father in me, especially since certain moments in his life seem to prefigure mine! He was not much older than I when this mystery of man, which now obsesses me, began to take hold of him."). And it reappears again in *The Voices of Silence* with the motif of creative continuity and heritage ("There is no master, no style, that does not emerge from the matrix of another.").

Destiny can be conquered only by a few, and only at that moment in which all the forces of man culminate. This is a world of heroic initiation, and there is a time for initiation. Which accounts for the character of the precursor, the shaper, the master, and even the leader. Malraux's work has been reproached with being proud. And doubtless it is. But this pride of the hero is not the instinctive complacency of the individual for himself; his confidence is a genuine defiance, the total proof of his strength. And so, even more deeply than he believes in himself, Malraux believes in those who have provided unquestionable examples of greatness—a singular capacity for admiration fills him. The tone of *The Voices of Silence* is one of admiration. And one might recall that beautiful passage in *The Walnut Trees of Altenburg* in which the narrator evokes "those classics whose dreams and human experience abounded in my father's memory . . . Goethe, Shakespeare, and the others, Stendhal, Tolstoi, Dickens . . . the Thousand and One Nights of the Western world. . . ." Has it ever been pointed out that Malraux only signs his name to laudatory critiques, and not only when writing on the classics (Nietzsche, Laclos), but when he writes on his contemporaries: Faulkner, Gide, Bernanos? One need only know him to know that he will only speak of those works or those men whom he considers important, and that no one is further removed from the spirit of the pamphlet, of denigration or of belittling. "Le contre n'existe pas," he likes to say.

Action, like creation, has its masters. In that universe, the leader plays an important role, not unlike that of the artist. The desire to serve? Not at all, and Malraux, from his viewpoint, could reply with these words of Garine, "Something I have always loathed." Opportunism oriented toward the desire to do something at any cost (in order to clarify the conjunction Malraux-de Gaulle, the lines of Vincent Berger on the subject of Enver should be recalled: "It is too late to act on something; one can only act on some one.")? Not that either. There is in Malraux a natural admiration for the man who has proven himself, who has gone beyond himself, or beyond whoever preceded him. The myth of the great individual compensates for the vanity of ideas. More than truth Malraux sought authority, truth incarnate: "Nietzsche turned into Zarathustra" as he has said himself à propos of Lawrence. Trotsky's prestige probably carried more weight during Malraux's revolutionary period than all the analyses of *Das Kapital*. [*It was less Trotsky than a mythical figure of the Russian revolution incarnated by Trotsky—the figure of an era in the Revolution.*] This quality of admiration preceded his confidence in himself, and the initial mistrust that one senses in him is the same as his mistrust of youth. One cannot know the worth of ideas that have not been lived, nor of men who have not performed. "This lightheartedness bestowed on the age of twenty by the exclusive knowledge of the abstract . . .": this quotation (referring to Garine) is an accompaniment to one from *The Psychology of Art*, "The artist has an eye, but not at the age of fifteen; and how many days does a writer need to write with the sound of his own voice?"

Unlike so many contemporary writers who tried to prolong indefinitely a charming or violent adolescence, Malraux indicates in his earliest writings something of impatience with his own youth. The fear of growing old (for old age is not only the proximity of death, but also the appearance of an involuntary perspective, of an ineluctable interior order, and Perken wishes for Claude an early death) is dominated by will and the eagerness to attain that moment in life that is the only meaningful one. [*However, the feeling of having aged is known to me.*]—when, between ignorance and lassitude, dream and action meet. Forging ahead of the narrator, the novels of adolescence project the anticipated image of an acquaintance with life, "truth incarnate": Garine and Perken. There is not a single novel which lacks this theme of the authority of older or deeper experience; corresponding to spiritual paternity (Tchen and Gisors, Tchen and the pastor) is the paternity of flesh and blood which is also a moral paternity (Kyo and Gisors, Vincent Berger and the narrator of *Altenburg*). "This lecture is my father's," Kyo writes in the margin of one of Gisors' lectures. And the narrator of *Altenburg* says, "Having had a father, I was happy, and at times proud, that it was he."

This is the authority of experience, not of ideas. In Malraux's universe, everyone knows what "the notion of a man" is. But what is the truth? "Vain thought, orchards of endless reflowerings . . ."? The common quest for greatness is expressed in the form of irreconcilable attitudes. Everyone wants to give a meaning to human existence—to make being out of nothingness. Multiple and inimical voices whose will unites them, but whose truth divides them. Malraux's universe is one of continuous conflict, and the great conflagrations of History only illumine the rival passions that struggle for possession of man.

The Royal Way (because the enemy is the jungle and the Moïs—pure destiny) and *The Days of Wrath* (because it is constructed around one character) are outside this conflict within man. But from *The Tempta-*

tion of the West, in which European pragmatism is pitted against Oriental wisdom in an unresolvable dialogue, to *The Walnut Trees of Altenburg,* in which the dialogue is no longer between historical ideologies but between concepts of history (Möllberg maintains the absurdity of the human adventure against those who support its continuity, and Walter, for whom man is no more than "a miserable little pile of secrets" made to nourish art works which assure to a few a separate greatness, argues against Vincent Berger, who thinks that man is what he does, and that the greatness of the few mysteriously testifies to the greatness of many); from *The Conquerors,* in which the destruction of revolutionary passion is revealed, to *The Voices of Silence,* in which the different styles of art appear as voices laden with irreconcilable truths and in which the opposition of styles replaces the rivalry of individual ethics ("Apollo, Prometheus, or Saturn; Aphrodite or Ishtar; the resurrection of the flesh or the Dance of Death")—Malraux never stops dramatizing inimical truths. Garine, in *The Conquerors,* works for the Revolution because "everything that is not the Revolution is worse than the Revolution," but above all, like Perken, he looks for "the most efficient use of his strength," something far greater than his own life. "Conquering revolutionary," he opposes Borodine, "a Roman revolutionary," as well as Cheng-dai, the idealist, and Hong, the terrorist, who are motivated by their love or loathing of bloodshed.

Brought together by action, the revolutionaries of *Man's Fate* are inspired by different and often conflicting passions: Kyo is a revolutionary through his will for dignity; Hemmelrich through humiliation; Tchen, because only heroism can cauterize the emptiness of a soul thirsting for the absolute ("What does one do with a soul, if there is neither God nor Christ?"); Ferral sees meaning in his life through the pure exercise of his yearning for power; Gisors contemplates life with opium; Clappique with fantasy. Of all the novels, *Man's Hope* is the one that vibrates most with discordant voices (and perhaps for that it is the greatest). In the fraternal communion of the Revolution, how many different gods, how many dissimilar hearts. There are those of the Apocalypse and those of the lyric illusion, those who "Want everything and immediately," who, like the Négus, want "to live as life should be lived, right now or perish" and for whom the Revolution represents "a vacation from life." These men want *to be.* And there are those who want *to do,* who know they must "organize the Apocalypse" in order to give it a future, and that "action is thinkable only in terms of action," whether they want justice or victory: Manuel, Garcia, Scali. But there is also Magnin who refuses to accept the conflict "between that which revolutionary discipline represents and those who do not understand its necessity"; there is Guernico, the Christian, who for the first time feels his church alive; Alvear and his distant sympathy, his skepticism toward the event, his certainty that "the notion of man" is determined by the perseverance of the individual, not by any collective solution.

A universe of debate, of torment, which remains the universe of the individual consciousness. Here the conflict is not between inner truth and its surrounding world. However different his characters may be, Malraux inhabits them all, and it is himself he confronts. In each one of them, he expresses either the part he momentarily prefers, or a part painfully sacrificed; his choices, his temptations, his regrets. Like Goethe before the definitive choice, who speaks simultaneously—and inconclusively—through the mouths of Orestes the demented and Iphigenia the confident, through Torquato Tasso the tormented and Antonio the wise, Malraux never ceases questioning and answering himself by means of those intense and feverish dialogues whose secret he possesses.

Not a single *accentuated* character who is not Malraux himself. He understands more than he represents; the universality of comprehension of his intelligence goes beyond his possibilities of artistic expression. Invincibly agnostic, he has an understanding of the religious attitude (which, by the way, grew steadily deeper) that permits him to write in a passage from *The Voices of Silence* that the saint does not escape from humanity; he assumes it. Nonetheless, no character endowed with religion was ever destined to become one of his true heroes: the pastor who raises Tchen is not Gisors; Guernico is not a Scali. And so, if he understands more than he demonstrates, he only demonstrates that which he is able to feel vitally, that which he is, that which he chooses, that which tempts him. Clappique and Gisors seem to indicate two evasions he rejects, and he repudiates Ferral's yearning for power within the framework of capitalism. However, he experienced the very things he rejects in them—the taste for action purely for power, and also the taste for fiction (it is easy to imagine that Clappique is the author of *Lunes de papier*), the taste, transitory but experienced, for alleviation through opium. As Garine says of Hong—"There are few adversaries I understand better than him," so Malraux is each of the adversaries he created. And how inseparable from himself are all these characters whose revolutionary motivation seems constantly to be the quest for their own fulfillment: the painfully sundered fragments of a kind of unity, not lost but inaccessible, in which being and doing have only one voice. Malraux is the very thing he condemns (the Négus, Hernandez, as well as Manuel and Scali), and we must seek him out in his rejections as well as in his choices.

All of these diverse voices unite in the one who animates their dialogue. All of these enemies are brothers. "A type of hero in whom culture, lucidity and an aptitude for action unite": through Garine, Malraux defines all his characters, and himself. All of them have the same language, the language of the intellectual; the same domain, that of action; the same accent, that of a passion all the more vehement because of its uneasiness about itself, and its even greater anxiety about other truths. Malraux, unlike Balzac or Proust, in no way seeks to give each character a personal voice, to free each character from its creator. [*You make very subtle distinctions, but I wonder if in your analysis there is not a notion of the specific nature of the novel, a notion that has always been suspect to me.*

You and I have both known the period in which the novel was La Princesse de Clèves, *later it was* The Mill on the Floss, *followed by the singularly important* War and Peace. *Those students who failed seventeenth century French composition were allowed to compete in nineteenth century English composition. Dostoevsky, whose presence over the last forty years is overwhelming, never played this role of model in the eyes of critics. Nor has Balzac, no matter what is said. Because the use of Balzacian devices, separated from what Baudelaire called his visionary nature, produces Zola novels more frequently than Balzacian ones.*

The autonomy of characters, the particular vocabulary given to each of them are powerful techniques of fictional action; they are not necessities. They are more evident in Gone with the Wind *than in* The Possessed, *non-existent in* Adolphe. *I do not believe that the novelist must create characters; he must create a particular and coherent world, just like any other artist. He should not compete with the world of vital statistics, but with the reality that is imposed on him, the reality of "life," seeming at times to submit to it, and at others to transform it, in order to rival life.*

Present-day theories on the novel seem to be related to theories of painting during the period of the primacy of three dimensions. And you can see why: the novelist, in order to create his universe, utilized material that he is forced to extract from everyone's world of everyday life. Moreover, this material is either a technique *of creation or nothing. Balzac is the great novelist, not Henri Monnier. It is the power to transfigure reality, the quality realized by this transfiguration, that makes for his talent; he is evidently a poet. And in that Zola is not Balzac's equal. Margaret Mitchell's novelistic techniques are not inferior to Dostoevsky's, but there is no common denominator between the imaginary world imposed by* Gone with the Wind *and that imposed by* Brothers Karamazov. *The greatness of Proust became evident after the publication of* Temps Retrouvé *gave meaning to the techniques that until then did not seem to surpass those of Dickens.*

The autonomy of language of Balzacian characters is purely relative. The jargon of Nucingen suggests no authentic voice at all. The Shakespearean outbursts that provide certain of Balzac's creations with a life truly liberated from their clay ("La loterie, c'est des bêtises," in La Rabouilleuse) *express their deepest passion through a common vocabulary.*

I believe that all through his life, Balzac was galvanized by the will to transfigure, inherited from history and the theater, that can be symbolized by "have you met César Birotteau? He was a remarkable type! The Napoleon of the perfume business." His novel is born at the very moment he conceives the scene in which a very ordinary César Birotteau is transformed into a historical personage. The accent of this parfumeur resembles the stories of Frédérick Lemaître and Barbey d'Aurevilly. Most of Balzac's accents are notes attuned to a period less polyphonic than one thinks.

As to Dostoevsky, you have read his Notebooks. *If anyone has discovered his genius while dialoguing with the lobes of his own brain it is certainly he. Certain major actions shift, in the process of editing, from one character to another. In the first notebook of the* Idiot, *the assassin is not Rogojin but Myshkin. Dostoevsky's creatures are the incarnation of an interrogative meditation whose underground course is fairly easy to follow. But he only seeks the flintstones in order to strike one against the other. Hippolytus (the tubercular in* The Idiot) *is created for the famous dialogue that sets him up against the prince, and for that reason hardly seems to me to be independent from Dostoevsky. And his mob of buffoons is a chorus that asks his heroes the eternal question "Why has God created us?"*

That the illusion of the autonomy of characters may be the privilege of genius, I do not doubt. We are less aware of this through relief than through its irreducible presence, in an apparently photographic figure of the mysterious dimension that is afforded by the reality of art. The more convincing the hero of a novel, the more convincing his life, which is not quite like that of other men. The potency of fictional illusion is not always born from the ability to attain an independent existence, transmitted as such. I believe that for a large number of playwrights and novelists, the characters grow out of the drama, not the drama out of the characters; and the heroes of Aeschylus, as well as Shakespeare, of Dostoevsky and Stendhal, are the "projections" for their authors, around whom, like the objects in certain surrealist paintings, a trompe-l'oeil mob assembles or disperses.] In the dialogue that opposes them, Ferral speaks like Gisors, Scali like Alvear, Walter like Vincent Berger. Their language was not overheard by Malraux while listening to other men. He arrived at it, if not by transcribing, at least by transposing his own language, but filtered and magnified. Filtered, because there is at least one vein that cannot pass into the novel, that is, the mocking irony that so often appears in his conversation. Magnified, because conversation (precisely through irony) often belittles what the novel extolls. But one recognizes in the dialogue of his novels the rhythm that is in his speech (and thought), the same rapidity, the same suddenness of attack, the quivering and fitful agitation, the same pathetic syncope, the same blend of lyric eloquence and elliptic sobriety. The same irrevocable aphorisms, the same impassioned formulation, the same fulgurating sentence that shim-

mers like a thin blade suddenly unsheathed and then dies out in the blaze
of an opposing formula.

What Malraux is not, to any degree whatever, he refrains from representing. In this universe that is not only one of interior conflict, but also
one of combat, the absence of the enemy is striking. Capitalists, oppressors,
Nazis, Falangists—all of them, the human adversaries of the novels'
heroes—are absent. It is symbolic that in *The Walnut Trees of Altenburg*,
the father is a German soldier in 1914, and the son a French soldier in
1940. Neither of them fights against the other nation, but both fight in
the name of man against the gods, and the German voices that are heard
from the trenches before the attack give off the same sound as the French
voices from the prisoners' camp.

In this refusal to represent the enemy, we must no doubt see the consequence of Malraux's anti-dogmatism. However deeply attached he may
be to his truths [*Perhaps it is something other than a truth*], he knows
that they are not universally evident, and that there are few roads indeed
on which human dignity cannot march. This fundamental anti-dogmatism allowed him, formerly, to write in the preface to *The Days of Wrath*,
at the very moment when he had bound his life and work to a particular
ethical and political attitude which he passionately defended, "There
are other human attitudes"; it recently permitted him to end a speech in
which he rejects Soviet totalitarianism, by saying "let everyone fight for
what he believes." Those values that are neither his choice nor his
temptations, that remain outside him, he knows he can only portray
negatively. ("If I had had to give to the Nazis the importance I give to
Kassner, I would evidently have done it in terms of their true passion,
nationalism.") He rejects introducing at the heart of the human world a
negative representation, as though everything that participated in man,
in Malraux's eyes, were endowed with a certain grandeur. He has represented neither the capitalist nor the Nazi. We would make a bet that in
the future he will not represent the Communist for, incapable as he is of
reducing him to a caricature, he could at best only recreate the face of
Kyo or Manuel. But the killers and torturers are there because, beyond
the human order, they merge, like the jungle and the Moïs, with the
impersonal, suffocating and opaque presence of destiny.

Like the sage or the believer, the political adversary is a human type
Malraux understands, because it is situated within the same domain as
intelligence and ethical exigency. The striking omissions in this universe
can thus not be attributed to the failure of communication. It is precisely because the adversary is, without being the author himself, too
similar to him for Malraux to represent him. But there are still other
omissions [*There are many more omissions than one would think even in
the most extensive works. Though some are perfectly natural, it would
be interesting to specify the others. The omission of the name of Christ
in Shakespeare (mentioned only once I believe) could orient a highly*

fertile investigation] and if Malraux avoids introducing into his novels the kind of man who participates neither intellectually or morally, it is because he refuses to communicate with such a man, or at least fails in trying to do so. "Intellectuals are a race apart," says Walter in *The Walnut Trees of Altenburg.* No character in Malraux's novels is anything else.

[Gide: *There are no imbeciles in your books.* Malraux: *I do not write to bore myself. As to idiots, there are enough in real life.* Gide: *That is because you are still too young. (Around 1938.)*]

In each book, however, the mob is present; and the quest for a fraternity far vaster than the one that unites the dialoguing intellectuals or the comrades in adventure extends through all his works. The mob seen is the one that surrounds the tragic hero and is dominated by him from the height of his solitary grandeur, not at all the kind of mob with which one communicates through love. Malraux is no doubt haunted by virile fraternity, particularly since it eludes him. Cantonese coolies, tortured prisoners of Shanghai, Spanish peasants, prisoners of the camp in Chartres: the populace always appears through an individual consciousness from which it is painfully and proudly separated. The fraternity known by the hero is not one that would make him emerge from himself—it only binds him to his equals. Rather than a communion between the hero and the people, there is, in the books of the revolutionary period, an exaltation of the hero above the myth of the people. In reality, Garine is related only to the narrator, Perken to Claude, Magnin to Scali or to Manuel, the narrator of *Altenburg* to the memory of his father; even Kassner is alone in his prison with a gilded legend.

In *The Walnut Trees of Altenburg,* Malraux admits that he has not yet discovered the true people: "I thought I knew more than my own culture because I came across the militant mobs of religious or political faith; I know now that an intellectual is not just a man for whom books are necessary, but is any man for whom an idea, however elementary, commits and orients his life. Those who surround me have lived from day to day for millenia." Fundamental humanity itself finally appears to him to be the primary fact, and he tries to become more intimate with it. [*Above all, I think, I try to understand it. In this book, it is above all the fundamental enigma.*] But does he succeed? For the first time he welcomes among his characters simple men, men without ideas or faith —the men with whom he fought in 1940, who had not chosen to fight, as had the others, to serve the Revolution. For the first time, he makes men speak in a language not his own. "For the first time, listening to that living darkness, my father heard the German people. Perhaps more simply, the people, men. Voices expressing age-old indifference and dreams, voices of trades. . . . The timber varied but the tone remained the same, very old, enveloped in the past like the shadow of this trench— the same resignation, the same false authority, the same absurd knowledge and the same experience, the same inexhaustible gaiety. . . ." Such pages enrich the work, just as the experience they translate enriches the author. However, by listening too long to voices in the trenches, Malraux risks losing his own, and he does not succeed in making of it an element of his fictional world as Balzac, Dickens, or Dostoevsky [*What a couple (the last two)*!] succeeded in blending their voices with the humblest echoes. This revelation of fundamental humanity Malraux did not incarnate in any one figure that might take its place among his heroes—it remains global, almost abstract. And the narrator of *Altenburg* could make the same avowal that was made by the narrator of *The Conquerors* [*And the one in* Man's Hope?]: "Never before have I ever felt as strongly as today the isolation Garine spoke to me about, the solitude which surrounds us, the distance that separates what is profound in us from the movements of this mob, and even from its enthusiasm. . . ."

In this intense and narrow universe in which Malraux speaks only of himself through his successive or contradictory faces, and of that which is compatible to him, there is no room for *that other species*. The human universe is limited to action and virile intelligence. No children are among his characters. The infrequency and clumsiness of female figures has been pointed out. In *The Conquerors, The Royal Way,* and *Man's Fate,* the figures of prostitutes appear, and the accent placed on such scenes indicates the importance that Malraux, at least for that moment, gave to eroticism. But eroticism is not love, and it is through love that communion with the individual being is achieved. Eroticism is no more than the anonymous revelation of the opposite sex: for men, it is a means toward the thirst for power (the study of Laclos amply reveals the bond between will and eroticism); for women, it is the "gratitude for former humiliations." Only two feminine figures are characterized: May and Valérie. Valérie, for Ferral, is only the other sex—an object humiliated, possessed, and in turn, humiliating. May (like Kassner's wife), who is above all a comrade in arms, escapes the anonymity of eroticism through her participation in the heroic order of virile combat.

Thus it is quite true to say that Malraux's works do not give us, as do the works of most great modern novelists, the representation of human diversity. The mysterious sympathy that animates the works of Tolstoy, Dickens, and Dostoevsky, and that opens them onto the existence of "the other one," we may as well not look for here. This causes an evident monotony and also a certain confusion over characters: we do not know Kyo or Manuel as we know Myshkin or Prince Andrey, Mr. Micawber or Anna. [*Are you sure of knowing Myshkin, and Stavrogin? Are you certain of knowing Fabrice del Dongo, in the sense that you know Mr. Micawber?*

The word "know" applied to beings has always made me wonder. I do not think we know anyone. This word conceals the idea of communion, of familiarity, of explanation—and many others. "To know men is to be able to influence them," says Stendhal, and for each one this knowledge would be clear. But what the novelist offers is a completely different knowledge—exterior, in the case of episodic characters, and not really interior in the case of heroes. It does not resolve the enigma of the individual; it suppresses it. Let us leave my own characters aside—you are right, by the way, about them. I want to propose a game. Tell yourself the story of three or four of the greatest novels, assuming that it all "happened"—really happened. You will notice the resistance offered you by the "magic" of the novel—the true creation. Highly variable, for the Sanseverina resists much more than Anna Karenina.

Let us not deduce from this a hierarchy. . . .] One character alone emerges—the author himself. Even more than a human universe in these works, there is the human presence of Malraux in a universe that has no other density than his own. The gift of sympathy seems to have been denied his proud and beautiful creation, a gift that appears to be a primary one for the novelist, who, in addition to his other aspects, forgets himself when faced with others, and dreams about what he sees. Is this a weakness? It is not the meagerness of an individual that fills Malraux's pages. The submission of the work to the personality is in this case submission to greatness. The novelist, Flaubert said, does not express himself in his characters, but is capable of becoming any one of his characters. But suppose greatness is cast aside by preferring others to himself? Let us recall the highly significant preface to *The Days of Wrath*: "Flaubert . . . in creating characters who are foreign to his passion could go so far as to write 'I would roll them all in the same mud . . . since I am just. . . .' We have here two essential ideas on art. Nietzsche considered Wagner a mountebank insofar as he placed his genius at the disposal of his characters. However, it is possible to choose as one of the meanings of art: 'to attempt to make men aware of the greatness in themselves that they ignore.' " Thus, Malraux justifies himself for having reduced his creation to himself.

Chronology of Important Dates

Note: Though his novels are markedly autobiographical, Malraux's actual biography is full of mysteries and conjectures. In the best account of it so far, Miss Janet Flanner (see bibliography) remarks that Malraux's birthplace and date comprise "one of the few simple facts known about his life. . . . Malraux," adds Miss Flanner, "is hermetic where his private life is concerned," and "the confusing legends about him have swelled like balloons to fill his silence." It is still uncertain, for example, whether Malraux was really in Canton (probably not) or in Shanghai (probably so) anywhere near the time of the events dramatized in *The Conquerors* and *Man's Fate*, though he was, of course, undoubtedly in the Far East during the period.

1901	George-André Malraux born on November 3 in Montmartre, Paris.
1919-20	Intensive study of art (Oriental art especially), archeology, and anthropology. First writings.
1923	Explores the ruined temples along the abandoned "Royal Way" of Cambodia, in Indochina. Brought to court by French colonial authorities for removing statuary and sentenced to three years in jail; then, because of bizarre legal confusions, is released and the case against him dismissed. Probable cause of French governmental hostility was Malraux's support of the Jeune-Annam independence movement.
1924	Back in Paris.
1925-27	To Indochina again, then to China. Works with the Jeune-Annam movement; then becomes agent of the Kuomintang (Nationalist People's Party of China) in charge of propaganda and information, eventually in Canton.
1928	Back in Paris, joins the Gallimard publishing firm as editor of art-books (a post he has held intermittently ever since).
1929-31	Extensive travels, mainly in pursuit of various art studies, in Japan, India, Persia, the United States, and elsewhere.
1934	Flight over the Yemen desert in search of "the lost city of the Queen of Sheba"; returns with reports (plus blurred aerial photographs) of some kind of ruined city, never identified.
1936	To Spain to join the Loyalists, two days after the outbreak of civil war. Founds the international air squadron, *Escadre España* (later *Escadre Malraux*). Flies sixty-five missions, occasionally as pilot.
1937	To United States to raise funds for the Loyalist cause.

1940   A volunteer private in the French tank corps. In June is captured and imprisoned in Sens; in November escapes and crosses into the Free Zone. A month later makes his first contact with the slowly forming Resistance.

1941-42   In Switzerland and the Free Zone, reading and writing and doing occasional liaison work with British parachutists.

1943-44   With the now well organized and supplied Maquis. In the spring of 1944—as *chef du Maquis* and using the *nom de guerre* of Colonel Berger—is again captured and imprisoned. Liberated after the seizure of Paris, becomes commander of the volunteer Alsace-Lorraine Brigade which pushes as far as Stuttgart, Germany, by April, 1945.

1945   In November becomes Minister of Information for General de Gaulle's short-lived provisional government.

1947   Is instrumental in forming the Rassemblement du Peuple Francais (R.P.F.), a political party dedicated to the leadership of de Gaulle. Malraux's official title: Director of National Propaganda.

1958   After several years devoted exclusively to art studies (following the disintegration of the R.P.F.), returns to public life as Minister for Information and then Minister for Cultural Affairs in the Fifth Republic.

Notes on the Editor and Authors

.. W. B. Lewis, the editor of this volume, is the author of *The American Adam* and *The Picaresque Saint* and of a number of articles on American literature and contemporary European fiction. He teaches at Yale.

EON Trotsky (1879-1940), one of the great figures in the history of Russian Communism, was himself a distinguished writer on history and literature.

DMUND Wilson is America's foremost man of letters. His books include *Tò The Finland Station, The Shores of Light,* and *Patriotic Gore.*

J. M. Frohock, Professor of French at Harvard, is the author of *The Novel of Violence in America* and of many critical essays, as well as his study òf Malraux. His most recent book is a study of Rimbaud.

EOFFREY T. Hartman is the author of *The Unmediated Vision* (on Wordsworth, Hopkins, Rilke, and Valéry) and of the forthcoming *Wordsworth,* a study of the poet's development. Among his many critical essays is òne on the fiction of Maurice Blanchot. He teaches English and Comparative Literature at Iowa.

oseph Frank, long known as the author of "Spatial Form in the Modern Novel," has recently collected his critical essays in a volume called *The Widening Gyre.* He is now completing a long critical and historical study of Dostoevsky. He is Professor of Comparative Literature at Rutgers.

RMAND Hoog has written several novels (including *L'Accident*) and was formerly editor of the French periodical *Carrefour.* His criticism covers the range of French literature. He is now Professor of French at Princeton.

cola Chiaromonte, co-editor with Ignazio Silone of the Roman quarterly *Tempo Presente,* has written many articles in several languages on modern literature and the modern theater.

aude-Edmonde Magny, one of the outstanding literary critics of her generation in France, is the author of *Histoire du Roman Français depuis 1918* and òf one of the best studies in print of the contemporary American novel, *L'Age du Roman Americain.*

ctor Brombert, editor of the volume on Stendhal in this series, is the author òf *Stendhal et la vóie oblique* and is completing a book on Flaubert. He eaches at Yale.

aurice Blanchot occupies an important position in the contemporary French iterary world. Accomplished and original as a novelist, essayist, critic, and ditor, his prevailing interest in all these media is the relation between hilosophy and literature, meaning and language.

étan Picon, the best known commentator on Malraux, is one of the foremost terary critics in France today. He deals especially with contemporary writing.

Selected Bibliography

1. Malraux's Principal Writings

I. FICTION AND RELATED WORK

Lunes en Papier (Paris: Simon, 1921).

La Tentation de l'Occident (Paris: Grasset, 1926). *The Temptation of the West*, tr. by Robert Hollander (New York: Vintage Books, 1961).

Royaume Farfelu (Paris: Gallimard, 1928).

Les Conquérants (Paris: Grasset, 1928). *The Conquerors*, tr. by Winifred Stephens Whale (New York: Random House, 1929). Paperback with new *Postface*, tr. by Jacques Le Clercq (Boston: Beacon Press, 1956).

La Voie Royale (Paris: Grasset, 1930). *The Royal Way*, tr. by Stuart Gilbert (New York: Harrison Smith and Robert Haas, 1935). Modern Library Paperback, 1955.

La Condition Humaine (Paris: Gallimard, 1933). *Man's Fate*, tr. by Haakon M. Chevalier (New York: Harrison Smith and Robert Haas, 1934). Modern Library edition, 1936. Also published in England as *Storm in Shanghai*, tr. by Alastair Macdonald (London: Methuen, 1934).

Le Temps du Mépris (Paris: Gallimard, 1935). *Days of Wrath*, tr. by Haakon M. Chevalier, with a foreword by Waldo Frank (New York: Random House, 1936).

L'Espoir (Paris: Gallimard, 1937). *Man's Hope*, tr. by Stuart Gilbert and Alastair Macdonald (New York: Random House, 1938).

Note: in 1938, Malraux himself made a film of the last section of *L'Espoir*, with scenes shot in the actual locales of fighting (and background music by Darius Milhaud). The film was not shown publicly until after World War II, when it won the French film critics' award.

Les Noyers de l'Altenburg, published as *La Lutte avec l'Ange*, I (Lausanne-Yverdon: Editions du Haut Pays, 1943); then as *Les Noyers de l'Altenburg* (Paris: Gallimard, 1948). *The Walnut Trees of the Altenburg*, tr. by A. W. Fielding (London: John Lehmann, 1952).

II. SELECTED ART STUDIES

Saturne (Paris: Gallimard, 1950). *Saturn, an Essay on Goya*, tr. by C. W. Chilton (London: Phaidon Press, 1957; distributed in the United States by Garden City Books, New York).

La Psychologie de l'Art: I, Le Musée Imaginaire; II, La Création Artistique; III, La Monnaie de l'Absolu (Geneva: Skira, 1947, 1949, 1950).

The Psychology of Art: I, *Museum without Walls;* II, *The Creative Act;* III, *The Twilight of the Absolute;* tr. by Stuart Gilbert (New York: Pantheon Books, Bollingen Series No. 24, 1949-51).

Les Voix du Silence (Paris: Gallimard, 1951). *The Voices of Silence,* tr. by Stuart Gilbert (New York: Doubleday, 1953).

Note: *The Voices of Silence* was planned as a compressed and less expensive version of *The Psychology of Art,* and Malraux began it by a line-by-line revision of the earlier work. In fact, however, the revised sections are substantially the same as the earlier ones they correspond to; but at the same time, Malraux added an entirely new section, "Les Métamorphoses d'Apollon." The long one-volume *Voices of Silence* divides as follows: *Museum without Walls, The Metamorphoses of Apollo, The Creative Process, Aftermath of the Absolute.* See "A Bibliographical Note on Malraux's Art Criticism," by C.F.R., in *Yale French Studies* No. 18 (1957).

La Métamorphose des Dieux (Paris: Gallimard, 1957). *The Metamorphosis of the Gods,* tr. by Stuart Gilbert (New York: Doubleday, 1960).

III. MISCELLANEOUS

"D'une Jeunesse Européene" (in *Écrits,* Paris: Grasset, 1927, pp. 129-54).

"Préface," *L'Amant de Lady Chatterley* (Paris: Gallimard, 1932). "Preface to *Lady Chatterley's Lover*" (*Yale French Studies* No. 11, 1953, tr. by the editors).

"Préface," *Sanctuaire* (Paris: Gallimard, 1933). "Preface to Faulkner' *Sanctuary*" (*Yale French Studies* No. 10, 1952, tr. by the editors).

"Laclos" in *Tableau de la Littérature Française* (Paris: Gallimard, 1939).

The Case for De Gaulle: A Dialogue between André Malraux and James Burnham (New York: Random House, 1949).

"Lawrence and the Demon of the Absolute" [on T. E. Lawrence] (*Hudson Review,* Vol. VIII, 1956).

2. *Writings on Malraux*

I. BOOKS

Jeanne Delhomme, *Temps et Destin, essai sur André Malraux* (Paris: Gallimard, 1955).

W. M. Frohock, *André Malraux and the Tragic Imagination* (Stanford, California: Stanford University Press, 1952).

Geoffrey H. Hartman, *Malraux* (New York: Hillary House, 1960—in the series "Studies in Modern European Literature and Thought.")

Claude Mauriac, *Malraux ou le mal du héros* (Paris: Grasset, 1946).

Gaëtan Picon, *André Malraux* (Paris: Gallimard, 1945).

———, *Malraux par lui-meme* (Paris: Editions du Seuil, 1953).

Marcel Savane, *André Malraux* (Paris: Richard-Massé, 1946).

Roger Stephane, *Portrait de l'aventurier* (Paris: Sagittaire, 1950).

II. SHORTER STUDIES

Rachel Bespaloff, "Notes sur André Malraux," in *Cheminements et Carrefours* (Paris: Librairie Philosophique J. Vrin, 1938).

Esprit No. 149, "Interrogation à Malraux": a colloquy on Malraux by André Rousseaux, Alber Béguin, Gaëtan Picon, and Pierre Debray, followed by essays by Roger Stephane, Emmanuel Mounier, and Claude-Edmonde Magny [the latter included in this volume] (Paris, October, 1948).

Janet Flanner, "The Human Condition," in *Men and Monuments* (New York: Harper & Row, 1957).

Irving Howe, "Malraux," in *Politics and the Novel* (New York: Horizon Press, 1957).

Lewis, R. W. B., "Epilogue," in *The Picaresque Saint* (Philadelphia: Lippincott, 1961).

Emmanuel Mounier, "André Malraux, le Conquérant Aveugle," in *L'Espoir des désespérés* (Paris: Éditions du Seuil, 1953).

Henri Peyre, "André Malraux," in *The Contemporary French Novel* (New York: Oxford University Press, 1955).

Rima Drell Reck, "Malraux's Heroes: Activists and Aesthetes," *The University of Kansas City Review*, Vol. XXVIII, No. 1 (1961).

———, "Malraux's Cerebral Eroticism," *Forum*, Vol. VIII, No. 9 (1962).

Pierre Henri Simon, "Malraux," in *L'Homme en Procès* (Neuchatel: Baconnière, 1950).

Yale French Studies No. 18, "Passion and the Intellect: or André Malraux," entire issue devoted to Malraux (New Haven, 1957).

TWENTIETH CENTURY VIEWS

American Authors

TWENTIETH CENTURY VIEWS

European Authors